MW01137309

Praise for *The Challenge of Creation*

"In this revised edition of *The Science of Torah*, Rabbi Slifkin addresses creation and evolution with courage and integrity. Eschewing apologetics, Rabbi Slifkin sets down a highly sophisticated and deeply religious account of how an informed contemporary Jew is to think about the biblical story of creation. Clear, cogent, and philosophically convincing, Rabbi Slifkin's *The Challenge of Creation* is an intellectual *kiddush Hashem* (sanctification of God's Name)."

Professor Yehuda Gellman
Department of Philosophy, Ben-Gurion University of the Negev
Author, *Experience of God and the Rationality of Theistic Belief*

"*The Challenge of Creation* is a wonderful and important book. Rabbi Slifkin demonstrates that cosmology and evolution are not a threat to religion and that Orthodox Judaism should not be hostile to modern science. On the contrary, educated Jews should embrace scientific progress as giving us a better understanding of and appreciation for the glory of God. Rabbi Slifkin writes with clarity and logic and with a firm grasp of the scientific issues. He provides extensive references to a wide range of Torah giants whose interpretations show that cosmology and evolution are not alien from our tradition. It is an invaluable resource for those of us in communities where the scientific ideas described in this book are known to be firmly established and where students, friends and colleagues constantly question us about traditional Judaism's views on modern science."

Professor Carl Rosenzweig
Department of Physics and Astronomy, Syracuse University

"No one could read this book without being aware of the author's deeply spiritual nature and his absolute devotion to the faith of his fathers. At the same time, one meets a man for whom the world is God's creation and it is for us, made in God's image, to go forward bravely exploring and trying to understand this creation. Rabbi Slifkin shows us that modern science is in the end a wonderful hymn to what God has wrought, and its appreciation enriches our lives and makes possible an even greater respect for, and love of, the Author of all things."

Professor Michael Ruse
Department of Philosophy, Florida State University
Author, *The Darwinian Revolution* and *Darwin and Design*

Praise for *The Science of Torah*

"...Shows convincingly that it is possible to debate these questions within the framework of modern science, while remaining completely loyal to the fundamentals of *emunah*... for its scope and depth of treatment I think it is the best book presently available on this subject."

Rabbi Aryeh Carmell
Author, *Masterplan*; Editor, *Michtav Me-Eliyahu*

"Rabbi Natan Slifkin examines currents of modern thought that others suspected to be hostile to traditional Judaism, and proves them to be more friend than foe... The author quickly wins the confidence of the reader with thorough scholarship, using restraint instead of hype, and giving full voice to positions that differ from his own. *The Science of Torah* is a considered discussion of issues, rather than a pitch for a quirky private theory. It is a book you will be proud to share with thinking friends—both traditionalists and skeptics."

Rabbi Yitzchok Adlerstein
Author, *Maharal: Be'er HaGolah*

"...Approaches these issues with sensitivity and with the respect that they deserve, spurned on by his deep appreciation of the Divinely created universe, the rare ability of illuminating contemporary and classical scientific thought in a Torah light, and by an unquenchable thirst to search for the truth and to draw others close to Judaism... This beautiful and ambitious work is to be commended to every serious thinking Jew as a Torah perspective and framework with which to approach and further delve into these important issues."

HaModia

"As a scientist and observant Jew I found this book to offer the finest reconciliation between what many see as a conflict between science and Torah... This book presents the most clear explanation I have ever read of how these two, the observation of the physical world, and the spiritual world recorded in Torah, may come together, for a greater understanding of God's creation."

Professor Tim M. Kusky
Paul C. Reinert Professor of Natural Sciences, Saint Louis University
Author, *The Encyclopedia of Earth Science*

THE
CHALLENGE
OF
CREATION

THE
CHALLENGE
OF
CREATION

Judaism's Encounter With
Science, Cosmology,
And Evolution

Rabbi Natan Slifkin

Zoo Torah/ Yashar Books

ISBN 1-933143-15-0

Published by:
Zoo Torah
http://www.zootorah.com

Distributed by:
Yashar Books/ Lambda Publishers
3709 13th Avenue
Brooklyn, NY 11218
Tel: (718) 972-5449
http://www.yasharbooks.com

Distributed in Israel by:
Judaica Book Centre
5 Even Israel Street
Jerusalem 94228
Tel: (02) 622-3215
http://www.jbcbooks.com

This volume is dedicated
upon the occasion of the
40th wedding anniversary of

Lee and Anne Samson

Beverly Hills, California

"I am pleased to dedicate this ground-breaking
work of Jewish philosophy and insights into
God's wondrous creations to my wife, Anne. I am
blessed to have as my life's partner a perfect wife,
an incredibly devoted mother, and the most loving
grandmother imaginable."

With love,
Lee Samson

Contents

About This Book   11

Foreword   13

Introduction   17

PART ONE: SCIENCE

Chapter One
  The Theological Foundations of Science   27
Chapter Two
  The New Teleology   39
Chapter Three
  Miracles and Nature   58
Chapter Four
  The Particulars of Providence   68
Chapter Five
  The Importance of Natural Law   76
Chapter Six
  Approaching Conflicts   85
Chapter Seven
  Departing from Literalism   103
Chapter Eight
  Conflict and Reinterpretation   123

PART TWO: COSMOLOGY

Chapter Nine
  Evidence for an Ancient Universe   137
Chapter Ten
  The Chaotic Approach   146

Chapter Eleven
 The Prochronic Approach 157

Chapter Twelve
 The Prior-Worlds Approach 169

Chapter Thirteen
 The Day-Age Approach 178

Chapter Fourteen
 Departing from Concordism 187

Chapter Fifteen
 Genesis as a Theological Text 203

Chapter Sixteen
 The Content and Sequence of Genesis 218

Chapter Seventeen
 Dinosaurs and Sea Monsters 231

PART THREE: EVOLUTION

Chapter Eighteen
 Untangling Evolution 241

Chapter Nineteen
 The Origin of Life 252

Chapter Twenty
 Common Ancestry 257

Chapter Twenty-One
 Evolutionary Mechanisms and Intelligent Design 276

Chapter Twenty-Two
 Darwinian Evolution and God's Attributes 302

Chapter Twenty-Three
 The Ascent of Man 317

Chapter Twenty-Four
 In Conclusion 344

Bibliography 347

About This Book

This book was written for those who are committed to the tenets of Judaism, but also respect the modern scientific enterprise and are aware of its findings, and who are therefore disturbed by the challenges that are raised for their understanding of Torah. It addresses these challenges by following the approach of Rambam (Maimonides) and similar Torah scholars towards these issues, which, while firmly within the framework of authentic Orthodox Judaism, is not the method of choice in many segments of the ultra-Orthodox community. But many have found that no other approach works as well in solving these difficulties.

Other people may not possess as extensive a background in the sciences or may dispute the validity of the modern scientific enterprise. They may therefore simply not be bothered by the questions discussed in this book, or they may have different ways of dealing with such conflicts. Such people are not the intended audience of this book and they are advised not to read it.

Foreword

by Rabbi Dr. Tzvi Hersh Weinreb

Many of our Sages and leaders through the generations have had the luxury of "preaching to the choir." Their constituents, followers, disciples, and students lived in the same intellectual world as they did, were willing to accept the teachings of their mentors without serious question, and indeed lived lives in which they were not exposed to ideological frameworks at odds with those of their master. However, throughout the ages, some of our leaders have had to cope with constituencies which did question them. These constituencies were exposed to different cultural and philosophical influences, often at odds with the core teachings of these great men. And so these men stepped forward courageously and often at the risk of their own reputations, to provide direction for those who were lost and answers to those who were puzzled, and even guidance and words of gentle rebuke to those who were rebellious and hostile.

The heroes of the latter category include Saadia Gaon and Rambam. In the post enlightenment era, the need for approaches modeled by Rabbeinu Saadia and Rambam, approaches which dealt head-on with challenges from outside normative Judaism, increased many times over. And great men among us rose to these new challenges, including men of great fame such as Rabbis Mayer Leibush Malbim, Samson Raphael Hirsch, Abraham Isaac Kook, Eliyahu Dessler, and Joseph B. Soloveitchik, and less known thinkers to whom Rabbi Slifkin's book introduces us, such as Rabbi Gedalia Nadel.

Today, too, there are leaders among us who are blessed with constituencies that are not exposed to ideologies alien to traditional Judaism, or who are oblivious, intentionally or otherwise, to the challenges of these alien systems. Fortunate are these leaders, for they can continue to teach and preach what they see as the unadulterated and pure message of the Torah. However, there are those among us who are confronted daily with Jews whose exposure to the culture and philosophy of our times stimulate probing and consuming questions about Judaism. Some of these Jews come from the ranks of the non-observant who wish to draw closer to Torah and mitzvos but who find it difficult to integrate the thought system with which they have grown up with the teachings of the Torah to which they are newly introduced. But also among these individuals are those who have been steeped from birth in a traditional education and in a traditional understanding of Torah but who are now confronted, either through formal secular education, general reading, or discussions with those in their everyday environment, with new challenges of doubt and perplexity.

The greatest merit of Rabbi Slifkin's newly revised and expanded edition of his earlier work *The Science of Torah*, entitled *The Challenge of Creation*, is that it faces squarely many of the questions which trouble even the most devout of our brethren who allow themselves to think seriously about the implications for the religion they revere of the science they learned in school. Recommending to those who are thus troubled that they desist from such questions is futile, and has disastrous spiritual consequences, which include disillusion with our tradition, paralyzing doubt, and painful inner conflict. Most tragically, suppressing these questions prevents the opportunity to discover depths of Torah that the questioner may not ever have imagined or anticipated.

This work demonstrates that grappling with issues such as evolution, the age of the universe, the literalism of our sacred texts, miracles, *hashgacha pratis*, and the scientific world view in general can result in a new appreciation of the breadth and depth of our Torah, which indeed has seventy facets and is more profound than the depths of the sea. Seekers, whether new to Jewish observance or born into the Orthodox fold, will find in this work a model of honest confrontation with serious challenges. *The Challenge of Creation* spells out these challenges articulately, analyzes them keenly, and refers to impeccable and authoritative traditional sources to address them.

Rabbi Slifkin's work has engendered controversy in the past, and no doubt will continue to do so. This is to be expected, because the issues he deals with are sensitive, and many will find his approach provocative. It is to be hoped, however, that those who choose to disagree with Rabbi Slifkin will do so politely and intelligently, as befits Torah scholars and men of good will. The issues discussed in this book deserve debate and discussion, but also deserve thoughtfulness and reasoned responses.

Rabbi Slifkin is to be commended for his contribution to our abiding faith, as well as for his courageous intellectual honesty. Hopefully others, similarly motivated and equipped with comparable erudition and Fear of Heaven, will continue along the trail he has blazed.

Tzvi Hersh Weinreb
New York City
12 June 2006/ 16 Sivan 5766

Introduction

Questions of Faith

There is much awareness of potential conflicts between religion and science. The topics of the existence of a Creator, the age of the universe and the evolution of life are the best known of these. But few realize the extent to which these conflicts cause problems for people. Many are severely bothered by these conflicts, and are desperate to find solutions. Even people for whom these are not burning issues are nevertheless often suffering from a quiet feeling of unease that Judaism is afraid or incapable of dealing with these topics.

Educators are often at a loss to deal effectively with these issues. In the course of lecturing on this topic, I hear how teachers have rebuffed those who asked about dinosaurs and evolution, or have given answers that good, observant students have found patently unsatisfying. One extreme story involved a child who was given a "Barney the Dinosaur" stuffed toy by a relative and had it confiscated and destroyed by her teacher. I have even heard of students on school trips to a natural history museum whose teachers stand in plain view of the dinosaur skeletons and inform their students that dinosaurs never existed!

Then there was the case of the chocolate milk. When the movie *Jurassic Park* was released, a food manufacturer in Israel decided to cash in upon the craze by depicting dinosaurs on its dairy products. The result was that the company was threatened with losing its kosher certification! While this threat did not materialize, and was issued by a single official in one kashrus agency, it illustrates the degree of the problem. The official stated that he was pressed into action by calls from angry parents of children who were looking up "dinosaur" in the encyclopedia.[1]

A serious problem occurs with many schools which are forced to study the topic of evolution as part of a science curriculum. Rare is the teacher that knows how to effectively deal with the religious ramifications of the topic. The result is situations that are tragically absurd. There are schools in which teachers preface their course by informing the students that everything which they are about to learn is false. Some even insist that their students answer the state examinations incorrectly. Other schools refuse to teach the topic of biology to begin with. All these approaches leave many students with the uncomfortable feeling that Judaism is anti-science and afraid of the world.

The Reasons for This Book

Although there are many people who are struggling with conflicts between Torah and science, several books have already been written on this topic. What need is there for another one?

This book was written for several reasons. First, I discovered that none of the works currently available on Torah and science, popular as they are, comprehensively deal with the issues at hand. For example, certain key issues, such as the Jewish significance of scientific endeavor in general, and the true nature of the "Argument from Design," have not been properly discussed in the contemporary literature. In some cases it is even worse, with one popular work intimating that we can prove God's existence from phenomena such as bird migration on the grounds of it (supposedly) having no scientific explanation. Of course, such an approach is liable to prove extremely harmful when the reader discovers that there are indeed adequate scientific explanations for bird migration. The sophisticated and

---

1   Herb Keinon, "Dinosaurs and Kashrut Certificate 'Incompatible'," *The Jerusalem Post*, Aug 13, 1993.

critical reader seeking to find a rational basis for believing in a Creator is left dissatisfied by popular works on this subject.

Another example is with the age and development of the universe. While there has been a large volume of Jewish literature dedicated to this issue, these works generally deal with it in a superficial manner that does not prove adequate for the discerning reader. The literature on evolution is likewise dissatisfying. Some books are quoting scientists completely out of context or are reprinting arguments from thirty years ago that have long been disproved. Additionally, no Jewish book that I have seen adequately distinguishes between different meanings of the term "evolution," a distinction that should become clear in its significance during the course of this work. Most importantly, most books seem to take the areas of conflict of evolution with religion as being obvious, without analyzing what they actually are and whether they are all as absolute as they seem.

Most other books on Torah and science fall into two categories. One is the "rejectionist" approach, which seeks to disprove the scientific theories that conflict with the simple understanding of Torah. While this approach has a long history, it is simply not satisfactory for most people who have a thorough grasp of modern science, and it causes Orthodox Judaism to lose intellectual credibility. Another is the "concordist" approach, which accepts the findings of modern science and claims (often with dramatic sensationalism) that they are entirely consistent with the literal reading of the Torah. This approach is very popular, but it often involves poor scholarship that does not stand up to careful scrutiny. This book takes a different approach, as will become clear.

A further reason for compiling this work is that some highly valuable insights on the topic from important Jewish thinkers have not received public attention. Incredibly, even Rambam's approach to the Genesis account of Creation, which is of unparalleled importance to anyone seeking to reconcile Genesis with science, is virtually unknown outside of narrow academic circles. The critically important essay from Rabbi Samson Raphael Hirsch dealing with evolution was not published until relatively recently and is still obscure, and the insights of the late Rabbi Gedalyah Nadel of Bnei Brak have been published in a book that is generally unavailable.

I am not an original thinker, and there is not a single significant idea in this book that is of my own creation. All the fundamental points of this book, as novel as they may appear, are taken from Torah scholars that are universally respected in the Orthodox Jewish community. What I have tried to accomplish is to bring some of these little-known writings to light and show how they assist in solving contemporary challenges. I cannot pretend to have found answers for all the questions on this topic, and there are some questions that still bother me. With subject matter such as this, it is perhaps inevitable that difficulties will remain. Nevertheless, I do hope that this work outlines a successful general approach.

Concerns

There are many fears and concerns that are voiced with subject matter such as this. Many of these are addressed in the course of the book. It is indeed true that there are people who are simply incapable of dealing with topics as complex and sensitive as those of this book, especially if these ideas contradict what they have always been taught. Even my own beloved mother was shocked to discover what I had written![1] Indeed, as we shall later explain, it is possible that one of the reasons that God did not explicitly present the scientific version of history in the Torah is that it would not have been suitable for many of the Torah's readers.

Nevertheless, I do not believe that these are grounds to refrain from publishing such a book. The people who cannot deal with this topic are not likely to purchase this book, much less to understand it. Books such as this are usually only read by those who need them—those who have studied science and are bothered by the challenges that it raises. In fact, there are many more of these people than is commonly assumed.

The introductory comments of Rambam (Maimonides) in his *Guide to the Perplexed* (a work that was denounced by some as heretical) are equally applicable to this work:

> Let the reader make a careful study of this work; and if his doubt be removed on even one point, let him praise his Maker and rest

---

1 She eventually quipped that she doesn't mind if I write that *I* am descended from a monkey, as long as I don't claim that *she* is!

contented with the knowledge he has acquired. But if he derives from it no benefit whatever, he may consider the book as if it had never been written. Should he notice any opinions with which he does not agree, let him endeavor to find a suitable explanation, even if it seem far-fetched, in order that he may judge me charitably. Such a duty we owe to every one. We owe it especially to our scholars and theologians, who endeavor to teach us what is the truth according to the best of their ability. I feel assured that those of my readers who have not studied philosophy, will still derive profit from many a chapter. But the thinker whose studies have brought him into collision with religion, will, as I have already mentioned, derive much benefit from every chapter...

Lastly, when I have a difficult subject before me—when I find the road narrow, and can see no other way of teaching a well established truth except by pleasing one intelligent man and displeasing ten thousand fools—I prefer to address myself to the one man, and to take no notice whatever of the condemnation of the multitude; I prefer to extricate that intelligent man from his embarrassment and show him the cause of his perplexity, so that he may attain perfection and be at peace.

Rambam, Guide for the Perplexed, preface

Changes in this Edition

I first published the basic ideas contained in this volume in 2001, in a book entitled *The Science Of Torah*. This work differs from *The Science Of Torah* in several significant ways. One is that it has been more clearly packaged for its intended readership, in order to alleviate the concerns discussed above. There are also numerous other changes from the earlier version. The text has been completely revised and numerous minor but sloppy errors have been corrected. There is also a wealth of new material in several sections, and the book is twice the length of the first edition. In particular, there are new sources corroborating some of the more "radical" concepts in this book. This new version also addresses several themes not adequately discussed in the first edition, such as the license for non-literal interpretation, the history of conflicts between Torah and science, and questions posed by the existence of ancient human civilizations.

For the first edition, Rabbi Aryeh Carmell recommended that I remove the speculative material dealing with mystical patterns. I put it in anyway, since some of my other rabbinic mentors were very much in favor of it, and many people greatly appreciated this material. But others disliked it and were distracted from the other parts of the discussion, as Rabbi Carmell had wisely predicted. I further realized that this book builds upon the rationalist approach of Rambam, which does not involve mysticism. In this edition I have therefore removed the majority of that material.

Further updates and corrections to this work will be posted online at my website, www.zootorah.com. I recommend that the reader refer to this webpage at regular intervals, or subscribe by e-mail to my newsletter (essays-subscribe@zootorah.com) for notifications of updates.

How to Read this Book

This book should be read in sequence from beginning to end. Some of the ideas in the later sections of the book will appear incomprehensible or implausible unless one has internalized the lessons and themes discussed at the beginning. (I am under no illusions that this request will be followed by all readers. There are people who like to skim books for sentences and paragraphs that are taken out of context. Regrettably, the number of readers of my books is far exceeded by the number of firm opinions about my books. Nevertheless, for the record, I must state my request that the book be read carefully and in its entirety.)

Extensive use has been made of quotations due to the controversial nature of the subject material. Thus, quotations from renowned scientists are provided on those points that those who are scientifically-oriented and skeptical would scorn, and quotations from renowned Torah scholars are provided on those points that those who are highly religiously dogmatic would scorn. In many works and essays dealing with issues of religion and science, it is unfortunately common practice to quote scientists selectively and out of context and, in doing so, to distort their views entirely. I have made every effort not to do so in this work.

Certain compromises of both content and style have been necessary in order to accommodate both the religious and secular reader; it is hoped that each will be understanding of these.

Acknowledgements

I am deeply grateful to the Creator for enabling me to produce this work, which includes providing me with the help of a wonderful group of people. First, I would like to thank the distinguished Torah scholars who assisted me with the earlier version of this work, including Rabbi Yitzchok Adlerstein, Rabbi Mordechai Becher, Rabbi Avraham Edelstein, Rabbi Mordecai Kornfeld and Rabbi Meir Triebitz. I am especially indebted to Rabbi Aryeh Carmell, who mentored me in a general approach to the entire topic and reviewed the first edition of this book in great detail; I am deeply saddened that his declining health did not permit him to review this edition of the book.

This new book benefited from some important new contributors. Professor Yehuda (Jerome) Gellman of the Department of Philosophy at Ben-Gurion University of the Negev reviewed the manuscript in detail and lent of his expertise in philosophy. Professor Carl Rosenzweig contributed his expertise for reviewing the scientific information. Rabbi Meir Triebitz further assisted with his encyclopedic knowledge of Torah sources. Rabbi Nesanel Neuman's sharpness and erudition was of great assistance. Most of all, I must express my deep gratitude to the multitalented Rabbi Gil Student of Yashar Books. Not only did he edit the manuscript with great care, but his support and encouragement for my work has been of inestimable value.

Additionally, I would like to express my appreciation to all those who attended my lectures and classes on these topics, and who have discussed and debated these topics with me. In particular, I am grateful to the students of Ohr Somayach Institutions, Yeshivat Lev HaTorah, and Midreshet Moriah College for Women, whose questions and comments helped further clarify the topic for me. I am also greatly thankful to all those readers who wrote in with their comments, compliments and criticisms, especially Ariel Segal. My deep gratitude also goes to Mrs. Bryna Epstein at the Bar-Ilan library for her generous assistance in locating and copying countless articles and books for me, and to Akiva Atwood for technical guidance with many aspects of the book's production.

I am indebted to my parents, Professor and Mrs. Michael and Marietta Slifkin, for their continued encouragement; I would especially like to thank my father for his guidance with the scientific methodology and details, and for his frank and expert assessments of the validity of different scientific theories. I am profoundly grateful to my parents-in-law, Mr. and Mrs. Lee and Anne Samson, for their invaluable guidance, support and encouragement with this and other projects; our closeness belies the nine thousand miles that separate us. It is a privilege to have this book dedicated upon the occasion of their fortieth anniversary. Finally, I would like to express my deep appreciation for my wife Tali, who is a living inspiration for me, a wonderful mother to our children, and whose support is precious beyond words.

Natan Slifkin
Ramat Bet Shemesh
June 2006/ Sivan 5766

Part One:

SCIENCE

Chapter One

The Theological Foundations of Science

The Call for a Creator

There are many paths to belief in God. Revelation is the easiest, but few are they that experience it. For the rest of us, faith is achieved via tradition, study of the Torah, contemplation of the providence in one's life, the sheer experience of religion, and so on. Another path is contemplation of the physical world:

> How manifold are Your works, O God! In wisdom You have made them all; the earth is full of Your creatures.
>
> Psalms 104:24

Rabbi Bachya Ibn Pakuda, an outstanding Spanish philosopher of the eleventh century, considered contemplation of the natural world to be the most basic path to enhancing one's belief in God:

> Reflection on the wisdom manifest in God's creations is the most accessible way of verifying His existence and the surest path to a true conception of Him.
>
> *Chovos HaLevavos, Sha'ar HaBechinah*, Introduction

God's existence seems to be most easily grasped in His role as Creator, rather than Torah-giver, Miracle-worker, or Providence-arranger. The "Argument from Design" was the title given to the argument that the universe demonstrates evidence of design and therefore must have had a

27

Designer. In the wider world, this was most famously put forward at the turn of the nineteenth century by the clergyman William Paley, in his book *Natural Theology: or, Evidences of the Existence and Attributes of the Deity, Collected from the Appearances of Nature*. His best-known example was that of someone finding a watch in the desert and concluding that it must have been made by a watchmaker. The Jewish version of the watchmaker argument was recorded nearly two thousand years earlier:

> A heretic came to Rabbi Akiva and asked, "Who created the universe?" Rabbi Akiva answered, "The Holy One." The heretic said, "Prove it to me." Rabbi Akiva replied, "Come to me tomorrow." When the heretic came to him on the next day, Rabbi Akiva asked, "What is that you are wearing?" "A garment," replied the heretic. "Who made it?" asked Rabbi Akiva. The heretic replied, "A weaver." Rabbi Akiva said, "I don't believe you! Prove it to me!" "How can I prove it to you?" replied the heretic, "How can you not know that a weaver made it?" Rabbi Akiva said, "And how can you not know that the Holy One made the universe?" After the heretic left, Rabbi Akiva's students asked him, "But what is the proof?" He said, "Just as a house attests to its builder, a garment its weaver or a door its carpenter, so too does the world attest to the Holy One Who created it."
>
> *Midrash Temurah* 5[1]

We also find the idea that discovering new phenomena in the natural world further enhances the honor of the Creator:

> There are many secrets of nature which are discovered in every generation by scientists… in doing so, they give glory to the Holy One…
>
> Netziv, *Haamek Davar*, Introduction to Genesis

None of this should be taken to mean that contemplation of the wonders of the universe automatically leads people to the God of the Jewish faith. For it does not necessarily direct people to the conclusion that there was a single designer, or that the designer still exists, or that the designer possesses the attributes that we ascribe to God (as opposed to those ascribed to God by Aristotle). Nevertheless, it certainly greatly enhances religious belief and helps ground it in a rational foundation.

---

1 While the main force of this argument is one from causality rather that the ingenuity of design, the latter point also seems to be present.

The Challenge of Science

One reason as to why deriving belief in a Creator from contemplation of the natural world was fairly straightforward for much of history is that people barely knew anything about how the world works. They contented themselves with saying that supernatural forces make things happen. For the pagan nations this meant a plethora of minor deities, while for the Jews, on the other hand, and then the Christians and Moslems, it meant the one God. "Why do the leaves on the trees change color in winter?" "Because God makes them change color." In early times, people did not grasp the idea that there could be physical mechanisms by which God accomplishes this.

Yet this line of reasoning came under ever-increasing attack as science progressed. True, if one were to find a watch in the desert, it must have been made by a watchmaker. But explanations were advanced as to why the universe is different. In terms of life, the theory of evolution was proposed. In terms of other phenomena, such as planetary motion, science provided highly effective explanations as to how these things came about.

The religious responses to these kinds of explanations were mixed. Many looked upon scientists as heretics who were negating God's work. Some invoked God to fill the gaps in scientific knowledge; but as these gaps grew ever smaller, the "God-of-the-gaps" grew ever less necessary. Thus, on the whole, science is widely perceived as reducing God's part in the picture, if not removing it entirely.

As the scientific method gained momentum in the last few centuries, many people, both scientists and non-scientists, assumed that God had been rendered superfluous. "Why do the leaves change color?" "Because the leaves contain tiny green chlorophyll molecules. These collect light, carbon dioxide, and water, which they use to make food for the tree in spring and summer. As winter approaches, the tree doesn't need any food, and the chlorophyll molecules break down. As a result, the other molecules in the leaves become more apparent and they provide the orange and yellow colors." Explanations of this sort seemed to threaten earlier arguments for the existence of a Creator, such as that offered by Rabbi Bachya Ibn Pakuda:

There are men who say that the world came into existence by chance, without a Creator Who caused it and formed it. I find this astonishing. How could any rational human being, in his right mind, entertain such a notion? If one who held such a view were to hear someone make a similar claim about a revolving water wheel—that it came about without the design of a craftsman who invested effort in putting it together, constructing it, and supplying all its parts so that it perform its intended function—he would be amazed by such a statement, speak slightingly of the one who made it, consider him a total ignoramus, and be quick to expose him and reject his claim.

Now, if such a claim is rejected when it is made about a petty and insignificant little water wheel, which can be made with limited skill and serves a small plot of land, how can one allow himself to make the same claim about the great celestial "wheel" which encompasses the entire earth and all of its creatures; which reflects such an intelligence that its essence is beyond the grasp of all human understanding; which serves the well-being of the entire earth and everything in it? How can one say that it came into being without the intent of a Designer, without the planning of an omnipotent Intelligence?

Rabbi Bachya ibn Pakuda, Chovos HaLevavos, Sha'ar HaYichud 6

Today, the celestial wheel is known not to be a wheel at all, but rather a vacuum populated by stars and planets. Its "intelligence" is well within our grasp, via the science of astronomy. And there are adequate scientific theories as to how it was formed. In general, much of that which had previously been seen as requiring a Creator could now be attributed to scientific explanations, and gradually a not-unreasonable belief emerged that all phenomena will ultimately be accounted for in this way. What room, then, for a Creator?

Forgotten Foundations

The great irony of all this is that while science is commonly viewed as replacing religion, it was religion—and specifically Judaism—which enabled science to develop in the first place. Paul Davies, professor of mathematical physics at the University of Adelaide, is one of the most respected writers on science, especially in the field of its interaction with philosophy. He calls attention to an aspect of science that is often overlooked:

> In the age of science we regard it as perfectly natural to seek mechanistic explanations of things… A given cause, usually in the form of a force, produces a later effect. But early cultures did not generally regard the world in this way. Some perceived nature as a battleground of conflicting forces… Other cultures, especially in the East, believed that the physical world was a holistic tapestry of interdependent influences… For the modern scientist, it is sufficient only that nature simply have the observed regularities we still call laws. The question of their origin does not usually arise. Yet it is interesting to ponder whether science would have flourished in medieval and Renaissance Europe were it not for Western theology.
>
> Paul Davies, *The Mind of God*, pp. 74-77

The entire scientific enterprise has its roots in religion, specifically monotheistic Judaism. The *Merriam Webster Dictionary* defines science as "knowledge covering general truths or the operation of general laws especially as obtained and tested through the scientific method." But the search for the laws of the universe only makes sense if it is assumed that such laws exist, that there is structure to the universe. If the control of the universe is subject to a battle of the gods or the universe is simply chaotic and random, then there is no reason to assume that there are any laws to be found.

Joseph Needham, the primary authority on Chinese scientific endeavors, makes this point very well, in explaining why science never developed in Eastern societies:

> There was no confidence that the code of Nature's laws could ever be unveiled and read, because there was no assurance that a divine being, even more rational than ourselves, had ever formulated such a code capable of being read.
>
> Joseph Needham, *The Grand Titration: Science and Society in East and West*

In the West, on the other hand, the necessary foundation for scientific investigation was established by monotheistic religion. As biologist Kenneth Miller writes:

This very Western idea of God as supreme lawgiver and cosmic planner helped to give the scientific enterprise its start. Many Eastern religions take the view that reality is entirely subjective, and that man can never truly separate himself from the nature he wishes to understand. Whatever the contemplative value of these ideas, the ancient Eastern intellectual was thereby relieved of any feeling that the workings of nature might reflect the glories of the Lord. The Westerner was not, and this is one of the reasons we can say—despite the extraordinary technical prowess of many Eastern cultures—that true empirical, experimental science developed first in the West. Hindu philosophers were left to contemplate the ever-changing dance of life and time, while Western scholars, inspired by the one true God of Moses and Muhammad, developed Algebra, calculated the movements of the stars, and explained the cycle of seasons.

Kenneth R. Miller, *Finding Darwin's God*, p. 196

It was only through Abraham's legacy of monotheism, and its later offshoots of Christianity and Islam, that the thought-patterns necessary for scientific inquiry were formed.[1]

Our Western religious tradition also endows us with the assumption that things are governed by a logic that exists independently of those things, that laws are externally imposed as though they were the decrees of a transcendent divine legislator.

John Barrow, *Theories of Everything*, p. 15

As R. Hooykaas, professor of history of science at the University of Utrecht in the Netherlands, writes:

Most scientists of the nineteenth and twentieth centuries… may have been unconscious of the fact that the metaphysical foundations of their discipline stemmed, in spite of all secularization, in great part from the biblical concept of God and creation.

R. Hooykaas, *Religion and the Rise of Modern Science*, p. 26

We are so used to the idea of laws of nature that it might all seem obvious to us. But ancient cultures did not conceive of such a thing. They believed that physical things contained purposes and acted in a way that

---

1   This lends new depth to Maimonides' statement that the "pillar of knowledge" is the awareness of the one God (*Yad HaChazakah, Hilchos Yesoday HaTorah* 1:1).

reflected their inner natures rather than following any laws. Water would "seek out" the lowest level, stones would fall because the "natural place" of ponderous objects was the Earth, and gases would rise because they "belonged" in the sky.

> Much of this early thinking was based on the assumption that the properties of physical things were intrinsic qualities belonging to those things... Set against this way of looking at the world were the monotheistic religions. The Jews conceived of God as the Lawgiver. This God, being independent of and separate from his creation, imposed laws upon the physical universe from without.
>
> Paul Davies, *The Mind of God*, p. 75

We tend to think of Judaism's contribution to the world in terms of the Bible and the concept of morality. But here we see that Judaism is also considered responsible for the remarkable phenomenon of the entire scientific enterprise. "The Jews conceived of God as the Lawgiver"—and thus laid the groundwork for the search for the laws that He gave.

> In the first place, there can be no living science unless there is a widespread instinctive conviction in the existence of an *Order Of Things*. And, in particular, of an *Order Of Nature*... The inexpugnable belief that every detailed occurrence can be correlated with its antecedents in a perfectly definite manner... must come from the medieval insistence on the rationality of God... the impress on the European mind arising from the unquestioned faith of centuries... My explanation is that the faith in the possibility of science, generated antecedently to the development of modern scientific theory, is an unconscious derivative from medieval theology.
>
> Alfred N. Whitehead, *Science and the Modern World*, pp. 3-4, 12-13

The same point is made by prominent naturalist and philosopher Loren Eisley, and he notes the strange irony of this:

> The philosophy of experimental science... began its discoveries and made use of its method in the faith, not the knowledge, that it was dealing with a rational universe controlled by a Creator who did not act upon whim nor interfere with the forces He had set in operation... It is surely one of the curious paradoxes of history that science, which professionally has little to do with faith, owes its origins to an act of

faith that the universe can be rationally interpreted, and that science today is sustained by that assumption.

> Loren Eisley, *Darwin's Century: Evolution And The Men Who Discovered It*, p. 62

The Holistic Universe

Another aspect of how science is based upon a belief in the unity of existence is in its growing awareness that nothing exists in isolation. When scientists discover something, they don't settle for knowing what it is; they also investigate how it fits in with everything else. Yet there is no logical reason to suppose that a particular phenomenon should have anything to do with other phenomena, unless one presumes an underlying unity and integrity to the universe.

> Again, we notice that this motivation is essentially religious. There is no logical reason why the Universe should not contain surds or arbitrary elements that do not relate to the rest.
>
> John Barrow, *Theories of Everything*, p. 8

This point essentially originates in Judaism, and indeed we find it discussed in the eleventh century by Rabbi Bachya Ibn Pakuda:

> A further [argument that God is One] is that we find that the world's stability and perfect balance rests on the interdependence of its parts. No part is complete unless complemented by another, just as links in chain armor, the parts of a bed, the organs of the human body, and the components of other composite things complement each other and need each other to function properly. One can see plainly that... the earth needs the sky and water; animals are dependent on one another, as some species—birds, fish, and beasts of prey, for instance—feed on others...
>
> *Chovos HaLevavos, Sha'ar HaYichud* 7

The same concept is also expressed by Rabbi Moshe Chaim Luzzatto (1707-1746), the prominent Italian rabbi and philosopher:

> One who looks at the components of creation according to their superficial appearance, will at first see nothing other than scattered and disparate parts. That is to say, they are not connected to a single purpose, but rather every one is distinct, for a special purpose... but

34

one who goes deeper in wisdom will find that all parts of creation are tied together with a proper knot, as they are all required to complete the concept that the Higher Wisdom intended with creation, and they are all united in a single purpose.

Rabbi Moshe Chaim Luzzatto, Da'as Tevunos 128

Everything in the universe is understood to fit together—which leads to a very significant search.

The Search for Ultimate Unity

We have seen that scientific inquiry is based on certain philosophical assumptions. The modern "holy" quest of science is the search for a grand unified theory of everything, a single theory that will unify the fundamental forces in nature, including the so-far incompatible theories of general relativity and quantum physics. This quest has even greater implications of philosophical underpinnings.

> The current breed of candidates for the title of a "Theory of Everything" hope to provide an encapsulation of all the laws of nature into a simple and single representation. The fact that such a unification is even sought tells us something important about our expectations regarding the Universe... Our monotheistic traditions reinforce the assumption that the Universe is at root a unity, that it is not governed by different legislation in different places, neither the residue of some clash of the Titans wrestling to impose their arbitrary wills upon the Nature of things, nor the compromise of some cosmic committee.

John Barrow, Theories of Everything, p. 15

The ultimate implication for science of monotheism, of the recognition of the God Who created all the diverse parts of the universe, but Who possesses the ultimate simplicity and Unity, is the grand unified theory of everything. Only with monotheism does such a search make sense.

> Where the ancients were content to create many minor deities, each of whom had a hand in explaining the origins of particular things, but might often be in conflict with one another, the legacy of the great monotheistic religions is the expectation of a single over-arching explanation for the Universe....

Ibid., p. 8

Of course, not every scientist will admit to this. Yet, admit to it or not, discoveries in this direction confirm everything that Judaism has worked so hard to teach. The distinguished biologist Waldemar Mordecai Wolff Haffkine (1860-1930), inventor of the cholera and bubonic plague vaccine, wrote as follows:

> Alone of all religious and philosophic conceptions of man, the faith which binds together the Jews has not been banned by the advance of research, but on the contrary has been vindicated in its profoundest tenets. Slowly and by degrees—passing through innumerable stages in an analysis of the life of animals and plants and of the elemental phenomena of heat, light, magnetism, electricity, chemistry, mechanics, geology, spectroscopy, astronomy—science is being brought to recognize in the universe the existence of one Power which is of no beginning and no end; which has existed before all things were formed and will remain in its integrity when all is gone; the source and origin of all; in itself beyond any conception or image that man can form and set up before his eye or mind... This sum total of the scientific discoveries of all lands and times is an approach of the world's thought to our *Adon Olam*, the sublime declaration of the creed by the help of which the Jew has wrought and will further work the most momentous changes in the world...
>
> Cited by Rabbi Dr. Isaac Herzog,
> "The Talmud as a Source for the History of Ancient Science,"
> in *Judaism: Law, and Ethics*, p. 171-172

In the words of Rabbi Samson Raphael Hirsch (1808-1888), the renowned German Jewish leader and thinker:

> It is true, of course, that most natural scientists today are satisfied to stop at the point where they have surmised some sort of unity at the foundation of all nature. They do not attempt to proceed upward from there to the one, sole Creator and Composer of that unity. They do not even suspect that, with every step they take toward the discovery of unity in nature, they add another step to the universal throne of the one, sole God.
>
> Rabbi Samson Raphael Hirsch, "The Educational Value of Judaism,"
> in *Collected Writings*, vol. VII, p. 258

Far from science being an alien challenger to religion, it is actually a child of religion, and one that is gradually returning to its roots.

The Ultimate Answer

At the conclusion of Yom Kippur, the Day of Atonement and purification, we proclaim that God is *Elokim*. *Elokim* is the name that describes God as the ultimate empowerment of all the forces that govern the universe.[1] The many diverse phenomena of the universe are all the result of the One God.

Rabbi Samson Raphael Hirsch

Science and religion must ultimately reach the conclusion that there is nothing besides Him. The Grand Unified Theory of Everything expresses the unity of God.[2] Rabbi Samson Raphael Hirsch phrases this with his customary eloquence:

> Do the findings of all the natural sciences to date not show similarities that would suggest the existence of the very Oneness that is the foundation of Judaism? Is it not possible that the astronomer in his observatory, the mineralogist in his pit, the physiologist with his microscope, the anatomist with his scalpel and the chemist with his flask will be forced to conclude that all their studies actually center on one and the same work of creation in the heavens and earth? Is it not possible that, with all their investigations, they find themselves on the track of one single Thought that inspires the creation of matter and energy, laws and forms, that even in the midst of the infinite variety presented by the universe here is an obvious single harmonious unity?
>
> In light of the foregoing, would Judaism not be justified in viewing this idea of a universal unity, which inquiring minds have already pieced together from the textbook of the universe and which man's

---

1 Cf. *Shulchan Aruch, Orach Chaim* 5.

2 While some might fear this to echo Spinozian or pantheistic doctrines, nothing could be further from the truth. See Responsa *Chacham Tzvi* 18, and Jakob J. Petuchowski, *The Theology of Haham David Nieto*, pp. 15-16.

consciousness yearns to express, as nothing less than the long-awaited triumph of the truth of Judaism? This is the truth with which, thousands of years ago, Judaism first appeared in the midst of a chaotic multitude of gods, proclaiming that there is only one, sole God in heaven and on earth, and that all the phenomena of the universe are founded upon His Law. This idea, the concept of the Unity of God, is the truth for which Judaism has endured a course of martyrdom without parallel in world history.

"The Educational Value of Judaism," in *Collected Writings*, vol. VII, p. 258

Chapter Two

The New Teleology

The Order of the Universe

The religious foundations of science have long been overlooked. Most scientists are caught up in the pursuit of discovering more and more about how the universe works. Yet as science becomes more and more advanced, and more and more rational laws are discovered which explain the mechanics of the universe, some people are beginning to ask why this should be so.

> You find it surprising that I think of the comprehensibility of the world to the degree that we may speak of such comprehensibility as a miracle or eternal mystery. But surely, *a priori*, one should expect the world to be chaotic, and not to be grasped by thought in any way... Even if the axioms of the theory are posited by a human being, the success of such a procedure supposes in the objective world a high degree of order, which we are in no way entitled to expect *a priori*. Therein lies the 'miracle' which becomes more and more evident as our knowledge develops. And here is the weak point of positivists and professional atheists, who feel happy because they think that they have pre-empted not only the world of the divine but also of the miraculous.
>
> Albert Einstein, *Lettres a Maurice Solovine*, 102

We take order for granted. We have been brought up with concepts of laws of nature. To us, it is obvious that the universe should make sense.

But Einstein considered it "miraculous" that the universe evinces order. Nor was he alone in thinking this. In the words of physicist Paul Davies:

> The success of the scientific enterprise can often blind us to the astonishing fact that science works. Although most people take it for granted, it is both incredibly fortunate and incredibly mysterious that we are able to fathom the workings of nature by use of the scientific method.
>
> Paul Davies, *The Mind of God*, p. 148

Nobel Prize-winning physicist Eugene Wigner (1902-1995) made the same point:

> It is, as Schrödinger has remarked, a miracle that in spite of the baffling complexity of the world, certain regularities in the events could be discovered... It is not at all natural that "laws of nature" exist, much less that man is able to discover them.
>
> Eugene Wigner, "The Unreasonable Effectiveness of Mathematics in the Natural Sciences," p. 225, 227

The eminent mathematician Richard Wesley Hamming (1916-1998) repeated this in a paper with a similar title:

> Mathematicians working in the foundations of mathematics are concerned mainly with the self-consistency and limitations of the system. They seem not to concern themselves with why the world apparently admits of a logical explanation... when all my explanations are over, the residue is still so large as to leave the question essentially unanswered... I am forced to conclude both that mathematics is unreasonably effective and that all of the explanations I have given when added together simply are not enough to explain what I set out to account for... The logical side of the nature of the universe requires further exploration.
>
> R. W. Hamming, "The Unreasonable Effectiveness of Mathematics"

This point cannot be emphasized enough. As we shall learn, the highest levels of recognition of God are reached through grasping that the workings of natural law are no less miraculous than the negations of these laws that are known as miracles.

We also find that the ordered structure of the universe is not expressed in an unusual or esoteric language. It is expressed in terms of the most simple and logical language of all: mathematics. This was noted by Pythagoras and Galileo, and the significance of it has recently come to light:

> ...the enormous usefulness of mathematics in the natural sciences is something bordering on the mysterious and... there is no rational explanation for it... it is difficult to avoid the impression that a miracle confronts us here... The miracle of the appropriateness of the language of mathematics for the formulation of the laws of physics is a wonderful gift which we neither understand nor deserve.
>
> Wigner, ibid., pp. 223, 229, 237

Objective Order

A counter-claim to all this has been raised, however. Some (called formalists or inventionists) claim that there is no objective reality to mathematics. Rather, mathematics is a purely human invention used as a tool to describe the universe—specifically, those aspects of the universe that can be described in terms of mathematics. Exactly why the human brain itself should be mathematically attuned is considered to be an evolutionary quirk that is not yet understood. According to this, there is no fundamental order to the universe, but rather man only notices the aspects upon which he can impose his mental picture of order.

Yet such a view is greatly flawed. Mathematical formulae are not invented but discovered. Platonism, as this is called, understands that mathematics has an objective reality.

> The notion of mathematical truth goes beyond the whole concept of formalism. There is something absolute and "God-given" about mathematical truth.
>
> Roger Penrose, *The Emperor's New Mind*, p. 112

Aside from the fallacy of the formalist view, it is doubtful that any serious scientist subscribes to it deep down anyway. As the prominent mathematician Reuben Hersh points out, it is a weak attempt to avoid the philosophical implications of there being an orderly nature to the universe:

Most writers on the subject seem to agree that the typical working mathematician is a Platonist on weekdays and a formalist on Sundays. That is, when he is doing mathematics, he is convinced that he is dealing with an objective reality whose properties he is attempting to determine. But then, when challenged to give a philosophical account of this reality, he finds it easiest to pretend that he does not believe in it after all... At present we merely record this as a generally accepted fact about the mathematical world today: Most mathematicians live with two contradictory views on the nature and meaning of their work.

Reuben Hersh, "Some Proposals for Reviving the Philosophy of Mathematics," *Advances in Mathematics*, p. 31

And from French mathematician Jean-Alexandre-Eugène Dieudonné:

On foundations we believe in the reality of mathematics, but of course when philosophers attack us with their paradoxes we rush to hide behind formalism and say, "Mathematics is just a combination of meaningless symbols..." Finally we are left in peace to go back to our mathematics and do it as we have always done, with the feeling each mathematician has that he is working with something real.

J. Dieudonné, "Modern axiomatic methods and the foundations of mathematics," *Great Currents of Mathematical Thought*, Vol. II pp. 251

The rational order of the universe is not a fictitious invention of human beings. It is an objective reality, as astonishing as that may be.

...It is important to point out that the mathematical formulation of the physicist's often crude experience leads in an uncanny number of cases to an amazingly accurate description of a large class of phenomena. This shows that the mathematical language has more to commend it than being the only language which we can speak; it shows that it is, in a very real sense, the correct language.

Eugene Wigner, "The Unreasonable Effectiveness of Mathematics in the Natural Sciences," p. 230

The Beautiful Universe

A further remarkable aspect of scientific discovery is that scientific laws are not only rational; they are beautiful. Beauty in science is often considered a more important factor than experimental accuracy.

> It is more important to have beauty in one's equations than to have them fit experiment... because the discrepancy may be due to minor features that are not properly taken into account and that will get cleared up with further developments of the theory... It seems that if one is working from the point of view of getting beauty in one's equations, and if one has really a sound insight, one is on a sure line of progress.
>
> Paul Dirac, "The Evolution of the Physicist's Picture of Nature," *Scientific American,* May 1963

This might sound bizarre, but it is not mere wishful thinking or the over-emotional characterization of a few people. It is a principle that has actually proven its own validity.

> All great scientists are inspired by the subtlety and beauty of the natural world that they are seeking to understand... In constructing their theories, physicists are frequently guided by arcane concepts of elegance in the belief that the universe is intrinsically beautiful. Time and again this artistic taste has proved a fruitful guiding principle and led directly to new discoveries, even when it at first sight appears to contradict the observational facts.
>
> Paul Davies, *God and the New Physics*, p. 220

But what is this beauty? Some describe it in terms of harmony or symmetry, but both relate to the other term used: simplicity.

> The beauty in the laws of physics is the fantastic simplicity that they have... What is the ultimate mathematical machinery behind it all? That's surely the most beautiful of all.
>
> J. A. Wheeler, *A Question of Physics: Conversations in Physics and Biology* p. 60

The belief that "the universe is intrinsically beautiful" has come about due to the discovery that so much of it clearly *is*, in terms of its reflecting simple principles. This is strongly connected to the search for a grand unifying theory, also based on the understanding that there is a fundamental unity and simplicity to the universe. That all scientists perceive such things as beautiful is interesting; it indicates that even those who do not acknowledge the theological implications of unity and simplicity are still emotionally in tune with it.

Perhaps the best example of how simplicity is a guiding force in science is with Occam's razor, the principle that if two theories exist to explain something, the simpler one is more likely to be correct and is the one that should be utilized. Although this has been empirically demonstrated, it is difficult to justify on philosophical grounds. Unless, of course, one believes that the universe was created by a Creator Who is simple—in that He possesses absolute unity and no disparate conflicting elements—and Who would then not unfold His creation of the universe into anything more complex than necessary.

The Comprehensibility of the Universe

> There is one qualitative aspect of reality that sticks out from all others in both profundity and mystery. It is the consistent success of mathematics as a description of the workings of reality and the ability of the human mind to discover and invent mathematical truths.
>
> John Barrow, *Theories of Everything*, p. 173

Even more astonishing than the rational order and mathematical basis of the universe is that it is an order which man is able to grasp with his two and a half pounds of brain cells. These two points are sometimes grouped together, but the latter is not at all obvious from the former.

That man can grasp the order of the universe itself contains two remarkable aspects. First, it means that man's thoughts and the universe's structure follow the same pattern. This is not at all to be expected, to put it mildly. Consider, for example, the way in which an artist's perception of a flower differs from a botanist's. And that is just within the class of human beings! Not only is there the wonder of the universe being based on order—it is order of the same type as man's thought patterns. In the words of one famous physicist:

> What has led me to science... is the not-at-all obvious fact that the laws of our thoughts coincide with the regularity of the flow of impressions which we receive from the external world, [and] that it is therefore possible for man to reach conclusions through pure speculation about these regularities.
>
> Max Planck, cited by Stanley L. Jaki,
> *The Road of Science and the Ways to God*

44

The second remarkable aspect of man's ability to grasp the order of the universe is that, even granted that the patterns of our minds and of the universe are the same, there is no reason to suppose that the former would be adequately intelligent to grasp the latter. A six-year-old might be mathematically attuned, but the gap between him and a mathematician would be so great that he would grasp nothing significant from him. And yet we are adequately intelligent to grasp the workings of the universe.

> It is enigma enough that the world is described by mathematics; but by *simple* mathematics, of the sort that a few years energetic study now produces familiarity with, this is a mystery within an enigma.
>
> John Barrow, *Theories of Everything*, p. 2

Man, with the use of his brain, has discovered the tools for unraveling many of the mysteries of the universe, and has been able to use them effectively.

> A study of mathematics and its contributions to the sciences exposes a deep question. Mathematics is man-made. The concepts, the broad ideas, the logical standards and methods of reasoning... were fashioned by human beings. Yet with the product of his fallible mind, man has surveyed spaces too vast for his imagination to encompass; he has predicted and shown how to control radio waves which none of our senses can perceive; and he has discovered particles too small to be seen with the most powerful microscope... Some explanation of this marvelous power is called for.
>
> Morris Kline, *Mathematics and the Physical World*, p. ix

The significance of this should not be overlooked. The universe is not only rational; it is rational *to man*. The secrets of the universe are open to us. There are those who would simply rate this as an extraordinary stroke of luck:

> How fortuitous that our minds (or at least the minds of some) should be poised to fathom the depth of Nature's secrets.
>
> John Barrow, *Theories of Everything*, p. 172

But others have found themselves thinking that it is almost as though the whole thing was carefully designed for man to be able to grasp with a reasonable degree of effort.

What is remarkable is that human beings are actually able to carry out this code-breaking operation, that the human mind has the necessary intellectual equipment for us to "unlock the secrets of nature" and make a passable attempt at completing nature's "cryptic crossword." It would be easy to imagine a world in which the regularities of nature were transparent and obvious to all at a glance. We can also imagine another world in which either there were no regularities, or the regularities were so well hidden, so subtle, that the cosmic code would require vastly more brainpower than humans possess. But instead we find a situation in which the difficulty of the cosmic code seems almost to be attuned to human capabilities. To be sure, we have a pretty tough struggle decoding nature, but so far we have had a good deal of success. The challenge is just hard enough to attract some of the best brains available, but not so hard as to defeat their combined efforts and deflect them onto easier tasks.

Paul Davies, The Mind of God, p. 148

The indication is that the universe was designed, with man as its purpose, and that one of his tasks is to attempt to understand the workings of the universe.

Where Does The Universe Come From?

Science aims to discover the mechanics of the universe. It finds the numerical constants of nature and the laws that govern phenomena. It produces theorems and equations. But it does not answer the question of "What makes it go?" Even the ultimate objective of science, the grand unified theory of everything, is incapable of doing this.

Even if there is only one possible unified theory, it is just a set of rules and equations. What is it that breathes fire into the equations and makes a universe for them to describe? The usual approach of science of constructing a mathematical model cannot answer the questions of why there should be a universe for the model to describe. Why does the universe go to all the bother of existing? Is the unified theory so compelling that it brings about its own existence? Or does it need a creator, and if so, does he have any other effect on the universe?

Stephen Hawking, A Brief History of Time, p. 192

One analogy given is of a kettle of water boiling on the stove. You might ask, "Why is the water boiling?" Someone might truthfully answer, "This water is boiling because the combustion of hydrocarbons has generated heat which has heated up the water until the vapor pressure is the same as the atmospheric pressure and so the kettle boils." That answer is correct. But the answer that is more useful is that the kettle is boiling because someone wants a cup of tea.

By the same token, describing *how* the universe works does not explain *why* there is a universe to begin with. This argument from causality has long been applied to the universe. But with the rise of modern science, we are now also in a position to apply it to science itself.

Where Do Scientific Laws Come From?

> The concept of law is so well established in science that until recently few scientists stopped to think about the nature and origin of these laws; they were happy to simply accept them as "given." Now that physicists and cosmologists have made rapid progress toward finding what they regard as the "ultimate" laws of the universe, many old questions have resurfaced. Why do the laws have the form they do? Might they have been otherwise? Where do these laws come from? Do they exist independently of the physical universe?
>
> Paul Davies, *The Mind of God*, p. 73

To some, the idea that "God makes the trees grow" has been rendered redundant by the idea that "biological processes, based on chemical and physical laws, make the trees grow." But the truth is that in formulating scientific explanations for things, we have not removed God from the picture; instead, we have discovered a new picture for Him to have drawn.

There is a story about a scientist (in some versions, the skeptical philosopher Bertrand Russell) giving a public lecture on astronomy. He described how the earth is an approximately spherical planet that orbits the sun, and how the sun in turn revolves around the center of an incredibly huge collection of stars called the galaxy, which in turn is one of countless galaxies in the universe. At the end of his speech, a little old lady stood up and said, "What you say is nonsense. The world is really a big flat plate resting on the back of a giant turtle." The scientist, smirking, replied, "And what is the turtle standing on?" Replied the old lady, "You think that you're very clever. But I have news for you: it's turtles all the way down!"

Most people believe that the chain of turtles cannot go on forever. Somewhere down the line there has to be a "superturtle," something that supports itself and has no prior cause. Some people think that an ultimate scientific theory is the superturtle—in the suggestion of Stephen Hawking, the unified theory might be "so compelling that it forces its own existence." But for those of us who do not subscribe to that curious philosophical idea, scientific laws are simply another turtle that needs to be dealt with. There must still be a superturtle. It is reasonable to conclude that there is an ultimate Creator.[1]

The discovery of scientific laws may have explained how the universe comes to have the form that it does. But it has not answered the question of "Where did the universe come from in the first place?" It has not even *replaced* the question with "Where did the scientific laws come from?" Rather, it has *created* the new question of "Where did the scientific laws come from?" It has enhanced the original question rather than resolve it.

> When the Darwinian hypothesis of natural selection was proposed, it provided a general and simple explanation for the contrivances of the natural world—the broken symmetries—but it had no consequences at all for the other form of the Design Argument based upon the laws of Nature themselves.
>
> John Barrow, *Theories of Everything*, p. 119

---

1 Some reject this approach because the next question is, "Who made God?" and the response that one can't ask such a question might as well be applied to the question of who made the universe. That is to say, if one is going to say that we can't ask who made God, then we might as well say that we can't ask who made the universe. This counterargument is, however, flawed. Somewhere down the line, it seems that there must be something that exists without a prior cause. Faced between attributing this quality to a physical universe or to a supernatural being, it is more reasonable to attribute it to a supernatural being. Another point to be made is that the fortuitous order of the universe must be taken into account; thus, even supposing it were valid to ask who made God, that would not be reason to conclude that "one might as well say" that this remarkable universe was not designed by God.

Lucky Laws

We have noted the wonder of the laws of the universe being structured and rational. But there is even more to wonder at. The laws of nature are not just any old laws—they are extraordinarily fortuitous ones. The universe does not just follow a rational system. It follows a very particular type of rational system, which is specifically good at producing matter, planets, and life.

That any physical matter exists at all rests on the fundamental nature of matter and energy. Things need not have been that way. There are stars and planets, for example. Life is inconceivable without the heat of the sun; yet the existence of that star is not to be taken for granted.

> It is particularly striking how processes that occur on a microscopic scale—say, in nuclear physics—seem to be fine-tuned to produce interesting and varied effects on a much larger scale—for example, in astrophysics. Thus we find that the force of gravity combined with the thermodynamical and mechanical properties of hydrogen gas are such as to create large numbers of balls of gas. These balls are large enough to trigger nuclear reactions, but not so large as to collapse rapidly into black holes. In this way, stable stars are born.
>
> Paul Davies, *The Mind of God*, p. 196

And then there is the biggest miracle of them all—life. There are so many ways in which things could have been different and there would have been no life.

> All the evidence suggests that this is not just any old universe, but one which is remarkably well adjusted to the existence of certain interesting and significant entities (e.g., stable stars)... The situation becomes even more intriguing when we take into account the existence of living organisms. The fact that biological systems have very special requirements, and that these requirements are, happily, met by nature, has been commented upon at least since the seventeenth century. It is only in the twentieth century, however, with the development of biochemistry, genetics, and molecular biology, that the full picture has emerged.
>
> Ibid., p. 198

We are not just lucky that the laws of nature and the structure of the universe exist in the form that they do; we are also fortunate that the very fundamental numerical constants of the universe have the precise values that they do.

> The numerical values that nature has assigned to the fundamental constants, such as the charge on the electron, the mass of the proton, and the Newtonian gravitational constant, may be mysterious, but they are crucially relevant to the structure of the universe that we perceive. As more and more physical systems, from nuclei to galaxies, have become better understood, scientists have begun to realize that many characteristics of these systems are remarkably sensitive to the precise values of the fundamental constants. Had nature opted for a slightly different set of numbers, the world would be a very different place. Probably we would not be here to see it.
>
> More intriguing still, certain structures, such as solar-type stars, depend for their characteristic features on wildly improbable numerical accidents that combine together fundamental constants from distinct branches of physics. And when one goes on to study cosmology—the overall structure and evolution of the universe—incredulity mounts. Recent discoveries about the primeval cosmos oblige us to accept that the expanding universe has been set up in its motion with a cooperation of astonishing precision.
>
> Paul Davies, *The Accidental Universe*, preface

Stephen Hawking, one of the world's leading physicists today, yet no believer in God, also concedes this point:

> The laws of science, as we know them at present, contain many fundamental numbers, like the size of the electric charge of the electron and the ratio of the masses of the proton and electron... The remarkable fact is that the values of these numbers seem to have been very finely adjusted to make possible the development of life... It seems clear that there are relatively few ranges of values for the numbers that would allow the development of any form of intelligent life.
>
> *A Brief History of Time*, p. 138-139

It is important to realize that many of these constants vary tremendously in order of magnitude. Within the four fundamental forces, for example, the nuclear force is greater than the gravitational force by a factor of

100,000,000,000,000,000,000,000,000,000,000,000,000,000. With such inconceivable disparities in the magnitude of the forces, the fact that a slight change in either would result in a chaotic universe is all the more staggering.

In recent years, an increasing amount of attention has been paid to these "fortuitous coincidences" that result in life. The full list is vast, far beyond the scope of this work. For example, the astronomer Fred Hoyle noticed that carbon, an essential ingredient of life, is formed by certain reactions in stars that can only be described as flukes. Further study revealed other lucky coincidences, and Hoyle eventually pointed out that the universe appears to be a "put-up job." More recently, Michael Denton has discussed many of these "coincidences" in his remarkable work *Nature's Destiny*. These include the fitness of light, water, the vital gases, the basic elements, and so on. We shall review a single example, that of light, by way of illustration.

Lucky Light

It is almost impossible to imagine complex life without the light and heat that we obtain from the sun. This is not merely due to the limitations of our own experiences. Scientists have determined that life simply cannot function without such things.

> It may form an interesting intellectual exercise to imagine ways in which life might arise and having arisen might maintain itself, on a dark planet; but I doubt very much that this has ever happened, or that it can happen.
>
> George Wald, "Life and Light," in *Scientific American* 201(4): 92-108

We are most familiar with radiant energy in its manifestations of light and heat, but the truth is that there are many types of radiant energy, including x-rays, microwaves, and gamma rays. All these types of electromagnetic radiation flow through space in the form of waves of energy, like the waves on the sea. The distance between the peak of one wave and the next is called the wavelength of the radiation. The difference in wavelengths between different types of radiation is, however, vastly bigger than the difference in size between different waves on the sea. The wavelength of the longest type of electromagnetic radiation that we have studied is an astonishing 10,000,000,000,000,000,000,000,000 times longer than the shortest!

Animal life requires certain types of electromagnetic radiation for at least five different reasons. The chemical reactions upon which life is based can only function if they are fuelled by electromagnetic radiation measuring between 0.32 and 0.80 microns.[1] Second, a certain amount of heat is required, which is primarily provided by infrared radiation. Third, vision requires electromagnetic radiation of a certain level that can be detected without being destructive, which is found in the region of the electromagnetic spectrum that we therefore call the visible region. Fourth, color vision is dependent upon the range of radiation levels in this region corresponding to those required for photochemical detection by biological systems. Fifth, maximizing the optical resolution within the constraints of the highly complex structure of an eye, together with the limitations of feasible size, requires radiation with a wavelength of about 0.5 microns.

Remarkably, a single small range of electromagnetic radiation—that between 0.3 microns and 1.5 microns—meets all these five delicate requirements. Even more incredibly, the majority of the radiation emitted by the sun falls within this range. Still more fortuitously, the sun does not emit any of the numerous utterly lethal types of radiation, such as gamma rays. This coincidence has been described by Ian Campbell in *Energy and the Atmosphere* as "staggering"—with considerable understatement. The delicate band of radiation that the sun emits, so extraordinarily fortuitous for the requirements of life, represents a subtle portion of one part in 10,000,000,000,000,000,000,000,000. To put it another way, imagine a stack of cards stretching halfway across the universe. Both the region of radiation that we require, and the region of radiation that the sun emits, is represented by the thickness of a single card.

The Response from Infinities

With such overwhelming grounds for concluding that the laws and constants of the universe were intelligently designed, one may wonder how

---

1   Ian Campbell, *Energy and the Atmosphere* (London: Wiley), pp. 1-2.

atheists respond to such things. A common response is that the universe is not extraordinary because there may be an infinite (or very large) number of universes.[1] Thus, some of them are bound to be fortuitously arranged, and it is even likely that there are other universes which are more amazing than ours. And it is only in one of the fortuitously arranged universes, such as ours, that people could exist in the first place to wonder why it is so fortuitously arranged.[2]

The confusion here is over what precisely is amazing about the universe, and also over what the infinite-universes theory means. The latter term is used in two distinct ways. Some use it to refer to an infinite number of universes which all have the same basic laws as ours, while others use it to refer to an infinite number of universes (either in space or time) with an infinite number of systems of law (or lack of laws).

If one is referring to an infinite number of universes (or regions of this universe) which all have the same basic laws as ours, then one has to understand what is being proposed to be amazing about the universe. It is true that such fortuitous coincidences as the size of the earth and the particular composition of its atmosphere would not be found in another universe. However, the main thrust of the argument from design is not from the particular circumstances, but rather from the very basic laws of science. The complexity, the order, the symmetry, and the beauty that we have described, would be present in all of these proposed universes. It is these that require a designer.

The other proposal is that there are an infinite number of universes with an infinite number of systems of law. This would certainly mean that there must be some universes with fortuitous systems of law such as our own, and that there is nothing remarkable in that. However, the

---

1 String theory seems to predict a huge, but finite, number of universes. As we shall see, however, such theories are highly speculative.

2 A common term used in these discussions is "the Anthropic principle"; sometimes a distinction is drawn between a "weak" version of this principle and a "strong" version. However, different works use the term in different ways; so much so that some use it to describe the argument for a Creator, while others use it to describe the argument against. I am therefore avoiding using this confusing term.

evidence for such a proposition (aside from the extraordinary nature of our universe) is precisely nil.

Even a mainstream publication such as the prestigious journal *Nature* acknowledges that that there are very real grounds for seeing the universe as being designed for its purpose:

> For two decades now, theorists in the think-big field of cosmology have been stymied by a mathematical quirk in their equations. If the number controlling the growth of the universe since the Big Bang is just slightly too high, the Universe expands so rapidly that protons and neutrons never come close enough to bond into atoms. If it is just ever-so-slightly too small, it never expands enough, and everything remains too hot for even a single nucleus to form. Similar problems afflict the observed masses of elementary particles and the strengths of fundamental forces. In other words, if you believe the equations of the world's leading cosmologists, the probability that the Universe would turn out this way by chance are infinitesimal—one in a very large number.
>
> Geoff Brumfiel, "Outrageous Fortune," *Nature* vol. 539, 5th January 2006

The article continues to describe how, in an effort to address this wonder and avoid its disturbing religious implications, scientists developed the idea that there are many millions of universes, in which case "it becomes more reasonable to assume that several would turn out like ours." But the article then admits that this is problematic in that there is absolutely no evidence for it:

> Because our Universe is, almost by definition, everything we can observe, there are no apparent measurements that would confirm whether we exist within a cosmic landscape of multiple universes, or if ours is the only one.
>
> Ibid.

Furthermore, on philosophical grounds, it seems more reasonable to propose that this universe was designed by a Creator than to propose that there are an infinite number of possible universes with an infinite number of possible scientific laws. As Paul Davies notes:

> ...The ordered regions in the infinite or oscillating model universes are separated by such huge expanses of space or time that no observer can ever verify or refute empirically the existence of many universes. It is

hard to see how such a purely theoretical construct can ever be used as an *explanation*, in the scientific sense, of a feature of nature. Of course, one might find it easier to believe in an infinite array of universes than in an infinite Deity, but such a belief must rest on faith rather than observation.

Paul Davies, *The Mind of God*, pp. 173-174.

And even Stephen Hawking, hardly a theist, concedes that the multiple-universe theory does not concur with the principles of science:

...In what sense can all these universes be said to exist? If they are really separate from each other, what happens in another universe can have no observable consequences in our own universe. We should therefore use the principle of economy and cut them out of the theory.

Stephen Hawking, *A Brief History of Time*, p. 139

Thus, mainstream science concedes that the universe is suspiciously fortuitous and that there is no independent evidence for multiple universes that would account for this.

There are still those who would argue with the conclusion that there must have been a designer, even in the absence of invoking multiple universes. Their argument is that it is only possible to wonder at life in the sort of universe where life arises. In all theoretically possible versions of the universe, there is a small quantity in which intelligent life will arise, and in those universes, the life-forms will marvel at the slim odds of their universe existing, and our universe is one of those possibilities. In other words, after the event, it is pointless discussing it having had a low probability, because it actually happened.

This argument is often put forward; the flaw involved depends on the understanding of the person using it. Some, who compare it to the odds of someone winning a lottery—the odds of any given person winning it are miniscule, but of course *someone* had to win it—are not acknowledging that the universe is qualitatively unique, in that it is rational and capable of producing galaxies, life and intelligence. It is therefore not to be compared to one person winning a lottery, the chances of which are 100% no matter how big the lottery, but rather to the same person winning thousands of lotteries, which is an extraordinarily unlikely event.

55

Others are aware of this point, but are simply claiming that after an event, it is pointless discussing its probability, because the fact is that it happened (and only in such a situation do people exist to think about it). Yet nobody works that way in other spheres of life. If there were to exist a person who wins every single lottery, you would not simply say that although such a thing is *a priori* unlikely, once it has already happened there is no point in discussing its probability—you would expect to see a police investigation! Likewise, the extreme fortuitousness of the laws of the universe leads to the obvious inference that the universe is, in the words of Sir Fred Hoyle, "a put-up job."

The New Teleology

We have explored the wonder of the system of natural law that governs the universe. The appreciation of this miracle becomes ever greater with the advancement of science.

> …The arguments from design and rationality have not disappeared in these last decades of the twentieth century. For whatever cause, valid or not, we still find inescapable the impression of a Mind behind the laws of this universe or inherent in them.

> Kitty Ferguson, *The Fire in the Equations*, p. 274

At the beginning of chapter one, we noticed that the traditional way of enhancing faith through contemplation of the natural world seems to have lost much of its power. Leaps and bounds in various fields of science have provided excellent explanations of how the universe came to exhibit the stunning beauty and complexity that it possesses. The discovery of the laws of nature has shown how the physical world came to be the way it is. It is no longer seen as something that calls for a designer.

But the evidence for design in its new manifestation, that of the design in the *laws* of nature, grows ever stronger. The more that science succeeds in discovering the laws of nature, the more their existence and design points to a Creator. As Rabbi Samson Raphael Hirsch puts it, it is what we expected all along:

> Indeed, each discovery in the natural sciences only confirms the fundamental truth first set forth by Judaism: There can be no thought

without a thinker, no order without a regulator, no law without a lawgiver, no culture without a creative spirit, no world without God and no man without the gift of free-willed morality.

Rabbi Samson Raphael Hirsch, "The Educational Value of Judaism, " in *Collected Writings*, vol. VII, p. 261

Ever increasingly, scientists are discovering evidence of the remarkable lawfulness of the universe, and the simplicity and elegance of these laws. Small wonder that we find the following view:

It might seem bizarre, but in my opinion science offers a surer path to God than religion.

Paul Davies, *God and the New Physics*, p. ix

Chapter Three

Miracles and Nature

The Ultimate Miracle

We are used to the idea that a scientific explanation is in conflict with divine explanation. But the truth is that, properly understood, science is itself a form of divine explanation.

> There is no blade of grass in this world below that does not have someone appointed over it in the world above, who smites it and tells it, "Grow!"
>
> *Midrash Bereishis Rabbah* 10:6

The laws of science are as much a creation of God as is the universe itself. Natural law is something that need not be the way it is, and could have been entirely different. Yet it does exist, and it exists in a particular form— a form that is incredibly fortuitous and beautiful, no less. The realization of this is the appreciation that natural law is no less a manifestation of God's will than is the suspension of natural law by way of miracles.

> One Shabbos eve, Rabbi Chanina saw that his daughter was upset. He asked, "My daughter, why are you sad?" She replied, "I confused a vessel of vinegar for a vessel of oil when kindling a light for Shabbos." He replied, "My daughter, why does it bother you? The One Who said that oil should burn can also say that vinegar should burn!" It was related that it burned all the way through the day until a light was taken from it for *Havdalah*.
>
> Talmud, *Ta'anis* 25a

Oil burns because the breakage of the carbon-hydrogen bond in one molecule causes both atoms to oxidize and produces heat that causes identical reactions in other molecules. But who said that the molecules should have these properties? Or that there should be such a thing as these particular molecules, or indeed any molecules at all? How did it happen that all these things in particular should exist such that they culminate in the remarkable phenomenon of fire? The One who determined that, can just as easily determine that vinegar should burn.

Everyday Miracles

The episode of the burning vinegar gives us an insight into another matter concerning kindling lights. The miracle of Chanukah was that a vial of oil, containing only enough oil for one night, burned for eight nights. In acknowledgment of this, we celebrate the festival of Chanukah for eight nights. The famous question on this is that there was surely only a seven-day miracle, since there was already enough oil to burn for one night. Why do we celebrate eight nights of Chanukah?

Over a hundred answers have been proposed to this question. But one simple answer is that when a miracle takes place, and oil burns for an additional seven nights, we realize that its burning on the first night is no less miraculous. A lesson of the Chanukah miracle is that natural law can be broken and therefore is not to be taken for granted in the first place. It teaches us that all nature is a miracle.

Having said all this, why are there miracles? In the case of Rabbi Chanina's daughter, there was a need for the miracle, as otherwise her kindling of lights for Shabbos would have been in vain. But there are many cases where God would have had ways of arranging matters without recourse to miracles. If God's greatness is revealed in natural law, why does He sometimes break it? The answer is implicitly contained in the story of the Chanukah miracle. Sometimes it is necessary to break the laws in order to show who made them in the first place.

Rabbi Yerucham Levovitz (1874-1936) of the Mirrer Yeshivah, in a series of profound lectures on the importance of natural law, explains that the greatest supernatural events of Jewish history were only a means to enable the appreciation of nature itself:

The purpose of the miracles of the Exodus, which were above the natural order of things, was so that the Jewish People should reach the spiritual level of the natural order of things. Namely, that in fulfilling and working according to the natural order of things, their faith in God should be clear and alive, and that they should be able to point with their finger and say, "This is my God" (as they did at the Splitting of the Red Sea) at the level of the natural order of things.

Rabbi Yerucham Levovitz

Rabbi Yerucham Levovitz, *Da'as Chochmah u'Mussar* 1:15[1]

Rabbi Joseph B. Soloveitchik (1903-1993), one of the seminal Torah personalities of the twentieth century, expresses this beautifully:

> The supernatural miracle is not very welcome in the covenant society. We prefer the regular flow of life... Yet the central theme of the Exodus tale is the miracle... We see that the Torah incessantly stresses the miraculous when reflecting on or recalling the redemption from Egypt... When the antithesis reached its climax and the historicity of the covenant came to a critical point, God wanted to demonstrate the unalterable necessity inherent in the charismatic historical occurrence. It cannot and will not be curtailed by any natural forces. If the need arises, the covenant will become a factum, even if other factors will have to be altered because of that. Miracle expresses the idea that whenever the covenant comes to a crisis in its eternal struggle with the forces of indifference, the historical motives will overcome the opposition of a cruel reality.

Rabbi Joseph B. Soloveitchik,
The Emergence of Ethical Man, pp. 188-189

---

1 See too Rabbeinu Bachya, Commentary to Numbers 33:1, introduction. This explanation stands in sharp contrast with Rabbi Chaim Friedlander, *Sifsei Chaim, Emunah VeHashgachah* vol. I p. 130.

The Downside of Miracles

The conclusion from all this is that since miracles are primarily tools that serve only to enable one to attain the higher level of perceiving God within nature, they are not necessarily seen in such a positive light. They are often no more than crutches which ought not be needed:

Rabbi Joseph B. Soloveitchik

> There was a case of a person whose wife died, leaving him a baby that required nursing, but he could not afford a nursemaid. A miracle happened for him, and he developed breasts like those of a woman and nursed his son.
>
> Rav Yosef said, "Come and see how great this man is, that such a miracle was performed for him!"
>
> Abaye said to him, "On the contrary! How degraded is this man, that the order of Creation was changed for him!"
>
> Talmud, *Shabbos* 53b

We can certainly understand Rav Yosef's verdict. A miracle such as this surely testifies that the person was on an extremely high spiritual level. Why did Abaye see it otherwise?

The answer is that God performed a miracle because the man was brokenhearted after his wife's death and needed to have his faith restored. Had he been on a greater spiritual level, he would have had no need of such proofs, and God would have found natural means for the child to be nursed.[1] The father would have appreciated these natural means as no less an example of God's kindness than a miracle.[2]

---

1 Rav Dessler, as cited by *Sifsei Chaim, Emunah VeHashgachah* 1, p.129.

2 *Michtav Me-Eliyahu*, vol. 1, p. 201.

In a similar vein, Ralbag (Gersonides) explains that the problem of miracles is that they indicate that God's system of natural laws is not good enough to accomplish what He wants to happen:

> When God wishes to perform miracles, He does so via causes that are the most appropriate according to natural laws.... This is because the natural order of existence was set by God in the most perfect way possible, and when necessity, due to providence, requires a change from this order, it is appropriate that God should divert from this as little as possible. Therefore God does not perform these miracles except via causes that divert as little possble from nature.

Ralbag, Commentary to Genesis, 6-9, HaTo'eles HaShevi'i

In an extremely important passage, Rambam explains that, due to this, one should try wherever possible to understand the events of the Torah in a non-miraculous manner:

> ...Our efforts, and the efforts of select individuals, are in contrast to the efforts of the masses. For with the masses who are people of the Torah, that which is beloved to them and tasty to their folly is that they should place Torah and rational thinking as two opposite extremes, and will derive everything impossible as distinct from that which is reasonable, and they say that it is a miracle, and they flee from something being in accordance with natural law, whether with something recounted from past events, with something that is in the present, or with something which is said to happen in the future. But we shall endeavor to integrate the Torah with rational thought, leading events according to the natural order wherever possible; only with something that is clarified to be a miracle and cannot be otherwise explained at all will we say that it is a miracle.

Rambam, Treatise Concerning the Resurrection of the Dead

Rambam and Ralbag are known for being extreme rationalists and were criticized by some for this. Yet the same view is also found in the writings of the fourteenth century kabbalist Rabbeinu Bachya ben Asher:

> God does not force nature not to pursue its assigned tasks unless there is an overwhelming and urgent need for this. The reason that He does not destroy the system is simply that He Himself created it. Why should God uproot His own handiwork?

Rabbeinu Bachya, commentary to Exodus 17:13

We see that there is considerable basis for seeing miraculous events as less prestigious displays of God's power than nature itself. There were other Torah authorities who were more ready to explain events in a miraculous manner, but even these authorities were often less inclined to the miraculous than is commonly assumed.[1] Natural law is itself one of the most miraculous of God's creations.

The Mechanics of Miracles

Now that we understand the very negative aspect of miracles, it should come as no surprise to learn that there is a strong tendency in Jewish thought to negate a supernatural element even in the most famous miracles.

> We already mentioned that our Sages did not believe that God miraculously alters nature on a regular basis. However at the beginning of Creation He created nature and the laws that it would follow. This included the rare occasion when there would be a miraculous divergence from natural events as well as the typical conduct of nature. Thus miracle was built into nature when it was created.... In fact all miracles are built into nature.
>
> Rambam, Commentary to the Mishnah, *Avos* 5:6[2]

Rambam believed that all miracles were not supernatural in the conventional sense of the term, but rather, no matter how extreme their nature, were "wired into" nature from Creation. However we

---

1 Ramban is the authority most commonly cited as supporting the interpretation of events as being miraculous. However, certain key statements of Ramban shed light on his general view and indicate that he only saw miracles as occurring in very narrowly defined circumstances. See Rabbi David Berger, "Miracles and the Natural Order in Nahmanides."

2 See too Rambam, *Shemona Perakim* 8: "God's will is that from the six days of Creation everything should function solely on the basis of natural law. This is stated in Ecclesiastes (1:9): 'What was, will be, and what has happened, will happen, and there is nothing new under the sun.' Because of this our Sages had to state that the miracles that are against nature—those that have happened as well as those that will happen—all of them were built into Creation. Thus the 'violations' of nature occur when they were programmed from the time of Creation. However when this miraculous 'violation' of nature occurs it is erroneously perceived as something new."

must remember that this belief was enabled by his being influenced by the Aristotelian worldview in general, whereby nature and the universe operates via "intellects." A modern scientific understanding of the universe would not seem to allow for such possibilities. Nevertheless, it seems clear that even were Rambam to be aware of modern science, he would still—perhaps all the more so—prefer to explain miracles as taking place within natural law as much as possible.[1]

Rambam, of course, was a strong rationalist. But even authorities less committed to rationalism stated that God works through nature as much as possible, and this is the case even where God is performing a miracle. After all, this is virtually explicit in the Torah itself, regarding one of the greatest miracles of all—the splitting of the Red Sea:

> And Moses stretched out his hand over the sea; and God caused the sea to go back by a strong east wind all that night, and made the sea into dry land, and the waters were divided.
>
> Exodus 14:21

The sea did not split with no discernible cause. Rather, there was a strong wind that blew all night, pushing the waters aside.

> The Holy One acted in accordance with the way of the world (*derech eretz*), that the wind dries out and parches the rivers.
>
> Rashbam, Commentary to Exodus 14:21

The subsequent verse states that the waters of the Red Sea were like walls. Even a wind probably cannot account for this, if it is to be taken literally. But the truth is that this does not actually break the laws of nature either. There's nothing which says that the violently vibrating molecules of the water should not leap to that position. Of course, the odds against it

---

1 Rabbeinu Bachya has a slight variation on this: "We can conclude from these *midrashim* that everything that was, is and will be has already been decreed from the first six days of Creation since there is nothing truly new since then. Thus everything that comes into existence is only a revealing of that which was created in the beginning. This is true also of the miracles. If you insist that G-d did not actually create them until they happened that would mean that something new was created, God forbid. In fact from Creation there has been no actual change in Nature because at the time of Creation it was implanted in Nature that it would happen according to God's wishes" (Commentary to *Avos* 5:8).

are extraordinarily great. But it does not violate a law of nature; it merely departs from the normal way of things.[1]

In this vein, Rabbi Joseph Soloveitchik notes that the Torah strongly downplays any supernatural aspect of miracles:

> What is a miracle in Judaism? The word "miracle" in Hebrew does not possess the connotation of the supernatural. It has never been placed on a transcendental level. "Miracle" (*pele, nes*) describes only an outstanding event which causes amazement. A turning point in history is always a miracle, for it commands attention as an event which intervened fatefully in the formation of that group or that individual.
>
> Rabbi Joseph B. Soloveitchik, *The Emergence of Ethical Man*, p. 187

Rabbi Soloveitchik proceeds to translate this in terms of the events of the Exodus:

> As we read the story of the exodus from Egypt, we are impressed by the distinct tendency of the Bible to relate the events in natural terms. The frogs came out of the river when the Nile rose, the wind brought the locusts and split the sea. All archaeologists agree that the plagues as depicted by the Bible are very closely related to the geographical and climatic conditions that prevail in Egypt. Behind the passages in the Bible we may discern a distinct intention to describe the plagues as naturally as possible. The Bible never emphasizes the unnaturalness of the events; only its intensity and force are emphasized. The reason for that is obvious. A philosophy which considers the world-drama as a fixed, mechanical process governed by an unintelligent, indifferent principle, may regard the miracle as a supernatural transcendental phenomenon which does not fit into the causalistic, meaningless monotony. Israel, however, who looked upon the universal occurrence as the continuous realization of a divine ethical will embedded into dead and live matter, could never classify the miracle as something unique and incomprehensible. Both natural monotony and the surprising element in nature express God's word. Both are regular, lawful phenomena; both can be traced to an identical source. In the famous Psalm 104, *Barkhi nafshi* ("My soul will bless"), the psalmist describes the most elementary natural phenomena like the propagation of light

---

1 Rabbi Aryeh Kaplan, *Faces and Facets*, p. 72-79.

in terms of wonder and astonishment—no different from Moses' Song of the Sea. The whole cosmos unfolds itself as a miraculous revelation of God. The demarcation line between revelation and nature is almost non-existent!

Ibid, pp. 187-188

Rabbi Soloveitchik concludes that the wonder of miracle is not in it departing from the natural order, but in it matching the natural order to the historical context:

In what, then, does the uniqueness of the miracle assert itself? In the correspondence of the natural and historical orders. The miracle does not destroy the objective scientific nexus in itself, it only combines natural dynamics and historical purposefulness. Had the plague of the firstborn, for instance, occurred a year before or after the exodus, it would not have been termed "with a strong hand" (*be-yad hazakah*). Why? God would have been instrumental in a natural children's plague. Yet God acts just as the world rule. On the night of Passover He appeared as the God of the cosmos acting along historical patterns. The intervention of nature in the historical process is a miracle. Whether God planned that history adjust itself to natural catastrophes or, vice versa, He commands nature to cooperate with the historical forces, is irrelevant. Miracle is simply a natural event which causes a historical metamorphosis. Whenever history is transfigured under the impact of cosmic dynamics, we encounter a miracle.

Ibid., p. 188

Even according to those authorities who consider that miracles do indeed fall within the domain of the supernatural, the miracles must themselves follow a certain order, both in terms of their occurrence and their execution:

Miracles also have an order and cannot be termed a perversion of existence... from the very beginning God designed the future order of miracles just as He designed the order of nature. The fundamental character of His design, however, is that natural order is not absolute, but rather leaves room for miracles which are a non-natural order, and eventually these miracles will occur. Just as nature is created with God's Name, so too by His Name He laid down an order in creation providing the ability for nature to change and make room for miracles. Therefore, we see that the occurrence of miracles is certainly no nullification of His order. Once more, we wish to stress that the miracles also follow His design and are not a change in the overall system; they possess a definite structure of their own, laid down since the beginning of creation, as does nature.

Maharal, Gevuros Hashem, second introduction

We see from this all the more strongly that order and structure are part of God's methods and indicative of His greatness. Laws—rational, structured laws—are the greatest expression of His wisdom. This is why the system of natural law is so important and is a superior order to the miraculous order.

Chapter Four

The Particulars of Providence

The Problem of Determinism

At this point in our discussion, there is an important matter that must be clarified. There was a good deal of legitimate opposition by the religious community to philosophers and scientists who theorized that the universe is entirely deterministic—that all events are scientifically explicable in terms of material causes. The philosophy of determinism, aside from its negative implications regarding free will, also negated the idea of God influencing the course of events. Some of those who saw God as working through natural processes, such as Deists, ended up with a picture of God as having designed the universe, but not subsequently being involved (except insofar as maintaining the universe's existence). God was seen as being like a craftsman who designs an intricate watch, winds it up, and then walks away.

Jewish philosophy regards it as fundamental that God utilizes Divine Providence to alter the events that happen in a person's daily life, in accordance with his good deeds or sins. Thus, whether or not a person recovers from a sickness is affected by his prayers, merits, and so on. The deterministic nature of the universe that science was discovering, however, indicated that the cause-and-effect system of natural law governs all events, which would mean that a recovery from sickness would be solely determined by the physical processes involved.

How, then, are we to reconcile our idea that God works through nature, with the concept of providence? (This is not merely of passing concern—we shall need to understand this issue later when discussing how God guides evolution.)

Limited Providence

Probably the simplest answer is that God sometimes simply overrides the laws of nature, tweaking things here and there in response to man's deeds. This would occur in as subtle a way as possible, so as to minimize the interference with nature, but at some level, it would still necessitate an override of natural law.[1]

This answer might seem to negate the significance that we have attributed to the laws of nature that God designed. After all, how sophisticated a system can it be, if God needs to constantly intervene? Furthermore, it is hard to imagine that "miniature miracles," whereby the laws of science are actually broken, are constantly taking place without ever having been detected.

However, this may not be anywhere near as great a difficulty as one might think—although the reason for this is one that will make some people uncomfortable. Despite the very common belief that "there's no such thing as coincidence (understood in its simplest sense)" and "it's all *bashert* (divinely ordained for one's own maximal growth)," such concepts are of relatively recent propagation and have only minor support in classical Jewish philosophy.

Amongst the Rishonim—the Torah scholars of the tenth to fifteenth centuries—we find prominently the view that Divine providence is of very limited application. Rambam's view, while subject to considerable dispute as to its true nature, certainly limits providence to only functioning with

---

1 Midrash *Koheles Rabbah* 3:17; Ralbag, Commentary to Genesis, 6-9, *HaToeles HaShevi'i*; *Sefer HaChinnuch* mitzvah 547; Ramchal, *Derech Hashem* 2:5:6; Malbim, Commentary to Genesis 2:1. See too the discussion of miracles.

people that maintain a certain intellectual relationship with God.[1] Ramban (Nachmanides), although popularly thought to maintain a view that miraculous providence is very widespread, is actually of a very different view. His opinion is that although providence does involve supernatural (albeit "hidden") intervention, it occurs only in very rare cases; for select righteous individuals and, under exceptional circumstances, for the Jewish nation in general. Most individual people's lives are run by natural law.[2] Rabbi Ovadiah Seforno explicitly states that the majority of the Jewish People are governed by natural law and do not enjoy specific divine providence.[3]

It was primarily due to the advent of Hassidism that an apparently different view developed, first propounded by Rabbi Yisrael Baal Shem Tov (1698-1760) and subsequently elaborated upon by the Habad movement.[4] This view stated that specific divine providence applies to all beings—even animals. It has been suggested that the propagation of this view may have been a reaction against the acceptance in the general culture of the deterministic scientific view.[5] But today it is probably due to the emotional comfort provided by universal providence ("there was a reason why I missed the train!") that it has become so widely accepted.[6]

However, it may be that there is no fundamentally significant difference between this view and the earlier view, but rather primarily a difference

---

1 *Guide For The Perplexed* 3:17-18,22-23,51. For extensive discussion, see Dov Schwartz, "The Debate over the Maimonidean Theory of Providence in Thirteenth-Century Jewish Philosophy."

2 See Ramban to Genesis 17:1, 46:15, Exodus 6:2, Leviticus 26:11, Job 36:7, and the important essay by Rabbi David Berger, "Miracles and the Natural Order in Nahmanides." A different view is found in Rabbeinu Bachya, in his introduction to Exodus 30:12. Rabbi Chaim Friedlander, in *Sifsei Chaim, Emunah VeHashgachah* vol. 1, interprets Ramban in line with the current mainstream outlook on divine providence, but his explanation appears somewhat forced.

3 Seforno, Commentary to Leviticus 13:47. See too *Sefer haIkkarim* 4:10 and Chafetz Chaim, in *Shem Olam, Nefutzas Yisrael* 8.

4 See too Rav Tzaddok HaCohen, *Sefer HaZichronos* 3, *Yichud Hashem*.

5 See Chofetz Chaim, *Shem Olam* 1:3 and 1:24.

6 In non-Hassidic circles, one can still find expression of the traditional view limiting providence to select individuals. See *Michtav Me-Eliyahu* vol. II p. 75.

in terminology. The limited providence discussed by Ramban and other Rishonim refers to an actual intervention in the natural order. The universal providence described in Hassidism refers to a deeper dimension in the system of nature itself.[1]

Predetermined Providence

One possible approach to reconciling providence with natural law is that God set up the natural order in such a way that it would "naturally" provide the correct responses. God set up the universe in the first place such that it would correspond to the choices that God knew man would make.

This concept is also an ideal way to resolve the conflict between one person's free will with another person's fate. If Frank, possessing free will, decides to kill Joe, what happened to Joe's destiny in life? One answer is that God, knowing in advance what choice Frank would make, arranged matters well in advance that he would target a person whose time was up anyway—Joe.

A potential difficulty with this approach is that it may be simply too far-fetched; but others will not see an omniscient God as being limited by this. It is certainly a possibility to be considered.

Quantum Providence

There is a radical proposal as to the mechanics of providence which hinges upon recent advances in science. It is suggested that, due to the quantum nature of matter, God can change the course of nature without actually breaking the laws of nature.[2] The astonishing discoveries of the

---

1 Cf. Rabbi Nachman of Breslov: "When a person performs good deeds, he is dealt with via providence. When he is not good… God leaves him to nature… In truth however we are not able to understand what is meant by nature and providence. This is because nature is actually also a manifestation of God's providence. It is impossible for a person to understand how two things are actually one, i.e. that nature is in truth God's providence" (*Likutei Mahran, mahadura basra* 17). *Shaar Ha-Yichud Ve-Ha-Emuna* by the *Ba'al HaTanya* explains Rabbi Yisrael Baal Shem Tov's radical beliefs to relate to sustaining every particle and force in nature at every moment, and not to causality.

2 Rabbi Aryeh Kaplan, *The Handbook of Jewish Thought* vol. II p. 286. For a very thorough discussion, see Robert John Russell (ed.), *Quantum Mechanics: Scientific Perspectives on Divine Action*.

twentieth century showed that even though the universe runs according to laws, this does not mean that it is deterministic.

> Among the many facets of the Western intellectual landscape inherited from the rise of modern science in the sixteenth and seventeenth centuries, the "received view" is of nature as a machine. According to classical physics, the universe is governed by a set of deterministic equations... In such a causally closed world, there would be little need or possibility for God to act in the special ways and on those particular occasions as the biblical witness had abundantly recounted—unless God intervened in natural processes.
>
> Now with the rise of quantum mechanics early in the twentieth century, a fundamental rethinking is taking place regarding our view of nature... if one interprets quantum mechanics philosophically as pointing to ontological indeterminism, then one can construct a robust bottom-up, noninterventionist, approach to objective, mediated, direct divine action. In this approach, God's indirect acts at the macroscopic level, understood as both general and special providence, arise in part form God's direct action at the quantum level... It does not reduce God to a natural cause; instead God's action is hidden from science.
>
> Robert Russell, *Quantum Mechanics:*
> *Scientific Perspectives on Divine Action* pp. vi, xxv

Advances in quantum physics revealed extraordinary facts, such as that light can act as either a wave or a particle, and that it is impossible to simultaneously know both the position of a particle and its momentum. The implications of this are bizarre. For example, a mirror reflects about ninety-five percent of the light hitting it, while the other five percent passes through it. This is easy to understand if we consider light to be a wave, but if, as certain experiments show, light is comprised of particles called photons, matters become peculiar. Five out of every hundred photons that hit the mirror will pass through it; but it is *impossible* to predict in advance what any given photon will do. One can construct machines based on quantum phenomena which perform actions that are inherently and absolutely unpredictable.

> Quantum reality is strange, troublesome, and downright illogical, but its unexpected discovery solves one of the key philosophical problems faced by any religious person: How could a world governed by precise

physical law escape a strictly deterministic future? …The indeterminate nature of quantum behavior means that the details of the future are not strictly determined by present reality. God's universe is not locked in to a determinate future, and neither are we.

Kenneth Miller, *Finding Darwin's God*, pp. 203-204

Chaotic Amplifications

It is not only on a quantum level that determinism is potentially undermined. The field of chaos mathematics revealed that the universe is structured in such a way that minute changes can have far reaching results. Some suggest that this is a way in which Divine Providence and free will can change the course of events without any large-scale intervention in nature.[1] When coupled with quantum phenomena, it might mean that this can be accomplished entirely within the boundaries of scientific law.

> A stochastic system is, roughly speaking, one which is subject to unpredictable and random fluctuations. In modern physics, stochasticity enters in a fundamental way in quantum mechanics. It is also inevitably present when we deal with open systems subject to chaotic external perturbations… For those, such as process theologians, who choose to see God's guiding hand rather than genuine spontaneity in the way the universe develops creatively, then stochasticity can be regarded as an efficient device through which divine intentions can be carried out.

> …We recognize patterns everywhere and codify them into laws that have real predictive power. But the universe is also far from being simple. It possesses a subtle kind of complexity that places it partway between simplicity on the one hand and randomness on the other… The order of the cosmos is more than mere regimented regularity, it is also organized complexity, and it is from the latter that the universe derives its openness and permits the existence of human beings with free will.

Paul Davies, *The Mind of God*, pp. 191, 192, 136, 139

---

1   See John Russell (Ed.), *Chaos and Complexity: Scientific Perspectives on Divine Action.*

The best example of this is with the weather. The weather, in particular the rain cycle, is perhaps the sphere of activity in which we most declare God's control. The Torah states that rainfall depends upon man's deeds; if they are good, then it will be bountiful, whereas if man sins, then the rain will be withheld. Early in the twentieth century, a challenge arose to this teaching. As computers became more advanced, they were employed for use with weather prediction. The great mathematician John Von Neumann predicted that it would soon be possible to construct a computer which could accurately forecast the weather. Most people accepted this. It seemed a reasonable idea; surely it was just a matter of programming in all the variables and their initial values. The rest would just be computation. Of course, there would be slight inaccuracies in recording the weather for the first setting, but these would be relatively insignificant.

This was proved spectacularly wrong. It was found that tiny variations would escalate to vast differences in just a few days. This is popularly known as "the butterfly effect," whereby the flapping of a butterfly's wings in China can have an escalating effect that results in a tornado in America. It is impossible, even at a theoretical level, to forecast the weather beyond a few days. God can control the weather in a spectacular way without requiring any large-scale intervention.

The Hidden Ways of God

The above discussions should not be taken as exhaustive explorations of what is an extremely complex topic,[1] but they do introduce possible different approaches to the matter. Yet all these ways of reconciling God's active involvement with the world with His system of natural laws can involve their own difficulties. It may be that in the future, improved understandings of physics will better reveal how God can interact with the world without breaking the laws of nature. But another alternative is that this may be something that can never be pinpointed by science. In the same way as the soul and free will are concepts that cannot be scientifically

---

1   A full discussion would have to include the concepts of *mazal* and free will as well as the distinction between general and individual providence and between direct and indirect causes of events.

ascertained to exist and are taken on faith, God's place in exercising His will in the world may be forever hidden from view.

> The honor of God is in the concealment of the matter, whereas the honor of kings is in the investigation of the matter.
>
> Proverbs 25:2

Chapter Five

The Importance of Natural Law

The Science of Creation

The Mishnah explains the significance of all the instances of "And God said, Let there be..." in Genesis:

> With ten utterances the world was created. What does this come to teach us—surely it could have been created with one utterance? Rather, it was to exact punishment from the wicked who destroy the world that was created with ten utterances, and to bestow goodly reward upon the righteous who sustain the world that was created with ten utterances.
>
> *Avos 5:1*

This explanation itself is difficult to understand. But Rabbi Moshe Chaim Luzzatto (1707-1746) explains that the concept of "ten utterances" refers to the world being created with a system of cause-and-effect, rather than with no discernible mechanism:

> It is undoubtedly true that The Holy One could have created His universe in an all-powerful way, in such a way that we could not have understood cause or effect in His deeds... But because the Higher Will desired that people should be able to understand some of His ways and actions—and indeed He wanted that people should engage in this and pursue it—therefore He chose the contrary, to act in the way of man; that is to say, in an intelligible and comprehensible fashion.
>
> *Da'as Tevunos 40*

Rabbi Chaim Friedlander (1923-1986) of the Ponovezh Yeshivah in Bnei Brak further elaborates upon this theme. Just as one better appreciates an innovative Torah insight if one understands the process that leads to the insight, so too one better appreciates God's role as Creator if one understands the creative process. Thus, there is a series of cause-and-effect—the laws of science—via which the natural world operates. However, this same system that leads some to better appreciate the Creator—the righteous people concerning whom the Mishnah stated that they benefit from these ten utterances—can lead other people in a different direction. If all they see is a general system of cause-and-effect, without ever tracing matters back to a First Cause, then the system has blinded them to the existence of a Creator. The atheist sees that everything follows a mechanistic system of cause-and-effect, and concludes that there is no God. The righteous person, on the other hand, traces back the system of cause-and-effect to the Prime Mover.[1]

Rabbi Friedlander's mentor at the Ponovezh Yeshivah, the influential Jewish thinker Rabbi Eliyahu Eliezer Dessler (1892-1953), translates this concept in terms of the development of the universe:

> Why was the world created in a way such that it appears as though it came about by way of evolution (seemingly referring to the general development of the universe rather than specifically biological evolution—N.S.)? However, this is the way of the revelation amidst the concealment. We see a long chain of cause and effect, which is the concealment. But it is up to us to mentally climb from the last to the first until we reach the First Cause, Blessed be His Name— and this is the revelation... The path of revelation is that we

Rabbi Eliyahu Dessler

---

1 *Sifsei Chayim, Moa'dim* vol. I pp. 421-422.

should choose to see how the entire chain of causes and effects unite at their root with the First Cause, Blessed be His Name, and the deeper that the concealment is, the greater that the eventual revelation, by way of our free will, will be.

Rabbi Eliyahu Dessler, *Michtav Me-Eliyahu*, vol. IV, p. 113

Mandrake Children

An example of the importance of working within nature is seen with the episode of Rachel and the mandrakes:

> In the days of the wheat-harvest, Reuben went and found mandrakes in the field. He brought them to Leah, his mother. Rachel said to Leah, "Please give me some of your son's mandrakes!"

Genesis 30:14

Why was Rachel so eager for these flowers? The fifteenth-century Italian commentator Rabbi Ovadiah Seforno states:

> These are a type of sweet-smelling herb which enable fertility.

Commentary ad loc.

Rachel had not yet been able to bear children to Jacob, and hoped that the mandrakes would help. But far from explaining matters, this only serves to complicate them further. After all, this isn't just an ordinary person that we are talking about, but Rachel, wife of Jacob, one of the matriarchs and a righteous person of the highest stature. Surely she was fully aware that it was God Who was withholding children from her rather than any physical problem! And it was surely just as clear that her salvation would be through prayer, not through fertility drugs!

Rabbi Ovadiah Seforno later adds:

> ...Since the intentions of the matriarchs appealed to God, in their efforts with bringing other wives and the mandrakes, their prayers were heard. For it is befitting for a righteous person to do all possible physical endeavor in order to attain his goal, and in combination with that, to pray that he will attain his goal...

Ibid. 30:16

So there clearly was an awareness that it would be God determining if she was to bear children. Why, then, the need for mandrakes at all? Why is it befitting to engage in physical endeavor, if it doesn't determine the outcome anyway?

The answer is as we have explained. Natural law is not to be seen as conflicting with God's authority. Just the opposite—it is a reflection of His authority and a manifestation of His wisdom. Working within the system of natural law, in combination with prayer, demonstrates that one acknowledges natural law to be God's law.

Levels of Awareness

Rabbi Dessler explains that there are different levels of appreciation of God's control of the world. The lowest level, on which many of us find ourselves, is that we profess to recognize the truth of it, but do not really do so at heart. The litmus test of this is whether we live our lives any differently. We might say, "God sustains us," but we wouldn't dream of actually entrusting Him to handle any of it. Because the person in this position does not really recognize God's control of the world, he will be treated strictly according to natural law, with no suspensions of it ever made for him. (It is in comparison to such a person that Rav Yosef praised the man who experienced the miracle of being able to nurse his child.)

A higher level is to recognize that God can do with nature as He pleases. A person at this level, however, might be distracted from this viewpoint if he never sees providence overriding the ordinary course of nature. He needs occasional proof that God controls his destiny. Such was the level of the man who miraculously nursed his child, which was why Abayey commented that it didn't place him in the best light. Another reason why this is not the highest level is that it still perceives nature as a tool—an extension of God, something one level removed from Him. This also implies a deficiency in God's abilities, as one only uses a tool if one can't do the job oneself.

The highest level is to see nature not as a tool of God, but as a representation of God Himself. It is not that matters are controlled by nature, which in turn is controlled by laws, which in turn are powered by God—God is present at every stage of the process. This is not, Heaven forbid, to imply a position of pantheism, or Spinoza's position that God is nothing more than a synonym for the laws of nature. It is not that God is really nature; rather, nature is really a concealed representation of God. He is not using tools.[1]

The Four Kings

Rabbi Dessler's point is demonstrated in a cryptic Midrash that contains an astonishingly profound lesson:

> There were four kings, each of whom requested different things: David, Asa, Yehoshaphat, and Chizkiyahu.
>
> David said, "I shall pursue my enemies, and overtake them..." (Psalms 18:38). God said to him: "I shall do so." And thus it is written, "David smote them from twilight until the evening of the next day..." (Samuel I 30:17).
>
> Asa stood up and said, "I lack the strength to kill them; instead, I shall pursue them, and You will do what is necessary." God said to him: "I shall do it." And thus it is written, "Asa pursued them... and the Kushim were overthrown... for they were destroyed before God..." (Chronicles II 14:12).
>
> Yehoshaphat stood up and said, "I do not have the strength either to kill them or to chase them; instead, I shall sing, and You will do what is necessary." God said to him: "I shall do it." And thus it is written, "And when they began with singing and praise, God set an ambush against the children of Ammon, Moab, and Har Se'ir..."(Chronicles II 20:22).
>
> Chizkiyahu stood up and said, "I do not have the strength either to kill them or to chase them or to sing; instead, I shall sleep in my bed, and You will do what is necessary." God said to him: "I shall do it." And thus it says, "And it was that night, an angel of God went out and smote the camp of Ashur..." (Kings II 19:35).
>
> *Midrash Eichah Rabbah 4:15*

There are many questions to be asked on this Midrash. What is David requesting from God when he states that he will chase his enemies? What does God mean when He says that He will do it? And if it is God doing it, why does the verse say that David did it? What did Asa mean when he

---

1   Adapted from *Michtav Me-Eliyahu* vol. I pp. 197-203.

said that he lacked the strength to kill his enemies? What did Yehoshaphat mean when he said that he only possessed the strength to sing, but not to chase or kill his enemies? And what on earth did Chizkiyahu mean when he said that he lacked even the strength to sing to God, and would go to sleep instead?

Furthermore, it would seem that this Midrash lists the kings in ascending order of greatness. After all, to conquer one's enemies by sleeping is surely more miraculous than to conquer one's enemies by fighting. Yet the Midrash is explained to be referring to descending levels of greatness!

Let us first understand that these four kings were on tremendously high spiritual planes. All were aware of God's control, to the degree that they all could have comfortably slept through their battles, secure in the knowledge that God would take care of matters. The matter at stake was whether they would reach even higher levels of faith. Was their faith strong enough that they would be able to proceed according to natural law, yet perceive it as having no innate power other than it being the will of God? Or would making use of natural law harm their appreciation of God's control?

> David said, "I shall pursue my enemies, and overtake them..." (Psalms 18:38). God said to him: "I shall do so." And thus it is written, "David smote them from twilight until the evening of the next day..." (Samuel I 30:17).
>
> Ibid.

King David handled his battles with the very highest level of faith. He could have comfortably slept through the night, and trusted in God. His greatness was that he was even able to wield his sword in battle, and yet attribute no innate significance to that act whatsoever. David fights his battles and understands that it is not military maneuvers, and not even laws of physics, that win his battles—it is simply the will of God. To David, the natural is no less the manifestation of God's will than is the miraculous.

> Asa stood up and said, "I lack the strength to kill them; instead, I shall pursue them, and You will do what is necessary." God said to him: "I shall do it." And thus it is written, "Asa pursued them... and the

Kushim were overthrown... for they were destroyed before God..."
(Chronicles II 14:12).

Ibid.

King Asa was on an extremely high level of faith. But not the highest.
He, too, could have comfortably slept through the night, and trusted in
God. He was even able to pursue his enemies and understand that such
actions would be irrelevant. But he was not able to actually physically
engage in battle and still attribute everything to God.

> Yehoshaphat stood up and said, "I do not have the strength either to
> kill them or to chase them; instead, I shall sing, and You will do what
> is necessary." God said to him: "I shall do it." And thus it is written,
> "And when they began with singing and praise, God set an ambush
> against the children of Ammon, Moab, and Har Se'ir..." (Chronicles
> II 20:22).

Ibid.

King Yehoshaphat was one level lower. Any physical action would have
harmed his comprehension that God alone determines the action. The most
effort that he was able to offer without harming his faith was singing.

> Chizkiyahu stood up and said, "I do not have the strength either to
> kill them or to chase them or to sing; instead, I shall sleep in my bed,
> and You will do what is necessary." God said to him: "I shall do it."
> And thus it says, "And it was that night, an angel of God went out and
> smote the camp of Ashur..." (Kings II 19:35).

Ibid.

Finally, King Chizkiyahu. Amazingly, he feels that even to sing would
harm his faith; it would cause him to attribute his victory to the innate
(spiritual) power of his singing, and not to God. He dares do nothing but
sleep, and simply trusts in God to win his battles.

From this remarkable Midrash, we see that the very highest level is
to fully comprehend that the laws of nature are no different from the
miracles; they are both raw expressions of God's will.

The Importance of Natural Law

Based on what has been said so far, one might take the perspective
that natural law is nothing more than an ingenious method of enabling

free will—something that can either lead man away from God or towards Him.[1] But the truth is that there is a very significant innate value to the system of natural law.

> Rabbi Elazar ben Azaryah said: If there is no Torah, then there is no *derech eretz*; if there is no *derech eretz*, then there is no Torah.

> Mishnah, *Avos* 3:21

Derech eretz has been translated in different ways, but Rabbi Yerucham Levovitz explains it to refer to natural law. Appreciating the role and rule of natural law is an essential prerequisite to appreciating the role and rule of Torah. For if one perceives the universe as a chaotic and random mess, one will never appreciate that there is a Controller of the universe Who runs it according to a higher law. Appreciating the system of cause-and-effect in physical terms enables one to comprehend that such a phenomenon can exist in spiritual terms.[2]

In the eloquent words of Rabbi Samson Raphael Hirsch:

> A thoughtful observation of the laws of nature is sufficient for the Jewish mind to recognize that there is a God. And as he realizes that all of nature is governed by an unchanging law, the Jew feels the need to discover the laws that are applicable to him and to all mankind. He seeks to uncover the laws that proclaim to him the Will of God concerning mankind, just as the laws of nature set forth the dictates of God's Will to the heavens and the earth and are evident from within these Divine creations.

> *The Educational Value of Judaism*, in *Collected Writings* vol. VII p. 254

Earlier, we learned that it was the recognition of a God that led to the discovery of the laws of nature in the first place; here we see that nowadays, the recognition of the laws of nature can lead one to discover God. Rabbi Hirsch later continues:

> ...Judaism is most anxious to make its adherents aware that all the phenomena of nature are subject to certain unchanging laws. Since

---

1 This is the popular view. See, for example, Rabbi Chaim Friedlander, *Sifsei Chaim, Emunah VeHashgachah* vol. I p. 130 (although he does make it clear elsewhere that there are other purposes for natural law).

2 *Da'as Chochmah U'Mussar* 1:14.

Judaism itself is a system of laws through and through, it attaches a profound ethical value to the study of the natural sciences. Judaism considers it vitally important for its adherents to become aware that their entire universe is governed by well-defined laws, that every creature on earth becomes what it is only within the framework of fixed laws, and that every force in nature can operate only within specified limits. Not by his whims of the moment but only by his own detailed knowledge of, and regard for, these laws can man make nature serve his purposes. Man himself, then, can exercise power only if he, in turn, obeys the laws set down for him and for his world.

Ibid. p. 263

Chapter Six

Approaching Conflicts

The New Convergence

For a considerable period, science was perceived as a threat to religion. But in the last few decades, many people have observed that instead of science diverging from religion, the two have begun to converge in profound ways. Henry Margenau, late Professor of Physics at Yale University, writes:

> There exists a widespread view that regards science and religion in general as incompatible. Let me therefore point out, first of all, that this belief may have been true half-a-century ago but has now lost its validity as may be seen by anyone who reads the philosophical writings of the most distinguished and creative physicists of the last five decades. I am referring here to men like Einstein, Bohr, Heisenberg, Schrödinger, Dirac, Wigner, and many others.
>
> Theories like the Big Bang, black holes, quantum theory, relativity, and the Anthropic Principle have introduced science to a world of awe and mystery that is not far removed from the ultimate mystery that drives the religious impulse. These twentieth century trends seem to call for new metaphor in describing the relationship of science and religion.
>
> "The Laws of Nature are Created by God," *Cosmos Bios Theos* p. 57

The primary examples of such a converging relationship is the very acceptance of scientific laws—the underlying unity of the universe—that we discussed at the beginning of this book. Another example of

85

convergence is with quantum mechanics. Although not directly confirming religious doctrine, this theory did challenge those who posited that the universe is purely deterministic, with no possibility of free will or Divine Providence.

What about regarding the Torah? Some scientific explanations have converged with the Torah's explanations of the universe. The most obvious example of this is the Big Bang Theory. The Aristotelian view of nature's permanence, with a universe that has never changed, was long a threat to the Jewish concept of creation and an actively involved God. This belief was carried over into science as the steady-state theory of the universe. The Big Bang Theory, on the other hand, while not explicitly religious, certainly pointed very strongly to the concept of creation. It was for this very reason that many scientists rejected the Big Bang Theory for years after its evidence came to light. In the face of overwhelming evidence, the consensus of scientific opinion finally accepted that the monotheistic concept of the universe having a beginning was true after all. Although not all scientists agree that this Prime Cause was God, they do admit that it is beyond the realm of science to say what it was.[1] Matters such as this demonstrated that science was now, at least in some ways, converging with religious tradition.[2]

---

1 Stephen Hawking argues in *A Brief History of Time* that the Big Bang does not necessarily imply a beginning. The mathematics of his theory are complex, but he conceptually depicts time as the globe, with the Big Bang at the North Pole. According to this model, there would be no beginning to time; the universe would simply "be." Asks Hawking, "What place, then, for a Creator?" However, rather than contradicting Judaism's view of things, Hawking has actually assisted it. Judaism states that there was no "before" the Big Bang, as time itself is a creation. As Davies puts it: "One can, of course, still ask: Why does the universe exist? Should the (timeless) existence of space-time be regarded as… 'creation'?… Most scientists… would agree that the existence of a mathematical scheme for the universe is not the same thing as the actual existence of that universe. The scheme still has to be implemented" (*The Mind of God*, p. 69).

2 On the other hand, some warn against attributing significance to the Big Bang. Physicist Howard J. Van Till writes: "Creation *ex nihilo* is a rich theological concept not merely about temporal beginnings but concerning the fundamental identity of the world and source of its existence at all times; the big-bang model is a theoretical scientific concept limited to the description of selected aspects of the formative history of the physical universe. A big-bang beginning and creation *ex nihilo* cannot be equated" ("The Scientific Investigation of Cosmic History," *Portraits of Creation* p. 114). A recent special

For the scientist who has lived by his faith in the power of reason, the story ends like a bad dream. He has scaled the mountain of ignorance; he is about to conquer the highest peak; as he pulls himself over the final rock, he is greeted by a band of theologians who have been sitting there for centuries.

Robert Jastrow, *God and the Astronomers*, p. 15

The Great Battles

Notwithstanding all this, it cannot be denied that despite the fact of science having emerged from monotheism, and the significant examples of the convergence of science with religion, the two disciplines are widely seen as being in conflict. Why is this so?

In part, it is due to the misunderstandings that we already discussed; common religious philosophy was that God is the direct cause of all phenomena in the simple sense, and science's revelation of natural causes was perceived by many, theologian and scientist alike, to contradict this. Although science was an outgrowth of monotheism, it forgot its roots. People were caught up in looking for scientific explanations for phenomena, and neglected to look for explanations for the scientific explanations. A deterministic view of the universe emerged in the seventeenth century, in which the universe functions like a machine, with its state at one moment determining its state in the next moment according to fixed laws. Science appeared to have conclusively ruled out Divine Providence and free will. Twentieth-century physics did much to counter such determinism, but providence and free will are still far from settled issues.

Historically, there were some famous conflicts which, although now largely settled, placed theologians and scientists at loggerheads. A famous example was with the Italian astronomer Galileo, who wrote about Copernicus's theory that the earth and other planets orbit the sun. The Catholic Church maintained a geocentric view of the universe, with the earth at a central point and everything revolving around it.

---

edition of *Scientific American* on the subject of time included an article by physicist Gabriele Veneziano arguing that the big bang was not the origin of the universe but rather the outcome of a preexisting state.

The Church declared Copernicanism "false and erroneous" in 1616 and ordered Galileo to never again proclaim that doctrine. There was considerable opposition to Copernicanism in Jewish circles too, as we shall later discuss.

But the best known conflicts between religion and science are the conflicts between the Bible and the scientific account of the world. The most famous of these, and the ones that we shall discuss in this book, are the conflicts regarding the age of the universe, the development of life, and the emergence of man. It is these issues that disturb most people; fortunately, as we shall discover, there are solutions.

There are many other conflicts and difficulties that need to be addressed, especially in the early chapters of the Book of Genesis. Most of these are beyond the scope of this work. However, in discussing various approaches to the development of the universe, life and man, the reader will better understand how to resolve other conflicts.

Seeking Solutions vs. Simple Faith

In seeking solutions that may harm deeply treasured and long-held beliefs, one may wonder if it is even worthwhile. Are we always supposed to follow our intellect? It is true that faith must sometimes be based upon emotional/spiritual grounds rather than intellectual grounds. However, most would agree that if there is no need to surrender our intellect in this way, then we should not do so.

Rambam admitted to this problem when he wrote *The Guide For The Perplexed*, yet he decided that it was outweighed by the importance of emphasizing that which is proven true, and of helping the intelligent person who is disturbed by conflicts between Torah and reason:

> When I have a difficult subject before me—when I find the road narrow, and can see no other way of teaching a well established truth except by pleasing one intelligent man and displeasing ten thousand fools—I prefer to address myself to the one man, and to take no notice whatever of the condemnation of the multitude; I prefer to extricate that intelligent man from his embarrassment and show him the cause of his perplexity, so that he may attain perfection and be at peace.
>
> Rambam, *Guide For The Perplexed*, preface

There are those who suggest that Rambam's approach was ultimately proved beneficial:

> Rambam was well aware of the effect his writings might have on the non-philosophic reader. Yet he persisted, working on the principle, "Let a thousand fools die, but let the one wise man live." Some see the current insistence on literalism at all costs as a reversal of this principle. "Let a thousand wise men die, so long as the unsophisticated can retain his simple faith." Yet it would seem that Rambam's foresight was vindicated. Eventually the unsophisticated tend to follow the intellectual's lead. If the intellect is won, all is won; the converse is also true.
>
> Rabbi Aryeh Carmell, *Challenge*, p. 259

In the same way, let us try to develop a more complex understanding of the account of creation. It may disturb certain people, as did the works of Rambam and Ralbag. But such people are not the target audience of this book. Our approach is aimed at those who accept the findings of science, appreciate that these pose a conflict with the account of Creation, and sincerely desire a satisfactory solution. Hopefully even those who do not take the approach that we are using will accept its legitimacy and necessity for others.

Rabbi Chaim Friedlander explains why discussing answers to questions involving sensitive areas is worth the risks involved:

> We are frequently faced with a dilemma in these topics: Is it worthwhile to enter into discussing them, and to know and understand what it is possible to understand and what it is not possible to understand, or to leave it all as a matter of simple faith? But on the other hand, it is likely that a person will raise the question and not know how to answer it, so it is appropriate to raise the question and the answer—especially in our generation, where there are many that are confused and have erred in their path. We have also merited, with divine assistance, to a generation of people who have returned to their religion, and have many questions about faith, and one should know how to answer them. (Editor's note—It should be pointed out that our teacher exerted himself in this area, of "Know what to answer," and would urge others and guide their approach in these areas.)
>
> Rabbi Chaim Friedlander, *Sifsei Chaim*,
> *Emunah VeHashgachah* vol. I, p. 337

"You Don't Die From a Question"

In today's era of instant gratification, people want to have answers to all their questions—preferably bite-sized, for easy consumption. Unfortunately, life does not work that way. No matter who we are, we never have all our questions answered.

At such times, there is an important Yiddish expression to bear in mind: *Fun a kashya shtarbt mon nisht*—"From a question, a person doesn't die." It expresses the concept that we should not be overly distressed when we do not find answers for all our questions. Even Moses remained with an unanswered question, and it was the most difficult one of all: Why do bad things happen to good people? Moses asked God Himself, and did not receive an answer. Talmudic literature is replete with questions that are left unanswered.

Unanswered questions should not cause a person to abandon his belief in God or Torah. There is no system of thought that is entirely free of questions and difficulties. Modern physics has many unanswered questions, yet it survives nonetheless.

"You don't die from a question"—indeed, we should even expect not to be able to find the answers to all our questions. There are always limitations on human knowledge. For example, at the beginning of the twentieth century, it appeared certain that the universe did not have a beginning. It was only in the mid-twentieth century that evidence for the big bang came to light. But until the evidence became available, the question seemed devastating. Some gave up on their faith; others said, "You don't die from a question," and in time, their children were able to discover the answer.

Unfortunately, however, while this approach has a very valuable place in Torah study, it is widely misused and abused. All too often, it is used to brush off important questions that can and should be answered. When a teacher is faced with a question with which he either does not appreciate its seriousness, is unaware of potential answers, or is personally uncomfortable with answers that exist, it is all too easy for him to wave it away by saying, "You don't die from a question."

For example, when a rabbi dismisses a question about a conflict between Torah and science, this is often for the implicit or explicit reason that he considers that the science is unreliable. But if, as sometimes happens, the questioner understands the science better than the rabbi, he will justifiably not be satisfied by the rabbi's dismissal of the question. He is left with the uneasy feeling that the question does not have a satisfactory answer.

The idea of having free license to say "you don't die from a question" is absurd. Imagine if you were trying to de-program someone who has been sucked into a cult. When you point out to him the flaws in the cult's ideology, he replies, "You don't die from a question!" But there are questions and there are Questions. Some Questions are so powerful that their target belief system does indeed die.

All too often, the teacher who tells a questioner that "You don't die from a question" does not adequately realize that although for him, it is only a question, for the asker it seems to be a Question. When the questioner is bothered by scientific evidence that seems to disprove the narrative of the Torah, he sees this as a Question. In his mind, the very authenticity of religion is at stake. When a rabbi dismisses this and tells him that "You don't die from a question," the questioner suspects (often correctly) that the rabbi is not aware of the seriousness of the question because he is not familiar with the extent of the scientific evidence. He also fears that perhaps this is indeed a lethal Question.

Telling someone that "you don't die from a question" carries serious risks and should be done as little as possible. The great Torah scholars of history did not use this approach. When Rambam encountered people who were struggling with difficult issues, he did not simply say, "You don't die from a question." Instead, he worked hard to write his *Guide For The Perplexed*. When Ramban was bothered with the new scientific explanations contradicting the traditional Jewish understandings of the Torah, he did not simply say, "You don't die from a question." He gave answers, and showed how the Torah must be reinterpreted, even though this undoubtedly caused difficulties for some people.[1]

Of course, the importance of giving answers does not justify giving any kind of answer; we cannot compromise the integrity of Torah. Even

---

1 We shall discuss examples from Ramban in the later chapter "Conflict and Reinterpretation."

legitimate answers sometimes require less-than-ideal compromises, and can involve certain risks. In some cases, their usage should be restricted to only those who are sincerely bothered by the questions. But this should not prevent us from taking questions seriously, and preparing ourselves for the possibility that sometimes we may indeed have to resort to an approach that makes us uncomfortable.

Avoiding the risks of giving less-than-ideal answers carries its own risks. All too often, telling someone "You don't die from a question" is accompanied by the implicit message that the questioner should not be asking such questions. But the unwillingness to seriously deal with questions can itself lead to a crisis of faith, as Maharal explains:

> A person should not reject something which is against his own views... especially if it is not presented as an attack on religion but is simply an honest expression of the other person's beliefs. Even if it is against his own religious beliefs and faith, he should not say, "Be quiet and shut your mouth," because there will not be a clarification of that person's religious understanding. In fact, in such cases we should tell a person to speak his mind freely and fully express how he feels, such that he should not feel that he has not been able to fully speak his mind. If sincere questions are silenced, this is indicative that the religion is weak, as discussed earlier. This attitude is the opposite of what some people think. They mistakenly think that forbidding people from discussing religion strengthens religious faith, but this is not the case. Suppressing of dissent and prohibiting people from speaking is a weakening of religion.
>
> Maharal, *Be'er HaGolah* 7

Maharal himself strongly attacked Azariah de Rossi for responding to difficulties in the Talmud with answers that Maharal deemed unacceptable. But—and this is a point that some people miss—Maharal provided alternate solutions! He did not simply dismiss the questions and leave the questioner with no answers.

Telling someone that "You don't die from a question" is an absolute last resort, when no answer can be found. It should not be used to casually dismiss the very significant issues that trouble people and for which answers, even if less than ideal, can be found. "You don't die from a question"—but you can fall very sick. And you don't die from getting it answered.

The Challenge of Rational Inquiry

There is an objection to be raised to our efforts in reconciling Torah with science and rational inquiry. Some people have engaged in rational inquiry and have reached conclusions that led them away from Judaism to a lesser or greater degree. Many therefore believe that the basic process of rational inquiry is a Pandora's Box that should not be opened.

Now, it is undeniably true that there are some people for whom rational inquiry has led them away from Orthodox Judaism, in belief or in practice. Torah and Judaism today face intellectual challenges that are hitherto unrivalled. But does this mean that one should close off rational inquiry? Absolutely not. One reason is that closing off all rational inquiry also causes people to leave Judaism. A survey of people who left observant Judaism found that 51% stated that they were not able to ask questions on intellectual issues when they were at school, and 64% felt that they were given unsatisfactory answers when they did ask.[1] In a book based around this survey, the author writes, in a section entitled "The Danger of Stifling Questions," as follows:

> Despite the history and importance of debate, we seem to have a hard time with questions today. Sometimes we do not accept them at all. At other times, we accept them only if they are "within the system," as long as they don't challenge the fundamentals of Torah. Students repeatedly express frustration and sometimes bitterness about this reality, and some go off the *derech* (the path of observance) because of it.
>
> Faranak Margolese, *Off The Derech*, p. 234

Sometimes, this result occurs because of a deep resentment engendered by the reluctance of educators and leaders to take these people seriously. At other times, it is because the students sense the lack of confidence that their rabbis possess. Another frequent scenario is that the questioners initially believe the weak answers given, and then have their confidence entirely shattered when they later discover the simple fallacies in these answers. While rational inquiry might be a Pandora's Box, stifling questions is a powder keg.

---

1 Faranak Margolese, *Off The Derech*, p. 386.

Thus, free inquiry can lead to problems, but so can the suppression of free inquiry. The best solution to this difficult problem would appear to be *measured* rational inquiry. One should be aware of one's limits and "red lines," one should be careful in the path that one takes in finding answers, and when dealing with others, one should be sensitive to their needs and capabilities.

When handled carefully, encouraging measured rational inquiry has positive results. Very few people (if any) make purely rational, objective decisions about their beliefs. Most people are affected to a considerable degree by their formative experiences in learning about these topics. A teacher who suppresses rational inquiry will cause his intelligent students to ultimately become extremely cynical, and they will be skeptical even of legitimate arguments supporting the Torah. But a teacher who encourages and guides rational inquiry, and who shows them a positive role model, will lead his students to have a healthy and confident attitude, able to recognize the good, and able to ignore the bad and be confident that satisfactory solutions will eventually emerge.

> Truth seekers, questioners and intellectually oriented people especially need a safe environment to express themselves. They, more than others, tend to need room to explore, search, and give voice to their doubt. If given a safe environment in which to do so, they may remain interested and engaged even if they never find answers to their questions. But if silenced by fear of rejection, they can suffer greatly.
>
> Faranak Margolese, *Off The Derech*, p. 235

The Reliability of Science

Some would assert that science is not a sufficiently powerful source of information to warrant adjusting our understanding of Torah. After all, they argue, scientists can't even predict what the weather will be like in two weeks' time; how can they be sure of what happened millions of years ago? They further claim that since science changes, it is therefore unreliable and we should not adjust our understanding of Torah to make it fit with science. Rambam rejected Aristotle's eternal universe—why can't we reject the cosmology of modern science? An additional point sometimes made is that scientists are influenced by a secular bias.

Such claims are mistaken on several counts. First, those who are truly knowledgeable about science understand that there is no comparison between the "science" of a few hundred years ago and the science of today. Modern methodology, coupled with the sheer numbers of people involved, and the ability of people to benefit from the research of others, means that modern science is on a very solid foundation.

> One can imagine a category of experiments that refute well-accepted scientific theories that have become part of the standard consensus of physicists. Under this category, there are no examples whatsoever in the past hundred years.
>
> Steven Weinberg, *Dreams of a Final Theory*, p. 102

The proof is in the pudding—science works. We have put men on the moon, we have cloned animals, we made predictions that came true. This also applies to the study of prehistory—for example, paleontologists can successfully predict what sort of fossils they will find depending upon which strata of rock they are digging in.

Of course, there are numerous minor "facts" of modern science that will be overturned. But there are major facts and minor facts. In the broad picture, science has a solid basis. In the same way that it will not one day be discovered that the world is standing still, it will not one day be discovered that the world is only a few thousand years old. True, not everyone may be qualified to distinguish between those aspects of science that can be considered adequately proven beyond reasonable doubt, and those aspects that may well be overturned in a few years' time. But that does not mean that nobody is capable of making those distinctions. Those who have studied science seriously can legitimately consider themselves capable of distinguishing between the two.

In cases where scientific knowledge does change, it is generally converging towards a more specific picture rather than entirely overturning previous pictures. For example, it used to be assumed that the world was flat, and then it was determined to be spherical. But later studies showed that it could not be a perfect sphere, and it must instead be somewhat flattened towards the poles. Later research refined this picture still further, and showed that it is more flattened towards the North Pole than towards the South. In such cases, later studies proved the earlier studies incorrect, but each stage was still a better approximation of the truth than was the previous stage.

It is true that scientists are as human as everyone else and are prone to making mistakes and being influenced by personal bias. But most of the issues that concern us here—the development of the universe and of life—are well-supported by broad lines of evidence that are evaluated by many different people and are not subject to the narrow perspective of a particular group.[1] Furthermore, the eighteenth-century scientists who originally determined that the literal reading of the Bible is not confirmed by the scientific evidence were themselves devout Christians who were strongly biased *against* this conclusion. It was with reluctance that they were forced to concede that science raises questions for traditional understandings.

True, Rambam provided arguments against Aristotle's eternal universe—but he was qualified to do so! One cannot compare Rambam's rebuttal of Aristotle with the unconvincing and naïve "science" of Biblical literalists today. Besides, for the most part Rambam did accept the Aristotelian worldview; the primary goal of his *Guide For The Perplexed* was to reconcile this with Judaism, not to refute it.

Living In The Present

A further reason why the argument that science is changing should not prevent reconciling it with Torah is that, even if one truly believes that it could fundamentally change, we have to work with what we know today. At the moment, the findings of science in these areas seem well proven to many people. We cannot expect people to suspend their beliefs on the improbable chance that there will be a future sea-change in science. We must try to understand Torah in terms of what we know today.

This point is expressed by the late Rabbi Gedalyah Nadel of Bnei Brak (1923-2004). A little-known but important personality, Rabbi Nadel was

---

1 There are some issues that can be argued to be subject to bias, such as the question of whether Darwinian mechanisms of evolution are sufficient to account for how life evolved. As we shall discuss, however, such issues are largely irrelevant from a religious standpoint.

one of the leading disciples of Israel's outstanding Torah authority, the Chazon Ish.[1] He was praised by his peers as a "wonder of the generation" in his studies and an "outstanding genius."[2] Unusually for a scholar immersed in the Torah-only city of Bnei Brak, Rabbi Nadel developed valuable insights regarding reconciling Torah with science that we shall later explore in detail. He explains why, notwithstanding the fact that one cannot attribute absolute truth to science, such reconciliations are necessary:

Rabbi Gedalyah Nadel

> One should realize that with intellectual knowledge of that which must be so, that which is impossible and that which is possible, one could fall into error. Human knowledge is developing, and there are things that were once considered true, and were later overturned... In general, no person has *definitive* knowledge regarding anything in the physical world... Even regarding certain things that Rambam thought to be correct from a scientific perspective, these are known today as mistaken, and (were he alive today) he would certainly admit this to us... [But] that which convinces the intellect, according to the knowledge and givens of a person in his respective situation, force a person.
>
> Rabbi Gedalyah Nadel, *BeToraso Shel Rav Gedalyah*, pp. 79-80

Such foresight is seen in the writings of the great Torah scholars throughout the generations who addressed such issues. Rambam, for example, explained that the Platonic view of the universe can be reconciled

---

1 "HaRav Gedaliah Nadel, *zt"l*," *Yated Ne'eman*, June 9th 2004.

2 Rabbi Michel Yehudah Lefkowitz, Rabbi Nissim Karelitz, and Rabbi Chaim Kanievsky, in a public notice warning against the possible falsification of some of Rabbi Nadel's teachings. I was fortunate to meet Rabbi Nadel before his passing, and I can attest to the authenticity of the posthumously published work *BeToraso Shel Rav Gedalyah*, which was based on recorded lectures.

with Torah, even though he considered it as yet unproved.[1] Rabbi Yehudah HaLevi felt that tradition trumped philosophical argument in showing the world to have had a beginning, and yet he added that if someone did rely on philosophy to conclude that the world had eternal elements, it would be possible to reconcile this belief with the Torah.[2] Rabbi Samson Raphael Hirsch was highly skeptical of the sciences of geology and evolution, which in his day were still in their infancy; and yet, he still daringly provided approaches to reconcile them with traditional Judaism. Furthermore, Rabbi Hirsch stated that reconciling evolution with Judaism would prove necessary "if evolution would ever be accepted by the scientific community." He did not state that it would be necessary when evolution is proven true beyond a shadow of doubt—rather, it would already be necessary when it is accepted by the scientific community.[3] And he provided this reconciliation even before that stage was reached! Rabbi Hirsch understood that when there is a scientific theory that is taken seriously by experts, one cannot simply expect people to abandon it and have faith. Solutions must be provided.

For many hundreds of years, great Torah scholars engaged in reconciling Torah with the prevalent wisdom of their era—from Rav Saadiah Gaon, to Rambam, to Rabbi Samson Raphael Hirsch. They did not dismiss science out of hand. Such an approach proved to be of essential importance in the past and is of no less importance today.

Teaching Genesis

The Mishnah places restrictions on the discussion of creation, that some may see as meaning that books such as this should not be disseminated:

> One does not expound the account of Creation to two people… And whoever considers four things, it would be better for him not to come into the world: what is above, what is below, what is before and what is after.
>
> Mishnah, *Chagigah* 2:1

---

1 *Guide For The Perplexed* II:25.

2 *Kuzari* 1:67.

3 I am indebted to Rabbi Matis Greenblatt for pointing this out to me.

There is a dispute regarding the definition of the "account of Creation." Many are of the view that it refers to the mystical wisdom of Kabbalah—in which case books such as this, discussing the physical history of the world, are not prohibited.

Rambam, on the other hand, is of the opinion that the Mishnah refers to the natural sciences. But while this would seem to mean that one should not study the physical sciences relating to the origins of the universe, this is not the case. First of all, one must remember that the science of Rambam was very different from that of today; were Rambam alive today, he would likely revise his entire interpretation of this Mishnah.

Furthermore, Rambam elsewhere makes it clear that these studies are very important. This, he notes, is in contrast to what is believed by certain people who look with disdain upon intellectual investigations. However, due to the shortcomings of the human intellect, intellectual inquiry must be subjected to careful limits:[1]

> The intention of these texts set down by the prophets and Sages [which warn against intellectual inquiry] is not, however, to entirely close the gate of speculation and to deprive the intellect of the apprehension of things that it is possible to comprehend—as is thought by the ignorant and idle, whom it suits better to regard their own deficiency and stupidity as perfection and wisdom, and to regard the perfection and the knowledge of others as a deficiency and a defection from Law, and who thus "regard darkness as light and light as darkness" (Isaiah 5:20). Rather, their purpose, in its entirety, is to make it known that the intellects of the human beings have a limit at which they stop.
>
> Rambam, *Guide For The Perplexed* I: 32

In commenting upon the Mishnah's prohibition against teaching publicly about the Torah's account of creation, Rambam explains that the

---

1 For a fascinating dispute as to the limits of rational inquiry, see Rabbi Yehudah Parnes, "Torah U-Madda and Freedom of Inquiry," *The Torah U-Madda Journal*, vol. I (1989) pp. 68-71; the response by Dr. Lawrence Kaplan and Dr. David Berger, "On Freedom of Inquiry in the Rambam—and Today," *The Torah U-Madda Journal*, vol. II (1990) pp. 37-50; and Rabbi Shalom Carmy, "The Nature of Inquiry: A Common Sense Perspective," *The Torah U-Madda Journal*, vol. III (1991-1992), pp. 37–51.

true nature of matters pertaining to Genesis are such that it can be harmful for those who are intellectually unprepared for them:

> We have already explained the reason for this in our introduction to this composition. It is that it is impossible for the masses to understand those matters, and they are [therefore] only transmitted from one individual to another with great care, for the masses understand very little of them. When a fool hears them, his faith becomes undermined and he thinks that they contradict the truth, while they are [actually] the truth.
>
> Rambam, Commentary to Mishnah ad loc.

The format of books, on the other hand, avoids this restriction—which is why Rambam was able to write his *Guide For The Perplexed*.[1] Likewise, a book such as this one is generally only read by someone who has a prior interest in this topic, a need to find answers, and the capability of comprehending them. Thus, even according to Rambam's understanding of the Mishnah's restriction, it does not apply to books such as this.

The Expectance of Comprehension

Despite the restrictions placed upon the study of Creation and the tradition that it is esoteric in nature, there is an expectation that, at least on some level, one ought to be able to understand the formation of the universe.

> It is undoubtedly true that The Holy One could have created His universe in an all-powerful way, in such a way that we could not have understood cause or effect in His deeds. And had He created it in such a way, it would have closed the mouths of everyone, who would not have been able to expound about creation at all, for it would have been utterly impossible for us to understand anything of His ways...

---

1 Rabbi Tzaddok HaKohen (who defines "the account of Creation" as referring to mystical wisdom) states that writing books on this topic or delivering lectures is permissible. The prohibition is regarding two or more students discussing it with their teacher. Teaching it in a discussion group is prohibited; reading a book or listening quietly to a lecture is permitted. (*Sefer HaZichronos* pp. 56-74, printed at the end of *Divrei Sofrim*.)

But because the Higher Will desired that people should be able to understand some of His ways and actions—and indeed He wanted that people should engage in this and pursue it—therefore He chose the contrary, to act in the way of man; that is to say, in an intelligible and comprehensible fashion… And the proof for this is the account of creation as written in the Torah. For there He attests that He created His world in divided periods of time, and distinct utterances, and in the order that He desired—and not all instantaneously, or in a single utterance with which He could have created it. Therefore it is up to us to understand all His actions and their reasons, and all the more so with their results—all the categories and species and their specifics…

> Rabbi Moshe Chaim Luzzatto, *Da'as Tevunos* 40

Such an understanding may not be attainable by everyone. Rambam gives a guiding principle regarding the nature of the account of Creation:

Now, on the one hand, the subject of Creation is very important, but on the other hand, our ability to understand these concepts is very limited. Therefore, God described these profound concepts, which His Divine wisdom found necessary to communicate to us, using allegories, metaphors, and imagery. Our Sages put it succinctly, "It is impossible to communicate to man the stupendous immensity of the Creation of the universe. Therefore, the Torah simply says, 'In the beginning God created the heavens and the earth' (Genesis 1:1)." Thus they pointed out that the subject is a deep mystery, as Solomon said, "It is elusive and exceedingly deep; who can discover it?" (Ecclesiastes 7:24). It has been outlined in metaphors so that the masses can understand it according to their mental capacity, while the educated take it in a different sense.

> *Guide for the Perplexed*, Introduction

Today, however, we are faced with a unique situation. At earlier times in history, when the masses had no difficulty in accepting the simple meaning of Genesis, there was no reason to confuse them by publicizing the deeper meaning. But today, many people are aware of the challenges that science raises to this simple understanding. Even if it is best not to think about "what came before," the fact is that people today *do* discuss it. In light of that, it is important to teach the topic so that people can learn about it in an appropriate way.

The Sages did not permit their investigations into creation to be made public, but since science has revealed all the results of its own investigations to everyone—results that are likely to shake faith in the truth of Scripture—we are obligated to bring the hints of the Sages to light, so as to present the word of God in its clear light and pure truth.

Rabbi Dovid Tzvi Hoffman, Commentary to Genesis, p. 48

Chapter Seven

Departing from Literalism

Literalism, Non-Literalism, and Allegory

We shall later be discussing Torah interpretations which accept the scientific account of the development of the universe and, to a lesser or greater degree, evolution. These are clearly not the simple ways of reading the Torah's account of creation. Before doing so, then, we must investigate whether it is at all acceptable to divert from the simple literal understanding of the Torah. A full discussion of this topic is beyond the scope of this work, but we shall survey the basic approaches.[1] There are important and little-known sources that will assist us in understanding Genesis.

It is extremely important to bear in mind that the possibilities in interpreting Torah are not limited to literalism and allegory. Many types of interpretation do not fall neatly into either category, at least according to the usual understandings of the term. For example, we shall explore an opinion in the Talmud that the entire story of Job did not take place. According to this view, the words of Job are still interpreted literally, but they refer to a fictional episode that serves to teach certain lessons. The book of Song of Songs, on the other hand, is traditionally understood to be a non-literal allegory—that is to say, the phrases appearing in it do not refer

1   For further discussion, see Joshua L. Golding, "On the Limits of Non-Literal Interpretation of Scripture from an Orthodox Perspective," *The Torah u-Madda Journal* vol. 10 (2001) pp. 37-59.

to that which a simple translation would indicate. There are interpretations that are not strict allegory, but are not the simple explanation of Scripture either, such as Rambam's explanation of several narratives in the Torah as referring to events taking place in dreams. Phrases such as "the hand of God" are interpreted in Kabbalistic thought not as a simple literary allegory to make God appear real to the masses, but rather as a reference to different plane of existence; these physical objects and events are embodiments in the physical world of other realities in a non-physical mode.

There is no black-and-white approach to literalism in the Torah. As with many topics, there have been heated debates regarding the extent of non-literal interpretation that it permitted. For example, Rambam and Ralbag interpreted many aspects of Creation and the Garden of Eden allegorically, but Abarbanel strongly disputed their approach. Several authorities give general principles or significant statements about allegory, which we shall now discuss.

I. The Mishnah and Talmud

One statement from the Mishnah is sometimes cited as basis for rejecting any non-literal explanation of Torah that is not part of the tradition:

> Rabbi Elazar HaModa'i stated, One who profanes the sanctified... one who embarrasses someone in public... and one who presents an interpretation (lit. "reveals a facet") of Torah against the law—even though he possesses Torah learning and good deeds, has no portion in the World-to-Come.
>
> Mishnah, *Avos* 3:11

Some claim that "presenting an interpretation of Torah against the law" refers to any interpretations which have no basis in the Written or Oral Torah and which contradict the tradition of the Midrashim and the commentaries. But the traditional explanations of this term are quite different. The Talmud[1] presents one view that it refers to someone who disgraces a Torah scholar, or who disgraces a person in front of a Torah scholar—certainly not relevant to our discussion. It also presents a view that it refers to the Torah interpretations of the wicked King Menasheh:

---

1 *Sanhedrin* 99b.

"And the one that acts high-handedly" (Numbers 15:30)—this refers to Menasheh son of Chizkiyah, who sat and expounded [Biblical] narratives in a disparaging manner. He said, Moses has nothing to write other than, "And Lotan's sister was Timna" (Genesis 36:22) and "And Timna was a concubine to Eliphaz" (ibid. 12) (i.e. he claimed that the Torah is discussing the lineage of a lowly person for no important reason); "And Reuben went in the days of the wheat harvest, and found mandrakes in the field" (ibid. 30:14) (i.e. he claimed that the Torah should not have included such a minor detail).

Talmud, *Sanhedrin* 99b

Accordingly, this is a specific condemnation of interpreting verses from the Torah as serving no positive purpose, not of interpreting verses non-literally. The classical commentaries offer further explanations of "one who reveals a facet of Torah in contrast to the law"; we shall later explore the views of Meiri. None of these apply to the non-literal interpretations of Creation that we shall be discussing.

The fifteenth-century Italian scholar Rabbi Ovadiah MiBartenura explains the case of one who "reveals a facet of Torah in contrast to the law" as follows:

It means that he displays a facet and explanation of Torah that is not in accordance with the law, for example that he translates "Do not give of your children to pass before Molech" as "Do not give of your children to intermarry." And this is not the simple meaning of the verse. Included in this [condemnation] is one who expounds verses in a disparaging manner (*derashos shel dofi*—the case of Menasheh discussed above). Another explanation of "displaying a facet" is that he is brazen-faced to transgress the Torah in public high-handedly, and has no shame.

Commentary to *Avos* 3:11

According to one view, the reference to Molech relates to the Mishnah which states that someone who interprets this verse as prohibiting intermarriage with a Molech-worshipping Aramean is excommunicated. The reason is that the person is giving the implication that intermarriage with a non-Molech-worshipping gentile is permissible.[1] Others give different explanations. However the point with all these explanations is

---

1 *Aruch*, referring to Mishnah *Megillah* 4:9.

that the person is interpreting the verse in a way that produces the wrong legal conclusions. The prohibition is against revealing a facet of Torah in contrast to the *law*. It has nothing to do with allegorical interpretations of non-legal parts of Torah.

Another potential source in the Talmud to prohibit non-literal interpretations is a principle in the Talmud which states that "a verse does not depart from its literal meaning" (*ain mikra yotzei midei peshuto*).[1] However, this is not as universal a principle as is commonly supposed. For example, it is not utilized in cases where the literal meaning of the verse is unreasonable.[2] There is no citation of it with regard to narrative portions of the Torah. And it is certainly not cited in reference to phrases such as "the hand of God." In addition, we shall see that even those who opposed allegory in various cases did *not* cite this principle as their justification.

There are precedents in the Talmud for interpreting Scripture non-literally. In discussing the book of Job, the Talmud cites a view that the entire book is not to be taken as a historical account in any way:

> One of the rabbis sat before Rabbi Shmuel bar Nachmani, and said: Job never existed and never was created, but rather was a parable.
>
> Talmud, *Bava Basra* 15a

When Rabbi Shmuel bar Nachmani proceeds to object to this view, he does not cite the principle of "a verse does not depart from its simple

---

1 See *Shabbos* 63a and the commentary of Maharsha ad loc. The usage of the concept here is to preserve the significance of the metaphor. While the purpose of the verse is for the allegorical message, the method used for that purpose is not to be ignored, but is to be used for further lessons.

2 The Talmud (*Yevamos* 11b) states: "Rabbi Yosi ben Kipar said in the name of Rabbi Elazar: It is forbidden for a man to remarry his divorced wife after she has been married to someone else, but it is permitted if she has been betrothed to someone else, for the verse says, 'after she has become defiled.' The Rabbis say that in either case, she is forbidden; and how do they fulfill the verse of 'after she has become defiled'? It refers to a *sotah* who has secreted herself with another man." *Tosafos* asks a powerful question: "How can the Rabbis make the verse depart from its straightforward meaning, which refers to a man remarrying his divorced wife?" He gives a remarkable answer: "They felt it was unreasonable that marrying a divorcee should be called 'defilement,' since the conjugal act was permitted." Here we see an important qualification to the principle. Although ordinarily a verse does not depart from its straightforward meaning, it does if the straightforward meaning is unreasonable.

meaning" as an objection. Instead, he states that the historical details given concerning Job indicate that it was an actual occurrence. Notwithstanding this objection, Rambam prefers to adopt this view.[1]

It should be noted that according to this view, the book of Job is not to be taken as an allegory (as, say, Song of Songs is understood). Rather, the book of Job is a fiction. This does not mean that it is a mere fairy tale. The Book of Job is ideally written on parchment, following specific laws as to its form, and possessing great sanctity. It was written to impart certain lessons of great importance. It contains many profound truths, despite not being historically true.

II. Rav Saadiah Gaon

Rav Saadiah Gaon addresses those who allegorized the verses describing the resurrection of the dead. In discussing the issue, he gives criteria by which to determine if the Torah is to be understood literally or allegorically:

> And I so declare, first of all, that it is a well-known fact that every statement in the Bible is to be understood in its literal sense except for those that cannot be so construed for one of the following four reasons: It may, for example, either be rejected by the observation of the senses... Or else the literal sense may be negated by reason... Again [the literal meaning of a Biblical statement may be rendered impossible] by an explicit text of a contradictory nature, in which case it would become necessary to interpret the first statement in a non-literal nature... Finally, any Biblical statement to the meaning of which rabbinical tradition has attached a certain reservation is to be interpreted by us in keeping with this authentic tradition.
>
> Rav Saadiah Gaon, *Emunos VeDeyos*, Book VII

Rav Saadiah proceeds to point out that it if were permissible to remove commandments from their simple meaning, there would be no commandments left, as it is always possible to find some sort of allegorical meaning. He then writes that if one were to allegorize the commandments in this way, one could also similarly allegorize the narrative portions of

---

1 *Guide For The Perplexed*, III:22. See too Rabbi Moshe Eisemann, *Iyov*, for a justification of this position.

the Torah, such as the splitting of the Red Sea. The Torah would thereby be fundamentally overturned. Rav Saadiah therefore concludes that one cannot interpret verses allegorically unless there is good reason to do so, as detailed in the four types of reasons that he gives. It seems that Rav Saadiah is not automatically opposed to allegorizing narrative portions— just to frivolous allegory, used without sufficient cause.

III. Rambam

Rabbi Moshe ben Maimon (1135-1204) was a controversial scholar. His *Guide For The Perplexed* was condemned by some and even burned. Rabbi Yaakov Emden (1697-1776) was so shocked by parts of it that he even doubted whether they could have been written by Rambam.[1] Yet Rambam's undisputed status as one of the leading Torah scholars in history grants authority to his work that cannot be denied. Even those who are opposed to his approach do not generally deny its legitimacy for those who wish to pursue it.

Ironically, it is Rambam himself who is generally regarded as giving the last word in defining what is acceptable and what is unacceptable in Jewish belief. His Thirteen Principles of Jewish Faith, although disputed by some authorities, are now almost universally accepted as binding, at least in theory.[2] In light of this current acceptance, while some frown upon the views of Rambam himself in certain matters, they can hardly be condemned as heretical.

Rambam's *Guide For The Perplexed* deals extensively with the theme of allegorical interpretations of Scripture. One of the areas where Rambam interprets Scripture differently from its traditional and literal interpretation is in cases involving angels. Rambam was of the belief that any such episode can only be referring to visions. Thus, since an angel stands in front of Balaam's talking donkey, Rambam asserts that the entire episode occurred in a vision—that is to say, the donkey did not talk in the physical

---

1 *Mitpachas Sefarim*, p. 56.

2 Marc B. Shapiro's book *The Limits of Orthodox Theology*, which lists numerous examples of authorities who argued on Rambam's principles, received a hostile reception in some quarters for this very reason.

world. Rabbi Yehudah Alfakar objects that Rambam is disputing an explicit statement in the Mishnah which says that the donkey's speech was created at the end of the six days of creation along with other miraculous phenomena that appeared in this world.[1] Yet apparently this did not dissuade Rambam from offering his view.[2]

Traditional portrait of Rambam

In the *Guide For The Perplexed*, Rambam also discusses the use of allegory in the Biblical account of creation. Rambam explicitly states that the account of creation is not supposed to be taken at face value:

> The account of creation given in Scripture is not, as is generally believed, intended to be literal in all its parts.
>
> *Guide For The Perplexed*, 2:29

Rambam proceeds, in a veiled manner, to state that the six days were not actually days or even time periods at all, and that various elements of the account of Adam in the Garden of Eden are allegorical, as we shall explore in detail later. Rambam's general approach is best summed up in a letter that he wrote:

> ...Know that these prophecies and similar matters that we say are allegorical—our words are not a decree, for we are not basing ourselves on a prophecy making it known that they are allegorical, and we did not find a received tradition for the sages from the prophets that the details of these matters are allegorical. Rather, I shall explain to you what brought us to this concept—and that is our efforts, and the efforts of select individuals, which is in contrast to the efforts of the masses. For with the masses who are people of the Torah, that which is beloved to them and tasty to their folly is that they should place Torah and rational thinking as two opposite extremes, and will derive everything

---

1   *Kovetz Teshuvos HaRambam*, part 3 [*Iggeros Kenaos*], p. 1b.

2   As we shall see later, it seems that Ramban may have also disputed this Mishnah, in explaining the rainbow to be a natural occurrence.

impossible as distinct from that which is reasonable, and they say that it is a miracle, and they flee from something being in accordance with natural law, whether with something recounted from past events, with something that is in the present, or with something which is said to happen in the future. But we shall endeavor to integrate the Torah with rational thought, leading events according to the natural order wherever possible; only with something that is clarified to be a miracle and cannot be otherwise explained at all will we say that it is a miracle.

Rambam, Letter Concerning the Resurrection of the Dead

IV. Rashba

Rabbi Shlomo ben Aderes (1235-1310), known by the acronym Rashba, is the authority most commonly cited by those opposed to non-literal interpretations. Rashba famously issued a ban against the study of philosophy (excluding the works of Rambam) by those aged under 25, specifically addressing those who were making use of allegory in interpreting the Torah.[1]

> …There are those who did not leave a single verse unturned, claiming that it is a parable. They render Abraham and Sarah as Form and Substance. They overstepped all boundaries in explaining the twelve sons of Jacob as referring to the twelve constellations, Amalek as the evil inclination, Lot as the intellect…
>
> Teshuvos HaRashba 1:414

However, Rashba's opposition to allegory is neither as straightforward nor as absolute as is commonly depicted. It seems that Rashba was condemning a school of thought that possessed two faults. One was that their allegories were unnecessary and frivolous; Rashba repeatedly describes the allegories as being "of no benefit and without cause."[2] There was no driving need to interpret the account of Abraham and Sarah as referring to form and substance. Second, this school of interpretation sought to fundamentally undermine Judaism:

---

1   *Teshuvos HaRashba* 1:414-419.

2   *Teshuvos HaRashba* 1:416.

> And these people, for no good reasons, make allegories out of all Scripture, overturning the commandments in order to ease their burden of suffering.... Some of them claim that everything from Genesis until the giving of the Torah is all allegory... in truth, they show that they have no loyalty to the simple meaning of the commandments.
>
> *Teshuvos HaRashba* 1:416

In perceiving a threat to the observance of the Torah's commandments, Rashba was following in the path of Rabbi Shlomo ben Avraham of Montpellier, who spearheaded the campaign against Rambam's *Guide For The Perplexed*. According to Rabbi Meir HaLevi Abulafia (1180-1244), author of *Yad Rama* and opponent of Rambam's philosophical approach, Rabbi Shlomo's concern was due to rationalists who sought to undermine the observance of the commandments by claiming that philosophical knowledge was all that mattered and that God did not really care about ritual observances.[1] This type of condemnation is echoed by later authorities, who also warned how such an approach could lead people to allegorize the Torah's laws and commandments.[2] Such allegories and resultant concerns bear no relation to our subject matter.

If we analyze one discussion of Rashba on this topic, we similarly see that his objection to reinterpretations of Scripture are likewise not as absolute as might be assumed:

> Know, that every wise man from amongst the wise and pious men of our Torah, when he sees a theory of the philosophers which appears correct in his eyes, and then comes across verses of Scripture which indicate the opposite, will reinterpret them in such a way which befits the philosophical theory, and rates the verse of Scripture to be an allegory, when the context is not obligatorily a matter of [literal] prophecy or commandment. But when he reaches [a philosophy at odds with] the Wise of Israel then he will interpret the verses literally, even if philosophy disagrees with them.
>
> For example, with the resurrection of the dead, where one cannot unequivocally prove it from Scripture, and all the verses [pertaining to this belief] can be explained by way of allegory (just like the verses

---

1 *Kovetz Teshuvos haRambam* (Leipsig 1859) vol. 3 pp. 6a-7a.

2 See *Akeidas Yitzchak, Shaar* 7 and Maharetz Chajes to *Shabbos* 63a.

that are even more explicit regarding the dead of Ezekiel). What forces [the interpretation supporting and demonstrating the belief of the resurrection of the dead] is the famously nation-wide received tradition. In such a case, it will be acknowledged that the received tradition negates the philosophical analysis, and it will teach us that we do not concern ourselves with such analyses when it stands against our received tradition. For God's wisdom is above and beyond our powers of investigation. Such is, by law, the fate [of philosophy that stands against] anything that is a received tradition in the hands of our elders, men and women. And we shall not forsake their tradition, *unless it proves impossible to uphold* (emphasis added), may such not occur...

Teshuvos HaRashba 1:9

In this passage, Rashba argues that a nationwide *tradition*, which is assumed to have been received from Sinai, takes precedence over a *philosophical* argument. This does not mean that a nationwide *assumption* that is not received from Sinai takes precedence over *scientific* proof, which is far more powerful than philosophical speculation. Furthermore, Rashba indicates that it is theoretically possible even for a tradition that is assumed to have been received from Sinai to be proved impossible to uphold—in which case the conclusion is presumably that it was not in fact actually received from Sinai.

In an illuminating paragraph, Rashba further notes that there are those who, in many cases, legitimately take a different approach than he in interpreting Scripture non-literally:

And I am not holding guilty any of the philosophers in negating these principles, as there is no statement of prophecy or tradition from their own scholars forcing them otherwise, just as I will not hold any of our own nation guilty in not explaining some of the Scriptural verses in accordance with their literal meaning such that he considers it necessarily an allegory, due to his intellectual judgment that it is far-fetched. Why should we hold him guilty for this? Indeed we are forced to admit in many places that Scripture spoke by way of allegory... but when there is something that is definitely the received tradition in our nation, why should we negate this received tradition.

Ibid.

Thus, Rashba is far from the absolute literalist, opposed to the rationalism of Rav Saadiah Gaon, that one might assume. Rabbi Tzvi Ashkenazi (1658-1718), in discussing how one person took the words of the Zohar to be allegorical, extended Rashba's position to the Zohar and presents it as congruent with the approach of Rav Saadiah:

> And that which [the person that he refers to] seeks to extract the clear words of the Zohar by way of allegory and parable—our fathers and rabbis have already taught us that one may not take any words of Torah literature from their literal meaning, even the hidden and sealed words of the Written Torah, just as they said, "Scripture does not depart from its literal meaning." And how much the father of Israel, the Rashba of blessed memory, was angered in his response 414, 415 and 416 against those who take verses out of the literal meaning, up to the point that his anger went out to smite them until excommunication. And this is not only with regard to matters of commandments and fundamentals of Torah, but with all the Torah in its entirety, for "the words of Torah are not given to divisions." *...Unless in an instance where our senses compel us, or there is evidence against the simple meaning, or the verses contradict each other, just as Rabbeinu Saadiah Gaon wrote in his book of beliefs...* (emphasis added; here he cites Rav Saadiah's four circumstances in which Scripture can be interpreted non-literally) *...*and if so, in our case, where none of these four criteria are fulfilled—and just the opposite, all four confirm the simple meaning of it, that one should not remove the words of the Zohar from their simple meaning
>
> Responsa *Chacham Tzvi* 77

In conclusion, Rashba did not pronounce a blanket ban on any non-literal interpretation of Scripture. Instead, he forbade those that were done without sufficient reason and that would undermine Judaism.

V. Meiri

Rabbi Menachem ben Shlomo Meiri (1249-1316) lived in Provence, where there were people that took rationalism to an extreme. In what appears to be a reaction to this school of thought,[1] he presents a comprehensive discussion on non-literal interpretations of Scripture.

---

1   See Moshe Halbertal, *Bein Torah le-Chochmah: Rabbi Menachem ha-Meiri u-Vaalei*

Meiri's discussion occurs in the context of the *megaleh panim b'Torah shelo k'halachah*, someone who "presents a view of Torah in contrast to the law."[1] He explains this to refer to someone who interprets one of the Torah's commandments as having an esoteric meaning in place of its simple legal requirement. It is not the esoteric meaning *per se* to which Meiri objects; rather, it is the idea that the commandment is not *also* a legal obligation at its simple level of meaning. He gives the example of someone explaining that the prohibition of eating pork actually means that one should not possess ignoble character traits. While there may be all kinds of deeper layers of meaning to this commandment, one can never know with certainty what the true reason is, and it certainly does not replace the strict prohibition of physically eating pork.

Meiri then elaborates and explains that there are three components to Torah. One is that which is only true at an allegorical level, and not in its simple literal meaning at all. In this category, he places verses such as those speaking of God possessing physical form, and stories of events that are physically impossible and which are not described as occurring by way of a miracle. Such accounts must be understood allegorically.

The second category is that of verses which should only be understood literally and possess no deeper meaning. This includes commandments which have a clear rational basis, such as the prohibition of harming someone. Meiri also mentions events that are described as occurring by way of miracles, and the concept of the beginning of the world (*chiddush ha-olam*). This category also includes historical details that have no ethical or philosophical significance.[2]

The third category is that which is true at both a simple and deeper level. This would include many of the commandments which contain deeper layers of meaning beyond their simple definition.

---

ha-Halachah ha-Maimonim be-Provence (*Between Torah and Wisdom: Rabbi Menachem ha-Meiri and the Maimonidean Halachists in Provence*), ch. 1 sec. 4.

1   Commentary to *Avos* 3:14.

2   This is in contrast to how Rambam might explain certain details in the prophetic writings; that they are written simply to "flesh out" the allegory. See *The Guide For The Perplexed*, prologue and 3:22, and the explanatory comments of Rabbi Moshe Eisemann, *Iyov*, p. xxii.

In analyzing Meiri's view, we see that events that are physically impossible are to be interpreted allegorically unless they are specifically described as occurring by way of miracle. One might think that this does not include the events of creation, which can be proposed to have occurred by way of miracles, and which Meiri appears to refer to as *chiddush ha-olam* and to group with the category of miracles as being literal. However, one can argue otherwise. The appearance of the world indicates that a non-literal understanding of creation is required even if one posits that miracles were involved. This is because, for example, although God is obviously capable of creating the world in six days, the geological record indicates that He did not actually do so. In light of this, Meiri's mention of *chiddush ha-olam* should probably be understood as referring to the fact of the creation of the universe *ex nihilo* rather than to the specifics of *how* it was created. This is a distinction that is also relevant to another authority that we shall soon study, Abarbanel.

In connection with this, it is important to briefly discuss the concept of *chiddush ha-olam*. For hundreds of years, this was a concept of paramount importance in the debate against non-Jewish philosophers. Aristotle maintained a belief in *kadmus ha-olam*, the antiquity of the world—that the universe has always existed in its current state, without a prior cause. Rambam argued for belief in *chiddush ha-olam*—that the universe was created *ex nihilo*. This is not merely a debate about cosmology; it was fundamental to a dispute about God's interaction with the universe. The paramount importance of *chiddush ha-olam* that we find amongst the medieval scholars was due to the fact that the alternative, in the philosophical framework of that era, was almost inextricably linked to the idea that God is not involved with the universe:

> The belief in eternity in the way that Aristotle sees it—that is, the belief according to which the world exists by necessity, that nature does not change at all, and that the ordinary course of events cannot be modified in any aspect—this uproots the Torah from its foundation, and utterly denies all the miracles, and erases all the hopes and threats that the Torah assures.
>
> Rambam, *Guide For The Perplexed* 2:25

For this reason, allegorizing *chiddush ha-olam*—the concept that the world was created—was seen as a rejection of God's interaction with the world. But this has little bearing on the contemporary issue of whether creation took six days or fourteen billion years.

VI. Ralbag

Rabbi Levi ben Gershon (1288-1344) continued the rationalist approach of Rambam, and in some cases took it even further. Like Rambam, he became highly controversial for some of his radical views, yet his status as an outstanding Torah scholar has not been challenged and his commentary is still printed in standard editions of Scripture. He explicitly states that there is a license for non-literal interpretations:

> We must believe what reason has determined to be true. If the literal sense of the Torah differs from reason, it is necessary to interpret those passages in accordance with the demands of reason.
>
> *Milchamos Hashem*, p. 98

His extensive use of allegory is illuminating. For example, he understands the episode of the Garden of Eden to be mostly allegorical:

> The "Garden" alludes to the material intellect... And the division of rivers from the garden alludes to that which the material intellect leads to other powers of the soul... And the snake alludes to the power of the imagination... "And God called to the man"—is by way of allegory, in the manner of "And God said to the Satan" (Job 1:7), "And God said to the fish" (Jonah 2:11); and so too is that matter with God's statement to the woman and with God's statement to the snake.
>
> Ralbag, Commentary to Genesis

Ralbag's final comments in his study of that episode are especially interesting:

> Some great later sages erred and devised allegories regarding Cain, Abel and Seth and lost the intentions of the Torah. You should know that it is improper to devise allegories with Torah matters except in places where it is compelling to be allegory, for if this measure was given over [freely] to men, the Torah would fall and we would not be able to derive from it the intended benefit.
>
> Ibid.

Like Rashba, Ralbag argues against frivolous use of allegory, as it can undermine the Torah. But he does state that it is appropriate to use allegory when one is compelled to do so. Ralbag found compelling reason to do so with much of the account of the Garden of Eden, due to his understanding of philosophy. For us, that which seems adequately proven from science provides the compelling reason—and it is much more compelling than philosophy.

VII. Abarbanel

Rabbi Don Isaac Abarbanel (1437-1508), in his famous and lengthy commentary on the Torah, lists various positions with regard to the account of the events in the Garden of Eden.[1] He first cites Rashi and Ramban as presenting a literal explanation, and he notes that even though a superficial reading of Ibn Ezra would give the same view, this is clearly not his true position. Abarbanel then cites Rambam, Ralbag, and the true position of Ibn Ezra that the episode is to be understood allegorically. He then criticizes the allegorical approach on several grounds.

First, Abarbanel discusses stylistic difficulties with such an allegorical explanation. Since Abarbanel understands the section preceding this story (concerning the creation of the world) and the section following it to both be literal, he asks how an allegorical episode can be inserted in the middle of a literal text. Abarbanel considers that this would be stylistically problematic, and that an allegorical text should be set aside in its own work, as is the case with the book of Job (according to some explanations). Abarbanel later adds that anything presented in the Torah as a factual account, without any internal indications that it is allegory, such as the story of the Garden of Eden, should be taken as literal.

Abarbanel then warns of risks involved with such allegorical explanations. First is that if one allegorizes the account of the events in the Garden of Eden, one may come to allegorize the six days of creation, which would lead to negating *chiddush ha-olam*, the creation of the universe *ex nihilo*. Second is that one may come to allegorize legal sections of the Torah.

Abarbanel then wonders how Rambam took license to make such interpretations, which could lead to an allegorical understanding of the

---

1 Commentary to Genesis p. 85 in standard edition.

Torah's commandments. He proceeds to explain how Rambam and those who followed his method can be judged favorably. First is that they never intended that one may apply this method of interpretation to the legal areas of the Torah. Second is that they never intended to allegorize the six days of Creation such that it would contradict the idea of *chiddush ha-olam*. Third is that regarding the story of the tree of knowledge, the formation of Eve from Adam's side, and the snake's conversation, both rational thought and the teachings of the Sages led them to interpret matters non-literally. He explains that the simple reading of this episode is something that includes many impossibilities, and since it is unthinkable that the Torah would teach us things that are false, there must be a different way of understanding the verses. He later adds that Rambam also took license from the fact that the Sages describe so many events as having taken placed in the Garden of Eden, which could not possibly all have occurred in one day.

There are several points to consider with regard to Abarbanel's discussion. One is that his objection to this method is not simply that everything in the Torah must necessarily be literally true. He does not, for example, cite the Talmudic principle that "a verse does not depart from its literal meaning." Rather, he rejects allegory due to stylistic difficulties and dangers of what it could lead to. Such objections can be countered and did not seem to concern the Rambam and others whom Abarbanel was criticizing. Abarbanel accepts that rational difficulties with understanding the Torah literally can create an understandable license for interpreting it allegorically, even though he himself does not take this approach.

A second point to note is that few people today would be able to fully agree with Abarbanel's position. His objection to Rambam's allegory rests in part on his repeated statements that everything in the earlier episode of the six days of Creation must be *entirely* literal. It is clear that Abarbanel felt that the six days themselves must have been ordinary days on earth as we know them—that is why he points out that all the events of the Garden of Eden according to their simple meaning could not possibly have taken place on the sixth day. Abarbanel's cited objection to allegorizing the six days is that it would/could lead to denial of *chiddush ha-olam*. This follows his position that there must be consistency in interpretation. The six days are either entirely allegorical or entirely literal; once one allegorizes even a part of them, one has potentially damaged the foundation for *chiddush ha-olam*. But almost everyone today, theist and atheist alike, accepts that the universe had a beginning. Furthermore, anyone who accepts that the universe is billions of years old must reject Abarbanel's premise that the six days are either absolutely literal or absolutely meaningless, and explain the word *yom* as either a long period of time or a spiritual concept. Thus, most people would not agree with Abarbanel that it is all-or-nothing.

A final point to note is that Abarbanel's opposition to Rambam's approach stemmed in a large part from his fears that it would lead to an Aristotelian view of the universe. Such concerns have no bearing upon a contemporary non-literal interpretation of Genesis.

Recent Authorities

In 1873, when the evidence for an ancient universe was just coming to light, Rabbi Samson Raphael Hirsch wrote that none of these discussions relate to the fundamentally important tenets of faith:

> Judaism is not frightened even by the hundreds of thousands and millions of years which the geological theory of the earth's development bandies about so freely... Our Rabbis, the Sages of Judaism, discuss (*Midrash Rabbah* 9; Talmud *Chagigah* 16a) the possibility that earlier worlds were brought into existence and subsequently destroyed by the Creator before He made our own earth in its present form and order. However, the Rabbis have never made the acceptance or rejection of this and similar possibilities an article of faith binding on all Jews. They were willing to live with any theory that did not reject the basic truth that "every beginning is from God."
>
> *The Educational Value of Judaism*, in *Collected Writings*, vol. VII, p. 265

The prominent German scholar Rabbi Dovid Tzvi Hoffman (1843-1921), a member of Agudath Israel's Council of Torah Sages, was himself highly skeptical of the ability of science to draw conclusions about the early history of the world. Yet he pointed out that, were one to accept its findings, there is certainly a basis for interpreting the episode of Creation non-literally:

> There are other ways to reconcile the Scriptural account with the findings of science. Even if it is not possible to adopt them within the

framework of the simple meaning of Scripture, one should remember that even with the legal portions of the Torah, there is an accepted tradition in our hands that sometimes the literal meaning is changed. All the more so, it is permitted to do so with the account of creation, an account in which the Sages found many things that cannot be identified from the words of Scripture, but which can be derived via deeper methods of investigation.

Rabbi Dovid Tzvi Hoffman, Commentary to Genesis p. 48

An important but little-known discussion of this point is found in the writings of Rabbi Dr. Isaac HaLevi Herzog (1889-1959). Rabbi Herzog, although underappreciated in some circles, was an outstanding scholar[1] whose brilliance in Torah was obscured by his quasi-political appointment as Ashkenazi Chief Rabbi of Palestine and later the first Chief Rabbi of Israel. He makes some valuable points about the interpretation of Genesis:

It is worthy of note that whilst now and again we hear a voice raised against the exclusive addiction to scientific pursuits, we hardly hear in the Talmud and Midrash an echo of a conflict between science and religion... The Talmudim and Midrashim have preserved very little, if anything, of the teachings of the ancient masters on many a matter dealing with the deepest and most abstruse aspects of both science and metaphysics. These were included in the two branches of esoteric lore known as *Ma'asei Bereshit* and *Ma'asei Merkabah*, which were never taught publicly...

The mysterious character which the *Ma'asei Bereshit* evidently bore, warrants the conclusion that the interpretations of the Pentateuchal account of the Creation included in that body of esoteric lore, was not of a literal nature. It may well be that questions affecting the

---

1   He was ordained by Ridvaz (Rabbi Yaakov Dovid ben Ze'ev Willowski; 1845-1913), who pronounced him one of the world's outstanding Talmudists. At his funeral, Rabbi Aharon Kotler of the Lakewood Yeshivah referred to him in his eulogy as a "prince," and spoke of his extraordinary Torah scholarship (*HaPardes* 34:1 pp. 41). Rabbi Herzog's elite group of disciples included several who would emerge as the leading Torah scholars in the nation, such as Rabbi Yechezkel Abramsky, Rabbi Shlomo Zalman Auerbach (whose work *Ma'adanei Aretz* bore the approbation of Rabbi Herzog), Rabbi Shmuel Wosner, and Rabbi Yosef Shalom Elyashiv. (See Rabbi Yisrael Meir Lau, *Al Tishlach Yadecha El Ha-Na'ar*, pp. 170-171.)

relation between science and religion received due treatment in those two departments of esoteric learning. The method pursued by the Jewish teachers of the Middle Ages is exemplified in Maimonides' *Guide*. They did not, in the first place, accept as true everything taught by Greek science and metaphysics.

Rabbi Isaac Herzog, "The Talmud as a Source for the History of Ancient Science," p. 170

Rabbi Isaac HaLevi Herzog

Rabbi Herzog proceeds to illustrate this point by pointing to Rambam's treatment of the doctrine of the eternity of matter. Rambam maintains that one version of this doctrine is compatible with Judaism in principle even though it conflicts with the letter of the Torah. Because he is not convinced of the truth of this doctrine, he adheres to the straightforward meaning of the Torah; but he states that, if he were convinced that this doctrine had been proven, he would reinterpret the Torah to accommodate it. Rabbi Herzog concludes:

> When, again, our medieval thinkers felt that attempts at harmonization were absolutely necessary, they did not hesitate to explain the words of the Torah in a manner deviating from the literal sense... it is well to bear in mind that already our ancient sages, to say nothing of our medieval theologians, would not seem to have insisted upon literalness in such transcendental matters as the account of the Creation.
>
> Ibid.

The Drawbacks of Non-Literalism

There are certain non-literal explanations of the Torah that undermine the very foundations of Judaism. For example, positing that the first three words of Genesis, *Bereishis bara Elokim*, mean that a super-deity called Bereishis created God, or arguing that sections concerning commandments are allegorical or not absolutely binding, fundamentally damage Judaism.

121

But positing that the descriptive parts of the account of creation are not to be taken literally does not contradict any of the thirteen principles of Jewish faith, or any fundamental concepts of the Torah. Why, then, do so many people insist upon utterly rejecting the legitimacy of such an approach?

There is a legitimate reason for being wary of non-literal understandings of the Torah, in that it puts one on a dangerous slippery slope. Where does one draw the line? This indeed was the reason why authorities such as Abarbanel were opposed to allegory. Tragically, history shows many who have taken non-literal understandings of the Torah too far. There were people who allegorized the commandments, and allegorized narrative portions in such a way as to fundamentally undermine Judaism.

However, while this is reason to avoid non-literal explanations as much as possible, it is not reason to avoid them in limited circumstances where there are overwhelming grounds for accepting such explanations. There are many cases where we definitely interpret the Torah non-literally, notwithstanding the slippery-slope risk. And there is good reason to state that the wealth of evidence concerning the history of the universe provides compelling reasons for interpreting Genesis in this way. Furthermore, the area of Torah that we are discussing is one that is the most open to allegory, since it is the most esoteric. As we shall see, such an approach to Genesis has been taken by some of the greatest scholars in Jewish history.

Chapter Eight

Conflict and Reinterpretation

A Tradition of Reinterpretation

For many people, the greatest difficulty with the idea of a universe that is billions of years old or the evolution of life, on both an intellectual and emotional level, is simply that there is no historical tradition of explaining Torah in this way. This is not an insignificant concern. Rabbi Moshe Sofer (1762-1839) famously commented that "anything new is prohibited by the Torah,"[1] and with good reason. Time and again, there have been individuals and sects that provided "new" explanations of Torah which resulted in fundamentally undermining Judaism. But it is more than that; any substantial new innovation in Torah interpretation by definition causes some harm to Judaism, which canonizes its traditional scholarship.

Certainly it is not desirable that a section of Torah should be explained entirely differently from how it was traditionally understood. However, we are not dealing here with the question of whether it is preferable or even whether it is acceptable as a mainstream view; we are dealing instead with the question of whether it can be at all legitimate.

The answer is that, certainly in cases where there are no legal ramifications, it is indeed legitimate. There are numerous cases where classical or recent commentators disputed the interpretations of the Sages

---

1 Responsa Chasam Sofer, *Orach Chaim* 28, 181 and *Yoreh De'ah* 19.

of the Talmud.[1] They were not offering additional insights; they were replacing the interpretations of the Sages of the Talmud.

Innovating new interpretations of Torah based upon advances in science is a slightly different matter; in some ways it is easier, in some it is more problematic. It is easier in that there is a stronger objective basis to license the new explanation. We would generally not be so presumptuous as to assume that we understand the Torah better than our ancestors, but science gives us insights that previous generations lacked. Yet this is problematic in that the reinterpretation is being done due to external pressures. Nevertheless, there are cases that have already occurred where, due to advances in our knowledge about the natural world, Torah authorities were forced to explain the Torah differently from the traditional understanding.

The Firmament

One example is with the *rakia*, the "firmament" created on the second day. The Biblical commentator Rabbi Meir Leibush (Malbim, 1809-1879) notes that there are several opinions amongst the traditional commentaries as to the nature of this firmament:

> With regard to the nature of the firmament, the commentaries were in confusion, and Rabbi Isaac Abarbanel brings five opinions: (a) that it is the upper sphere which encompasses everything, (b) that it is the totality of heavenly bodies, (c) that it is the concave area of the lunar sphere, (d) that it is the strong spherical body which is made of the element of water and is established as the space of the world,[2] and (e) his own opinion, which found favor in his eyes, that a great, thick and heavy sphere was made on the first day, and the other surrounding spheres were made from it on the second day. And all these opinions were built on strands of spider's silk that were spun by the early

---

1 For a list of examples, see Rabbi Chaim Friedlander, *Sifsei Chaim - Pirkei Emunah u-Bechirah*, vol. 2 pp. 257-272. For example, the Midrash (*Bereishis Rabbah* 89:11) and *Tosefta* (*Sotah* 10:9) state that the famine in Egypt ended five years early when Jacob entered the land. But Ramban (Genesis 47:18) disputes this and writes that the famine lasted for seven full years. See too Ibn Ezra in his introduction to his commentary on the Torah, where he writes that one may offer alternate interpretations to those of the Sages in cases unrelated to law.

2 Rambam, *Guide For The Perplexed* II:30.

authorities, that there are actually spheres, but in our time it was been well clarified that all the host of the heavens are floating in a fine and pure substance that is called "ether"…

Malbim, Commentary to Genesis 1:6

Of course, the existence of ether has since been disproved, and the Malbim's explanation of *rakia*—that it refers to the atmosphere—is not without its own difficulties. But the point is that Malbim dismissed all the earlier explanations of *rakia* on the grounds that the traditional belief in cosmic spheres had since been disproved by science.[1]

The Rainbow and Ramban

Although Ramban was a prominent Kabbalist, he was also a rationalist.[2] In discussing the Torah's account of the rainbow appearing after the deluge, he notes that science forces us to revise the traditional understanding of this topic:

> "This is the sign of the covenant that I give"—It would seem from this sign that the rainbow which appears in the clouds is not part of the acts of creation, and only now did God create something new, to make a rainbow appear in the sky on a cloudy day… But we are compelled to believe the words of the Greeks, that the rainbow is a result of the sun's rays passing through moist air, for in any container of water that is placed before the sun, there can be seen something that resembles a rainbow. And when we look again at the wording of the verse, we will understand it thus. For it says, "I have set My rainbow in the cloud," and it did not say "I am setting it in the cloud," (in the present tense) as it said, "this is the sign of the covenant that I am giving." And the word "My rainbow" indicates the rainbow previously existed.

Ramban, Commentary to Genesis 9:12

---

1   Malbim proceeds to state "No spheres exist, as our Sages already noted." Possibly, he is referring to *Midrash Bereishis Rabbah* 6:8. If the Sages did indeed deny the existence of spheres, this would indicate that the medieval scholars rejected the opinion of the Sages in light of the science of *their* day.

2   See Asher Bentzion Buchman, *U-Madua Lo Yeresem*, in *Hakirah: The Flatbush Journal of Jewish Law and Thought* (Fall 2005) vol. II.

We see that although the simple understanding of the verse indicates that the rainbow was created after the deluge, as a message from God—which is indeed how several traditional authorities explain it[1]—Ramban explains it differently. He does so not because of his understanding of the text, but because of the conclusions of the Greek philosophers that the rainbow is a natural phenomenon.[2] It is only after proving that such must be the case that Ramban explains how the words of the verse can be understood accordingly and provides textual support in that direction.

There is a second occasion where Ramban notes that modern science would force us to divert from traditional understandings of Scripture:

> "When a woman conceives seed (*tazria*)" (Leviticus 12:2) …They said with regard to the meaning of this, "If the woman emits seed first then she will give birth to a boy…" (Talmud, *Niddah* 31a). Their intent was not that the child is formed from the seed of the woman, for a woman, even though she has generative organs (i.e. ovaries) like those of a man (i.e. testicles), these either do not produce any seed, or the seed is not thick and does not contribute anything for the embryo. Rather, they said "she emits seed" with regard to the blood of the womb that is collected at the conclusion of intercourse in the mother and attaches itself to the seed of the man. For according to their opinion the fetus is formed from the blood of the woman and from the white substance of the man, and these two together are called the "seed"… and the opinion of the doctors regarding formation is likewise. But according to the opinion of the Greek philosophers, the entire body of the fetus is formed from the woman's blood; the man contributes nothing other than the force that is known as *hyuli* in their language, which gives form to the substance… and if so, the word *tazria* is like, "[as a garden that] sprouts forth its seedlings" (Isaiah 61:11)…[3]

> Ramban, Commentary to Leviticus 12:2

---

1 Ibn Ezra; Maharal (*Gur Aryeh* Bereishis 9:12-9). Cf. Mishnah *Avos* (5:6), which includes the rainbow in the list of miraculous phenomena that were built in potential at the end of creation, ready to be manifest at the appropriate time.

2 Cf. Rashba to *Berachos* 59a, s.v. *mai*. See Rabbi David Horowitz, "Rashba's Attitude Towards Science and Its Limits," in *The Torah U-Madda Journal*, Vol. III, pp. 52-81.

3 Ramban proceeds to note that Onkelos follows this interpretation. However he seems to be citing Onkelos as secondary support, rather than claiming that Onkelos alone

While Ramban does not openly rule in favor of the Greek philosophers, he plainly would not have cited them to begin with, along with an explanation as to how their view fits with the verse, if he did not think that it was a view to be taken seriously. And according to the view of the Greek philosophers, one is forced to understand Scripture differently from how it was understood by the Sages of the Talmud.[1]

The Copernican Revolution

One of the most significant cases of science trumping tradition is with heliocentricity versus geocentricity. The traditional view was that the earth is the stationary center of the universe, around which the sun and all the luminaries revolve. It was not only the Church that strongly opposed the insights of Copernicus. With few exceptions,[2] the rabbis of the seventeenth and eighteenth centuries condemned Copernican astronomy as being opposed to Scripture and as being scientifically flawed.[3] It contradicted the simple meaning of the Scriptural statement that "the world stands forever," as well as the account in Joshua of time halting by the sun miraculously standing still (as opposed to the earth standing still).

Some still maintain the earlier belief that the earth is at the center of the universe, purporting to base themselves on Einstein's theory of relativity. This is the position taken by the late Lubavitcher Rebbe and his followers.[4] However, this can be rejected on at least three counts.

---

justifies this explanation.

1   I am well aware that some read both of these discussions by Ramban differently so as not to accept that Ramban was using science to reinterpret Torah. However I believe that such interpretations are contrived.

2   Such as Rabbi Yosef Shlomo Delmedigo (1591-1655).

3   Chacham David Nieto, *Matteh Dan*, IV, 104-135 (pp. 127a-129b); Maharal, *Nesivos Olam, Nesiv HaTorah* 14; Rabbi Tuviah Katz, *Maaseh Tuviah*, 43b-44b (*Olam ha-Galgalim* 4); Rabbi Yonason Eybeshitz, *Ya'aros Devash* 1:4. See Andre Neher, *Jewish Thought and Scientific Revolution of the Sixteenth Century: David Gans (1541-1613) and His Times*, Hillel Levine, "Paradise Not Surrendered: Jewish Reactions to Copernicus and the Growth of Modern Science," in *Epistemology, Methodology and the Social Sciences*; and David Ruderman, *Jewish Thought and Scientific Discovery in Early Modern Europe*.

4   *Mind Over Matter*, p. xlvi. A favorite citation for these people is the following: "The relation of the two pictures [geocentricity and heliocentricity] is reduced to a mere

First, since the movement of the sun and planets is due to the gravitational force that they exert upon each other, it is the sun, with its overwhelming mass, that causes the planets to move in the way that they do. Thus, it is still more meaningful to speak of the sun being at the center of the solar system.

Second, relativity does not mean that one can equally definitively state that the earth is at the center of the universe. On the contrary; it means that one *cannot* say that any one viewpoint is more objectively significant than another.[1]

Finally, one should note that the original Torah authorities to oppose Copernicus did not feel that both viewpoints were equally correct; they felt that geocentrism was objectively correct and heliocentrism was objectively false. They fought against Copernicus with arguments such as that if the earth were to be moving, we would feel the wind. Such arguments have not only been shown to be mistaken, but also show that their proponents felt that the earth could not be said to be moving in any sense at all.

Interestingly, the reservations about Copernicanism were similar to those about evolution. In removing earth from the center of the universe, many people feared that man's importance was being diminished, just as people fear happens with the concept that man evolved from animals. In describing the orbits of planets as elliptical rather than circular, many people saw God's work as less than their ideal of perfection, just as people perceive the trials-and-errors of evolution. In stating that the earth moves around the sun, many people saw a contradiction to Biblical accounts of the earth standing still and the sun moving, just as people perceive conflicts between evolutionary and Biblical accounts of man's origins. And in explaining mechanistic laws to govern planetary motion, many people

---

coordinate transformation and it is the main tenet of the Einstein theory that any two ways of looking at the world which are related to each other by a coordinate transformation are entirely equivalent from a physical point of view ... Today we cannot say that the Copernican theory is 'right' and the Ptolemaic theory 'wrong' in any meaningful physical sense" (Sir Fred Hoyle, *Nicolaus Copernicus*).

1 Thus, the corollary of Hoyle's statement above is that today we cannot say that the Ptolemaic theory is 'right' and the Copernican theory 'wrong' in any meaningful physical sense, either.

saw an attack on the idea that the heavens proclaim the glory of God's handiwork. In both cases, those with a more scientific understanding had to fight to show why no such theological conclusions are to be drawn.

The Six Days

As we shall later see, a number of recent and contemporary Torah authorities have explained that the six days of creation were eras rather than 24-hour days. Explaining that each day was billions of years long is thought to reconcile the Biblical age of the universe with that discovered by science. Later, we shall explore the difficulties with this approach; but for our purposes here, let us merely note that this approach is very widely accepted.

And yet, although there is basis for interpreting the word "day" to refer to an "era," there is certainly no traditional precedent for explaining the six days of creation as referring to fourteen billion years. Historically, these were generally understood to be six regular 24-hour days, just as the Shabbos that we observe in commemoration of the original Shabbos is 24 hours long.[1] There are some traditional sources that interpret them as longer periods, but none in terms of billions of years. Yet this has not prevented people today from interpreting the word "day" in this way. Rabbi Gedalyah Nadel explains that this is because, unlike earlier authorities who were not confronted with dinosaur bones and such, we have reason to do so:

> ...The expression "one day" that the Torah uses, according to its literal translation, refers to one [conventional] day. Rambam and the other early authorities truly held of this view, that each of the six days of creation lasted for one [ordinary] day, because they had no reason to believe otherwise.[2] However, for us, there are indeed such reasons...
>
> Rambam, in his introduction to the Guide, describes the heartaches of someone who knows with clarity, from rational proofs, that the Creator does not possess physical form, and yet he finds expressions of

---

1   See Rashi to Talmud, *Chagigah* 12a, s.v. *midas hayom*.

2   As we shall later see, Rambam did not actually believe that the six days of Creation were periods of time at all. Nonetheless Rabbi Nadel's point, that none of the medieval authorities believed the six days to be billions of years, holds true.

physical form in Scripture. Rambam tells him: Do not be confused—explain the verses by way of borrowed terminology, by way of parable and allegory, according to that which the rule and styles of language permit, and this is the correct explanation, according to the truth of Torah. There is no doubt that the verses did not intend that which is proved to the contrary by the intellect. So, too, we say: There are many different scientific proofs, by exacting methods that are tested by experience, which happen by natural processes, that from the time they began to happen, millions of years have elapsed… What is the problem—that in the Torah it writes "six days"? For this, Rambam wrote his book, in order that you should know that it is possible to explain the Torah's expressions differently from their literal meaning. And if the intellect requires it, and the styles of language permit it—it is obligatory upon you to explain it in borrowed meaning, by way of allegory… You are not able, and it is prohibited for you, to throw your intellect behind you.

Rabbi Gedalyah Nadel, Be Toraso Shel Rav Gedalyah, p. 91

The Hyrax and the Hare

The Torah seemingly states that the hare brings up the cud. Zoological studies of hares show that this is not true. Thus, several authorities who have studied the topic concluded that the phrase "brings up the cud" should be interpreted idiomatically to refer to the hare's habit of producing special pellets for reingestion, a phenomenon sometimes known as pseudorumination. Others have reinterpreted the description of the hare bringing up the cud as a colloquial description given to the hare by virtue of its superficially appearing to ruminate. No authorities have expressed reservations about interpreting the phrase non-literally and in conflict with the traditional understanding.[1]

Licensed With Care

The cases that we have discussed refute the claim advanced by some that Torah can only be reinterpreted to conform to science if there are

---

1 For a detailed discussion of this topic, see *The Camel, The Hare and the Hyrax* by this author.

internal justifications from tradition for doing to. This is clearly not what happened in the past. And there is a much more pressing need to develop such interpretations today, when the challenges are far greater and are more widely known. We see a precedent from the time of the Rishonim, the great medieval Torah scholars, of interpreting Torah to render it compatible with that which is considered proven, and we have a responsibility to continue in their path.

> The solution that Rambam gives to the aforementioned perplexed person is that there are things in the Torah that are not as their simple meaning, but rather need to be understood by way of allegory and parable... We never have to choose between relying on the intellect and relying on the Torah....

> The perplexity that Rambam presents in such a beautiful and emotional way is due to the difference between the verses which according to their literal meaning give physical form to the Creator and the philosophical knowledge that the Creator has no physical body. Nowadays, we have already forgotten this. Distancing ourselves from attributing physical form to God, which in those days was not so clear to everyone (see the words of the Raavad), does not pose a problem today. We have different problems, and these are the contradictions between the simple meaning of Scripture and scientific knowledge...

> Rabbi Gedalyah Nadel, *Be Toraso Shel Rav Gedalyah*, pp. 79-81

It cannot be stressed enough that this should not be taken as a free license for anyone to interpret Torah in whichever way they see fit. One must exercise extreme caution in any such interpretation. There must be sufficient cause for doing so, especially if the new interpretation is highly innovative or far-reaching in its implications. In the approaches discussed in this book, the causes for such reinterpretations are the firm conclusions of the scientific community reached by an overwhelming convergence of evidence; the consequences are mitigated by the subject matter not being fundamental matters of faith; and all the insights are taken from the works of universally respected Torah scholars.

A reservation voiced by some people is that many of the greatest Torah scholars today have not endorsed such views. However, this is not entirely accurate. While modern scientific cosmological explanations have not reached mainstream "official" acceptance in some Orthodox circles, there have been important rabbinical figures who have legitimized reconciling these with Torah, including Rabbi Samson Raphael Hirsch, Rabbi Yitzchak Herzog, Rabbi Avraham Yitzchak Kook, and Rabbi Gedalyah Nadel. Although these scholars were controversial in certain circles of Orthodoxy, few would deny their credentials as outstanding Torah scholars. Many Torah scholars privately endorse these approaches, even if they will not do so publicly due to the inability of much of the general public to accept it.

We have a responsibility to try to understand Torah according to what our knowledge and intellect tells us to be true. We have a right—indeed, an obligation—to adopt the tools of interpretation presented by the early Torah authorities and adapt them to the problems that face us.

The Resistance to Reinterpretation

In the previous chapter, we showed that there is authoritative license to reinterpret Torah based on scientific discovery. In this chapter, we showed that there is precedent for doing so. Why, then, is there so much resistance to doing so?

There are actually several factors involved. First, there are many people, including rabbinic authorities, who are simply unaware of the overwhelming scientific evidence that compels these approaches. Without such knowledge, it is natural and easy to reject any such reinterpretation.[1]

Second, many are likewise unaware of the prominent rabbinic authorities who have endorsed and proposed such reconciliations. Perhaps unsurprisingly, these writings have received little publicity.

Third, there are many unsophisticated people who take a black-and-white, all-or-nothing outlook. For them, the traditional understanding of Torah must be 100% perfect, or they lose faith in all of it.

Fourth, even those who do not take such a black-and-white approach pragmatically acknowledge that there are many who do. There is a legitimate fear of destabilizing Judaism. Certainly the concept of tradition

---

1 Thus, for example, Rabbi Yaakov ben Yosef Rischer (1670-1733), one of the greatest *halachic* authorities of his era, was able to reject science due to its position that the earth is round, which contradicted the Talmud (see Responsa *Shevus Yaakov* 3:20).

is destabilized when any part of it is shown to be less than perfect.[1] Many feel that any previous reinterpretations of Torah, such as those listed in this chapter, should be swept under the carpet.

While these concerns are justifiable, there are also counter-concerns. Insisting upon traditional understandings when modern knowledge indicates that they are untenable likewise causes problems. When people are convinced that science has indeed disproved certain traditional views of cosmology, then if they are to still maintain faith in Judaism, they must be shown that tradition has indeed shown itself in the past to be somewhat flexible to reinterpretation in such areas. A letter that I received from a person who left Judaism demonstrates why this is so critical:

> Maybe if I had been taught at the outset that there is no conflict between evolution and Judaism then I would have stayed observant. I don't know! All I know for certain is that my frustration with the fact that I absolutely knew that my rabbis had it wrong as regards evolution made me feel that the whole system was nonsense!

In this catch-22 solution, the best approach would seem to be that solutions which require diverting from traditional views be presented cautiously and often downplayed. But they must be made available for those that need them.

---

1 Cf. Michael Berger, *Rabbinic Authority*, p. 141, in discussing the tendency of some in the ultra-Orthodox community to reject the historical-critical method of studying Talmud, through which textual corrections render much medieval interpretation redundant: "It is not primitive narrow-mindedness but understandable self-preservation for an interpretive community to defensively reject a premise that threatens to undermine a large portion of its revered canon—and form of life. Few communities would act differently."

Part Two:

COSMOLOGY

Chapter Nine

Evidence for an Ancient Universe

Overwhelmed by the Evidence

There are two topics that have formed the focus of heated dispute between scientists and religious groups: the age of the universe, and the development of life on Earth. Unfortunately, these topics are sometimes confused with each other and are thought inseparable. The truth is that they are only inseparable insofar as evolutionary theory requires the world to be millions of years old. However, it is perfectly possible to accept the scientific evidence for the age of the universe and to reject evolution. Thus, those people who, for whatever reason, feel compelled to reject evolution, need not think that they must necessarily also reject the idea of an ancient universe.

In this part of the book, we shall discuss the age-of-the-universe controversy, which can be summarized as follows. People who follow the literal reading of the Bible believe the world, and the universe, to be less than six thousand years old (literalist Christians assess it as being closer to ten thousand years). Mainstream science, on the other hand, puts the age of the Earth at about five billion years, and the age of the universe at about fourteen billion years.[1] The conflict is obvious.

---

1 Data from the WMAP satellite has established that 13.7 billion years have elapsed since the Big Bang. Other estimates range between eleven and nineteen billion years, but these differences are irrelevant for our purposes.

For our purposes, there is no need to prove that the universe is fourteen billion years old or that planet Earth is five billion years old; these involve complex calculations. Rather, we shall simply present easily graspable firm evidence that the universe is much, much older than several thousand years. It makes no difference then if it is fourteen thousand years old or fourteen billions years old; as long as it is more than the conventional understanding of Genesis would dictate, a different approach is required. (There are those who claim that the universe merely looks *as though* it is extremely old and was created to look that way. That approach is discussed in a later chapter. In this chapter, we are simply establishing that the universe does indeed appear to be extremely old.)

The scientific evidence for an ancient universe is vast. It was first observed by devoutly religious Christian geologists in the eighteenth century who were initially trying to confirm the truth of the Bible according to a literalist reading. They tried to interpret their findings so as to make them fit with the Bible and invoked the deluge in order to account for aberrations. Ultimately, however, they reluctantly recognized that this was impossible. The evidence for the great age of the world was overwhelming.

> Every effort over the previous two centuries to make Scripture, literalistically interpreted, and geological data conform to one another to the satisfaction of the geological community eventually failed.
>
> Davis A. Young, "The Discovery of Terrestrial History,"
> in *Portraits of Creation* p. 57

Of course, there are always some people who will not be swayed by the scientific evidence, no matter how much is presented. For many, belief in a universe that is a few thousand years old is a deep-seated religious and emotional conviction, not subject to being evaluated on the basis of empirical investigation. However, this book is designed for those who, like many great Torah authorities, have a basic acceptance of the legitimacy of scientific endeavor. Before discussing the responses of Torah authorities to these issues, we shall review the scientific evidence.

The most common misconception about the evidence for an old earth is that it is solely based on radiometric dating which can be waved away by saying that rates of radioactive decay have changed over history. This is untrue. Not only are there independent lines of evidence that rates of radioactive decay have remained constant; there are also many entirely independent types of evidence for an old earth, from many different fields of science. Thus, although radioactive decay is the most oft-discussed dating technique, we shall dwell on other methods instead. This is because these other methods are very simple to understand and there is less to argue about. There are those who would quibble with some of the details or accuracy of these dating techniques, but while this may raise questions on the exact precision of the figures that they give, it is still clear that the earth is much older than a few thousand years.

Eras of History

The simplest evidence that the earth is far more than a few thousand years old can be detected by the naked eye and without any special scientific skills. At thousands of locations in the world, one can find remains of extinct creatures. Such remains may include fossilized skeletons, eggs, and footprints. But in every one of these places, distinct groupings of creatures are found, depending upon which layer of rock they are found in. This shows that there were many eras of different types of animal life on the planet.

For example, consider ammonites—primitive snail-like aquatic creatures that are long extinct. Fossil ammonites can be found in many places in the world; they are especially abundant in the Ramon Crater in Israel, which has many thousands of them. But there are no fossils of contemporary aquatic creatures in these places. Likewise, there are no ammonites amongst the fossils of contemporary aquatic creatures that are found elsewhere. This shows that ammonites lived in a different era than contemporary aquatic life. And even within the category of ammonites, there are many different types of species from distinct periods.

An ammonite from the Jurassic era

There are numerous places where one can find remnants of mammoths, in locations as diverse as Siberia and the La Brea tar pits in Los Angeles. However, there are no remnants of dinosaurs in these places. Conversely, amongst all the dinosaur fossils that one finds in different parts of the world, there are no fossils of mammoths. This shows that dinosaurs and mammoths did not live at the same time.

A mammoth skeleton at the La Brea tar pits

None of the thousands of locations where dinosaur fossils and footprints have been found have ever included human fossils or the remains of human civilizations. Similarly, none of the countless archeological excavations of ancient human civilizations have ever included traces or records of dinosaurs. Dinosaurs clearly lived in a different era than humans.

Even amongst dinosaurs, different layers of rock reveal distinct eras. Stegosaurus, Brachiosaurus and Allosaurus are never found in the same layers of rock as Tyrannosaurus rex, Triceratops, and Velociraptor. The conclusion is that each existed in a different period; the former lived in a period which has been termed the Jurassic, while the latter lived in the Cretaceous period.

The same conclusion emerges from studying the plant kingdom. We find fossilized plants and trees, and we can even sometimes find fossilized plants in the stomachs of fossilized dinosaurs and in fossilized dinosaur dung. They reveal that plants, too, have gone through many different phases. We find that grass only appears with certain latter groups of dinosaurs and never amongst the creatures that preceded dinosaurs, which tells us that grass only appeared much later in history. On the other hand, an enormous number of fossilized cycad trees are found in the layers of rocks containing dinosaur fossils, whereas only a small number of different species of cycads are found today.

Thus, there were distinct eras of animal and plant life on this plant. These would have required much, much more than a few thousand years in which to take place.

Dendrochronology and Creosote Bushes

Dendrochronology refers to dating events through studying tree rings. Every year, trees add layers of wood to their trunk, thus creating the annual rings that we see when viewing a cross section. The number of rings is therefore equal to the age of the tree.

These rings are not uniform in width. They vary in thickness depending on many factors, such as sun, wind, temperature, and snow accumulation. The result of this is that one can correlate the patterns of wide and narrow rings between different trees, thus working back farther than the age of a single individual tree. In other words, the outer pattern of rings on some long-dead trees may match the inner pattern of rings on some live old trees, which means that the long-dead trees lived the last years of their lives at the same time as the beginning of the lives of the current trees.

One place that this has been measured is in the White Mountains of California and Nevada. These are home to the oldest living trees, bristlecone pines. The oldest of these is more than 4,770 years old, and dead trees have been matched with live ones, extending the scale of bristlecone pine tree rings of known age back almost nine thousand years before the present.[1]

There is also a sequence of oak trees from Europe that yields a continuous chronology from the present back to about ten thousand years ago. A pine chronology of two thousand years in duration overlaps the end of the oak chronology. This results in a total chronology going back nearly twelve thousand years.[2]

---

1 Charles Ferguson, "Dendrochronology of bristlecone pine, *Pinus aristata*: Establishment of a 7484-year chronology in the White Mountains of eastern-central California, U.S.A." *Radiocarbon Variations and Absolute Chronology* (ed. I.U. Olsson) (New York: John Wiley & Sons 1970) pp. 237-259, and "Dendrochronology of bristlecone pine: a progress report," *Radiocarbon* 25:2 (1983) pp. 287-288.

2 Bernd Becker, "A 11,000-year German Oak and Pine dendrochronology for radiocarbon calibration," *Radiocarbon* 35 (1993) pp. 201-213. The chronology was corroborated by radiocarbon dating; see Bernd Becker and Bernd Kromer, "German Oak and Pine 14C

The conclusion that clearly emerges from this data is that a figure of less than six thousand years is certainly insufficient to account for the tree-ring record. Again, the claim that trees were created in a mature form is addressed in a later chapter. In this chapter, we are simply proving that the world does indeed look much older than a few thousand years.

While discussing the plant kingdom, it should be noted that it is not only dendrochronology that points to the world being more than six thousand years old. A type of bush known as the creosote bush sends out stems that form rings around it and gradually break off from the central stem. This process takes a known period of time. One such ring of creosote bushes in the Mojave Desert called King Clone, measuring nearly seventy feet in diameter, is estimated to have originally germinated 11,700 years ago.

Varve Analysis

Varves are annual layers of sediment laid down on the base of lakes. In the spring and summer, melting snow causes streams to flow with greater volume and speed, enabling them to carry coarse sediment such as sand which settles on the base of the lake. In the winter, when there is less run-off from the mountains, the streams only carry finer sediment. This is a process that can easily be observed in freshwater lakes today. Each varve therefore consists of a thin layer of light (coarse) sediment and an even thinner layer of finer dark sediment.

Depending on the climate and environment, there may be different numbers of layers per year, but in any case they cycle as two, three or four distinct types of sediment and then repeat the same cycle again. In Lake Van, Turkey, there is a continuous varve record extending to nearly fifteen thousand years ago.[1] In Lake Suigetsu, Japan, a 250-foot core sample

calibration, 7200 BC - 9400 BC," *Radiocarbon* 35 (1993) pp. 125-135, and Marco Spurk, "Revisions and extension of the Hohenheim oak and pine chronologies: New evidence about the timing of the Younger Dryas / Preboreal transition," *Radiocarbon* 40 (1998) pp. 1107-1116.

1   Günter Landmann, "Dating Late Glacial abrupt climate changes in the 14,570 yr long continuous varve record of Lake Van, Turkey," *Palaeogeography, Paleoclimatology,*

revealed a varve chronology of forty-five thousand years.[1] In the Green River formation of Wyoming, there are places with twenty *million* thin layers of sediment; thus, the varves of the Green River formation must have formed over a period of millions of years.

Ice Cores

In places such as Greenland and Antarctica, the annual snowfall compresses that of previous years into layers of ice. By removing a core sample of ice, one can count these annual layers. The layers can be distinguished with a variety of independent techniques. A visual counting can be done with the upper layers because crystals from summer snow are larger than those from winter snow, which results in a distinctive banding in the ice. Another method of counting layers is to look for dust particles, which are far more numerous in spring due to the greater winds. A third method is to measure the acidity of the ice, which is higher for summer snow. These measurements can be performed independently in order to corroborate each other. There are techniques which confirm that the layers correspond to years, and not seasonal effects; for example, one can find ash from known volcanic eruptions in certain layers.

The Greenland Ice Sheet Project 2 drilled to a depth of two miles in order to remove core samples. 110,000 layers of ice were visible, and this count was correlated via the other techniques mentioned above. Beyond this depth, it was too difficult to measure the layers. But this measurement alone reveals that the ice layers were deposited over a period of at least 110,000 years.[2]

Palaeoecology 122 (1996) pp.107-118.

1 H. Kitagawa and J. van der Plicht, "Atmospheric Radiocarbon Calibration to 45,000 yr B.P.: Late Glacial Fluctuations and Cosmogenic Isotope Production," *Science* 279 (1998) pp. 1187-1190.

2 D. J. Meese, A.J. Gow, et al., "The Greenland Ice Sheet Project 2 Depth-Age Scale: Methods and Results," *Journal of Geophysical Research*, 102(C12):26, pp. 411-26, 423; Richard B. Alley and Michael L. Bender, "Greenland Ice Cores: Frozen in Time," *Scientific American* 278 (2) pp. 80-85.

The Ancient Stars

Aside from dating methods that demonstrate the great age of planet Earth, there is also some simple evidence that the universe as a whole is even more ancient.

The sun is 92,000,000 miles away from earth. We know that light travels at a speed of approximately 186,000 miles per second. The light from the sun therefore takes eight minutes to reach the earth. In other words, when we see the sun, we are really seeing the sun as it was eight minutes ago.

The stars, however, are much further away than the sun. We know approximately how far away they are, using a variety of straightforward techniques. Our galaxy, the Milky Way, measures 12,614,400,000,000 miles across. The stars at the far end of the galaxy are so enormously far away that the light of them would have had to leave many hundreds of thousands of years ago in order to reach us.[1]

Despite its vast size, the Milky Way is only one of many vast galaxies that populate the known universe. One of the largest optical telescopes in the world, the 387-inch Keck Telescope at Mauna Kea Observatory in Hawaii, has revealed galaxies around ten billion light-years from the earth. This means that the light of them, seen through the telescope, has taken ten billion years to reach the earth.

Conclusion

These various types of measurement, as well as many others, show that there is a good deal more than radiometric methods available to establish that the earth is much more than a few thousand years old. Furthermore, these methods reinforce each other, as the correlation between the results produced by each is much too high to be dismissed as coincidental.

---

1 The constancy of the velocity of light is a basic axiom of Einstein's theories of relativity, which are well supported. There are some suggestions in the scientific community that the speed of light may have changed since the beginning of the universe. However, these are extremely speculative. More importantly, there is certainly no suggestion that the speed of light might have changed to anywhere near the magnitude required by a universe that is only a few thousand years old.

All the evidence therefore shows that the world is much, much more than the few thousand years old given by a simple Torah-based chronology. It is thus irrelevant whether it is fourteen thousand years old, fourteen million years old, or fourteen billion years old. Since it is much more than a few thousand years old, there is a conflict with the simple chronology of the Torah that we must address.

In the next few chapters, we will survey various popular solutions that have been proposed for this problem, and we will explore the difficulties with these approaches. Following that, we will present a different approach that satisfactorily resolves the fundamental conflicts.

Chapter Ten

The Chaotic Approach

Extrapolation

In the previous chapter we examined several diverse lines of evidence for a universe that is much more than a few thousand years old. But some people argue that since these measurements are based on extrapolating from the present to the past, and physical conditions in the universe may have been different then, the evidence is therefore meaningless. Rambam is sometimes cited in support of this argument:

> …The nature of something after it has been generated and achieved a stable final state does not permit any inference whatsoever as to the condition of it while this process began. Nor does the condition of something while it moves towards being generated permit any inference regarding its state before it began to do this. If you make this mistake, and attempt to prove the nature of something while in its potential existence from its properties when actually existing, you will fall into great confusion.

> …The essential point is that when something is in a state of perfection and completion, there is no indication as to what have been its properties beforehand. We therefore do not reject as impossible the opinion of those who say that the heavens were produced before the earth, or the reverse, or that the heavens have existed without stars, or that certain species of animals have been in existence while others were not in existence. For all this applies to the state of the universe while it was being generated.

> Rambam, *Guide For The Perplexed* 2:17

146

At first glance, Rambam's argument might seem to support the idea of challenging scientific arguments for the antiquity of the universe. But upon closer study, we see that Rambam is saying something quite different.

Rambam was arguing against Aristotelian "proofs" for the eternity of the universe. Their claim was that the universe and everything in it had always existed in the same form. To this, Rambam responded that one cannot conclude a past constant history from a present constant state, just as watching a frog remain a frog for a year does not preclude the possibility that it was once a tadpole.

However, when one sees *evidence* of an earlier history, one can certainly draw conclusions regarding it. If you find a scar on the frog, you can deduce that it once had a wound. If you find a skeleton of an animal, you can deduce that there was once a live animal. Rambam's argument was that condition of something in this moment does not *necessarily* show what its previous condition has been. But in cases where we do indeed find evidence of its previous condition, there is no reason not to accept it.

It is true that Rambam did not believe that natural laws functioned during the six days of creation.[1] However, this should not concern us. In Rambam's worldview, the only conceivable frameworks were stasis and raw primordial chaos. There was no conceivable natural mechanism by which the universe could be formed. Today, not only are we aware of natural mechanisms by which the universe could be formed, and philosophically open to such possibilities, we also see from geology and paleontology that such was indeed the case, i.e. that natural laws have indeed been functioning for a very long time, and that natural processes were indeed involved in the formation of the world.

Finally, one should note that Rambam's words immediately following the above discussion are most significant:

> All these assertions are necessary if the Scriptural account of the Creation is to be taken literally. But in fact it should not be taken literally, as will be explained when we shall discuss this subject at length.
>
> Rambam, *Guide For The Perplexed* 2:17

---

1 See *Guide For The Perplexed* 2:30.

Orders of Magnitude

Rabbi Menachem Mendel Schneerson (1902-1994), the late Lubavitcher Rebbe, was adamant that the universe is only a few thousand years old. One of his arguments was that scientific views about the forces operating at the beginning of the universe were highly speculative:

> We may now summarize the weaknesses, nay, hopelessness, of all so-called scientific theories regarding the origin and age of our universe:
>
> a. These theories have been advanced on the basis of observable data during a relatively short period of time, only a number of decades or, at any rate, not more than a couple of centuries.
>
> b. On the basis of such a relatively small range of known (though by no means perfectly) data, scientists venture to build theories by the weak method of extrapolation, and from the consequent to the antecedent, extending to many thousands (according to them, to millions and billions) of years.
>
> c. In advancing such theories, they blithely disregard factors universally admitted by all scientists, namely, that in the initial period of the "birth" of the universe, conditions of temperature, atmospheric pressure, radioactivity, and a host of other cataclysmic factors, were totally different from those existing in the present state of the universe.
>
> d. The consensus of scientific opinion is that there must have been many radioactive elements in the initial stage which now no longer exist, or exist only in minimal quantities; some of them elements that cataclysmic potency of which is known even in minimal doses.
>
> e. The formation of the world, if we are to accept these theories, began with a process of colligation (binding together) of single atoms or the components of atoms and then their conglomeration and consolidation, involving totally unknown processes and variables.
>
> In short, of all the weak "scientific" theories, those which deal with the origin of cosmos and with its dating are (admittedly so by the scientists themselves) the weakest of the weak.
>
> Rabbi Menachem Schneerson, Mind Over Matter pp. 32-33

Yet it is difficult to see how these points are relevant to the issue at hand. It is true that some of the constants or conditions may well have been different during the incipient stages of the universe's formation. But this only means that the scientific estimate for the age of the universe, at about fourteen billion years, might be wrong by a few billion years. It certainly does not mean that the universe is just a few thousand years old! None of the scientific theories about the conditions during the birth of the cosmos are relevant to phenomena such as tree-rings, sedimentary layers in rivers, ice layers, and fossils.

Fossils and the Effects of Chaos

Rabbi Naftali Tzvi Yehudah Berlin (also known as Netziv, 1817-1893) wrote that dinosaurs lived before the deluge and were the results of cross-breeding experiments by that generation:

> "And all existence was obliterated" (Genesis 7:23)—the carcasses were obliterated, and the verse is careful to say "that were on the face of the earth." I.e. it is specifically these that were on the face of the earth [which were obliterated], but many carcasses remained on which much earth fell due to the flooding of the waters, and the bodies were thereby preserved. Those are the bones that the diggers of the earth find, and they find the bones of creatures that do not exist in the world today.

> ...It appears that these bones are from before the deluge, and even though they are found in climates where they do not live today, this is due to the fact that they changed their ways upon the earth before the deluge and went to other places. And that which they find unusual creatures is due to their having hybridized different animals, which gave birth to unusual offspring, just as the mule results from the crossbreeding of the horse and donkey.[1] It was providentially arranged that these bones should remain so that later generations would come and recognize the secrets of nature, and this is the Honor of the Blessed One... but at that time it was the Divine Will that they should be obliterated from the earth, so that they should not be seen at all such that people would endeavor to engage in such crossbreeding again and bring about such creatures a second time. Therefore it is written again, "And He obliterated them from the land"; the providence was that these unusual bones should not be found in that generation or many generations later, so that they should not try to renew them, therefore their remembrance was erased from the land.

> Netziv, *Haamek Davar*, Genesis 7:23

---

1 The original text reads "camel," which is presumably an unintentional error.

This creative approach explained the evidence as it was known to Netziv. However, were Netziv alive today and able to see the range of fossils that have now been discovered, he would likely not present such an idea. It is inconceivable that creatures such as tyrannosaurus or pterodactyl were the results of hybridization between contemporary animals. Furthermore, the evidence shows that the dinosaurs lived long, long before the deluge. Were Netziv alive today, he would likely have proposed an answer that explained all the evidence we currently have.

Some people claim that the chaotic acts of creation, and/or the deluge, had the effect of making the world look older than it actually is. There are various statements in the Midrash which seem to state that the laws of nature were different during the six days of creation.[1] Other statements indicate that the seasons and human physiology were different in the antediluvian era,[2] or that it affected nature in a very fundamental way.[3] While there are different traditions regarding how to interpret such Midrashic statements, some fully accept their literal meaning and argue that all scientific methods of dating the earth are therefore invalid. Rabbi Chaim Halberstam of Sanz (1793-1876) was the first to record such an explanation:

> ...The scientists found a star whose orbit takes 36,000 years, yet the world only has a duration of 6,000 years... how was this star created? So the scientists ask. I have heard that a wealthy man once asked this to my holy mentor of Ropschitz (Rabbi Naftali Tzvi Horowitz), who answered him in accordance with the attitude of the questioner, "Why must you examine hidden things? Our job is simply to serve God based on our knowledge, and we have no business with hidden things." However, subsequently I found in a book by a great man—who was of the holy ones in the days of the Arizal and perhaps even much earlier than that—who brings this question and answers it as follows: It is

---

1 *Midrash Bereishis Rabbah* 10:4 states that the constellations moved quicker before Adam's sin; *Midrash Bereishis Rabbah* 22:2 states that biological processes were wondrously sped up on the sixth day, in that Eve conceived and gave birth on the same day.

2 *Midrash Bereishis Rabbah* 34:11.

3 *Midrash Bereishis Rabbah* 28:3 speaks of its devastation and *Midrash Bereishis Rabbah* 32:7 speaks of God altering the course of nature in the way that the waters of the deluge came.

known that the universe was once in its most perfect state, but Adam corrupted it and caused a weakness in all of creation. And therefore, at the time of creation, if not for the sin of our father the first one, the movement (orbits) would have been fast; but now, because of the flaw caused by the sin [of Adam], the orbit has to wait 36,000 years. The *Yaaros Dvash* writes similarly.[1]

Rabbi Chaim Halberstam, Divrei Chaim al HaTorah, Chanukah, p. 90

In the nineteenth century, Malbim developed this explanation with regard to dinosaur fossils:

"And they were erased from the land"—that even though the mighty bones of many remained like iron javelins and were not erased, nevertheless they were erased from the [surface of the] land, for the flooding of water transported the carcasses into the depths, and most were swallowed up in the bottoms of the watery depths... such that when Noach emerged from the ark, he did not find any sign of the carcasses of these animals, or the giant bones and the huge creatures that were before the deluge. And "the testimony of God is trustworthy, making the simple one wise" (Psalms 19:8), to respond to the scholars of geology who dig in the depths of the earth and find large bones from giants and huge animals that were destroyed from the earth and have not existed since the days of the deluge, and they prove the antiquity of the world from this...

Malbim, Commentary to Genesis 7:23

Malbim seeks to account for why fossils of dinosaurs appear to be in a lower and older layer than remains of contemporary creatures. His explanation is that while smaller creatures were entirely destroyed by the deluge, the bones of larger creatures (i.e. dinosaurs) remained whole, to be transported into the depths of the earth by the waters of the deluge. One problem with this approach is that although in Malbim's time it was only large extinct creatures that had been discovered, since then we have discovered countless fossils of tiny dinosaurs and other extinct forms of life.

---

1 Rabbi Yoel Teitelbaum in *Divrei Yoel* (*Simchas Torah* p.613) identifies this as referring to *Yaaros Devash* vol. I *drush* 1 and 15.

An updated version of this claim was presented by the Lubavitcher Rebbe:

> The argument from the discovery of fossils, is *by no means* conclusive evidence of the great antiquity of the earth, for the following reasons:
>
> (a) In view of the unknown conditions which existed in "prehistoric" times, conditions of atmospheric pressures, temperatures, radioactivity, unknown catalyzers, etc., etc. as already mentioned, conditions, that is, which could have caused reactions and changes of an entirely different nature and tempo from those known under the present-day orderly processes of nature, one cannot exclude the possibility that dinosaurs existed 5722 years ago, and became fossilized under terrific natural cataclysms in the course of a few years rather than in millions of years, since we have no conceivable measurements or criteria of calculations applicable to those unknown conditions.
>
> Rabbi Menachem Schneerson, *Mind Over Matter* p. 34

The most glaring problem with this approach is that, if dinosaurs lived at the same time as contemporary creatures, then one would find dinosaurs fossils in the same rock layers as fossils of other creatures. The fact that we do not find this shows that they lived at different times. While some people may argue in return that Creation or a global flood had chaotic effects on the natural world and made it impossible to draw any conclusions from examining it, this is not what we find when we study the world. Instead of finding chaos, we find a very neat arrangement of fossils and sedimentary layers, with clearly distinct eras of animal life. This is why the early Christian geologists, who likewise had assumed that the deluge could account for their findings, were forced to reject this belief.

Similar ideas are quite prevalent. There are suggestions that the continents were still joined immediately before the deluge, or that the planet's axis was not tilted at that time, and so on. While such ideas might have been reasonable to the nineteenth-century thinkers who first proposed them, they no longer have any serious basis. They could say such things, but we cannot.

These ad hoc explanations demonstrate an unfortunate naiveté regarding science. It is easy for someone lacking knowledge in the natural sciences to toss out a theory regarding the earth's history. But it is rather like someone lacking knowledge of Torah saying that although the Torah prohibits working on Shabbos, it is nevertheless permitted to drive, because that is not "work." The educated Jew, on the other hand, knows that the prohibition of *melachah*, loosely translated as "work," has a very precise definition, and he understands that one cannot change the law about driving on Shabbos without fundamentally altering the entire framework of *melachah* and Jewish law. It is equally true that one cannot casually posit that fossils were artificially aged, or that the continents split in recent history, or that the earth's axis was not tilted before the deluge, without undermining the entire scientific enterprise. All such suggestions have enormous ramifications that can be tested and would be extremely noticeable. Yet nothing has ever been discovered that would lend credibility to such speculations.

Of course, people will respond that God can do anything, and indeed He can create a universe in which changing one aspect of nature does not affect other parts. Yet the question is not whether He *can* but rather whether He *did*. And what we see is that He created a universe in which altering one aspect does necessarily have implications for other aspects.

Rabbi Samson Raphael Hirsch was one of the earliest figures to be skeptical about the scientific evidence for the antiquity of the universe due to the extrapolation involved:

> Judaism would have nothing to fear from that theory even if it were based on something more than a mere hypothesis, on the still unproven assumption that the forces we see at work in our world today are the same as those that were in existence with the same degree of potency when the world was first created.
>
> Rabbi Samson Raphael Hirsch, *The Educational Value of Judaism*, in *Collected Writings*, vol. VII, p. 265

In the nineteenth century, when Rabbi Hirsch wrote this, the antiquity of the universe may well have reasonably been thought to be based upon mere hypotheses and unproven assumptions, especially to somebody like Rabbi Hirsch who, for all his brilliance in theology, was not a geologist. Since then, however, it has been verified beyond reasonable doubt. And perhaps the most important point to bear in mind is that which we noted earlier: that despite his personal skepticism of science, Hirsch nevertheless realized that other people took it seriously and therefore provided ways of reconciling it with Torah.

All Sped Up

Rabbi Shimon Schwab (1908-1993) maintained that the universe could not be billions of years old, and yet did not discount the scientific evidence in that direction. Instead, he posited that billions of years during the era of creation were equal to six regular days today. His explanation for this is that all the events of those fourteen billion years were sped up such that they took place in only six days:

> During the period of creation.... The earth could have turned around its axis much more rapidly... the billions of years which science claims to have calculated, all actually occurred during six ordinary days.
>
> Rabbi Simon Schwab, "How Old Is The Universe?" in *Challenge*, p. 169

An instant difficulty with this, and its resolution, is discussed by Rabbi Schwab:

> ...It is obvious that if all motion were uniformly multiplied all radiation, for instance, would become lethal. The accelerated speed would turn every particle into a deadly missile. Also a multiplication of the rapidity of all motion would upset the balance of mechanical forces which function differently at different speeds. Therefore, we should rather think of a uniform nexus of changes in the entire system of the natural order which is observable today, a uniform variation in all functions within the framework of natural law in conformity with the new universal velocity, not upsetting the intricate balance of all physical phenomena and the orderly cooperation of all parts within the whole.
>
> Ibid., p. 171

Although this solves the technical difficulties, it now raises another type of difficulty—if the entire system has sped up, in what way is it significant to say that any of it has sped up? Again, Rabbi Schwab raises the question and provides an answer:

> In fact, without having at least one exception somewhere in the universe, the simultaneous uniform acceleration of all motion is in

itself a meaningless concept. The fixed reference point which might give meaning to this whole concept is the Creation Light.

Ibid., p. 170

The Creation Light to which he refers is the light that appeared on the very first day, before the sun shone on the earth. This formed the basis of the calendar during the week of creation.

> The Torah gives us a clear definition of the length of a creation Day, namely the time from the appearance of the creation Light until its reappearance.

Ibid., p. 168

This is the reconciliation of the fourteen billion years with the six days explained by Rabbi Schwab. It retains the concept of six days meaning six days according to the current concept of time, and alters the laws of the universe during creation to fit fourteen billion years within that time.

Yet while there can be no scientific evidence against Rabbi Schwab's explanation, there is ample room to disagree with his description of the conclusion. If *all* physical phenomena as we know them were sped up, then the speeding up is irrelevant. The Creation Light, even with Rabbi Schwab's understanding that it had a physical manifestation, is an insignificant point of reference in comparison to the revolutions of the earth, the movement of the planets and suchlike. If the earth is rotating on its axis billions of times, the sun rising and setting billions of times, and countless millions of generations of animals are living their lives, then how is it meaningful to speak of this taking only six days? Imagine if last week was sped up by God so that it only took five minutes on the Cosmic clock—would this be detectable or even meaningful in any way? If fourteen billion years equal six Creation days, then it is fourteen billion years as *we* understand it, and the six days are being understood differently from the simple understanding. If virtually everything is being sped up, then effectively nothing is being sped up.

Conclusion

Postulating that the scientific evidence for an ancient universe is unreliable, due to the early universe being chaotic and subject to different laws, involves two fundamental problems:

155

(a) If the early stages of the world involved chaotic processes, then when we explore the earth's history we would see chaos. But we do not see this. Instead, we see neatly separated eras of life and a correlation of different dating methods.

(b) If all or most physical phenomena were sped up, then effectively nothing is sped up.

Some people will nevertheless argue that *somehow*, various processes were sped up or subjected to different chaotic phenomena to make the earth appear older, while other processes that actually dictate the age of the earth remained constant. But such speculations are vague, far-fetched and unconvincing. All the different available dating techniques point to the same results. How could changes in the universe have altered them all in synchronization to give the same misleading result, while leaving the phenomena that truly dictate its age as unchanged? That could only happen if God were deliberately out to fool us—an argument that we shall challenge in the next chapter.

Chapter Eleven

The Prochronic Approach

A Ready-Made History

One suggested reconciliation of the Biblical account with the scientific evidence for an old universe is that the universe was created a few thousand years ago with an aged appearance, looking as though it is fourteen billion years old. This seems to account for all the scientific evidence concerning the antiquity of the universe. Many consider this to be a very good explanation. But is it?

Adopting this approach implies that all scientific research in this field is indeed valid, since for all intents and purposes, the universe is fourteen billion years old. Yet many who propose such an approach are nevertheless uncomfortable with all the scientific evidence for an ancient world and attempt to refute it. This odd phenomenon perhaps indicates that this approach stems more from a distrust of science than from a serious belief in its viability.

Support for this position is claimed from a statement in the Talmud:

> Everything in the work of creation was created in its full form...
>
> Talmud, *Rosh Hashanah* 11a, *Chullin* 60a

The commentary of Rashi explains that this accounts for the verse stating that God created every "fruit-bearing tree"—it means that the trees were instantly ready to bear fruit.[1] The commentary of *Tosafos* explains that every creature was made in its final form.[2] Another Midrash states that Adam was created as a twenty year old man.[3] Likewise, people claim that the entire universe was created in a mature state. Thus, it was created less than six thousand years ago in such a way that it appears to be billions of years old.

The Modern Presentation

This approach was most prominently put forward by the late Lubavitcher Rebbe, Rabbi Menachem Mendel Schneerson:

> The argument from the discovery of fossils, is by no means conclusive evidence of the great antiquity of the earth, for the following reasons:
>
> …b. Even assuming that the period of time which the Torah allows for the age of the world is definitely too short for fossilization (although I do not see how one can be so categorical), we can still readily accept the possibility that G-d created ready fossils, bones or skeletons (for reasons best known to him), just as he could create ready living organisms, a complete man, and such ready products as oil, coal or diamonds, without any evolutionary process.
>
> As for the question, if it be true as above (b), why did G-d have to create fossils in the first place? The answer is simple: We cannot know the reason why G-d chose this manner of creation in preference to another, and whatever theory of creation is accepted, the question will remain unanswered. The question, Why create a fossil? is no more valid than the question, Why create an atom? Certainly, such a question cannot serve as a sound argument, much less as a logical basis, for the evolutionary theory.
>
> What scientific basis is there for limiting the creative process to an evolutionary process only, starting with atomic and sub-atomic particles—a theory full of unexplained gaps and complications, and excluding the possibility of creation as given by the Biblical account?

---

1 Rashi to *Rosh Hashanah* 11a.

2 *Tosafos* to *Chullin* 60a.

3 *Midrash Bereishis Rabbah* 14:7.

For, if the latter possibility be admitted, everything falls neatly into pattern, and all speculation regarding the origin and age of the world becomes unnecessary and irrelevant.

It is surely no argument to question this possibility by saying, Why should the creator create a finished universe, when it would have been sufficient for Him to create an adequate number of atoms or subatomic particles with the power of colligation and evolution to develop into the present cosmic order? The absurdity of this argument becomes even more obvious when it is the basis of a flimsy theory rather than based on sound and irrefutable arguments overriding all other possibilities.

Mind Over Matter, pp. 34-35

There are several difficulties with this general approach that we shall soon discuss. Particularly problematic is Rabbi Schneerson's statement that the question, "Why create a fossil?" is no more valid than the question, "Why create an atom?" This is a strange statement; a fossil is directly misleading in a way that an atom is not. Asking "why create an atom" is a pointless philosophical speculation, but asking "why create a fossil which appears to be a dead dinosaur if no such creature ever lived" is a very reasonable and obvious question.

Testing Faith?

Some claim that God might have implanted such a false history in order to test our faith in the truth of the Torah. There are, however, considerable theological difficulties with such a theory. First, although dinosaurs might have *de facto* become a test of faith for people, there is certainly no innate reason for them to be a test; as we shall see, there are plenty of ways in which the age of the dinosaurs is easily understood in light of the Torah.

Second, while we cannot definitely know God's mind, the Torah's description of Him indicates that He does not act in that way. Scripture is full of instructions to contemplate the universe and use it as a way to perceive religious truths. Nature points towards God, not away from Him. We are told, "Lift your eyes upon high and perceive Who created these!" (Isaiah 40:26); and that "The heavens speak of God's glory, and the sky tells of His handiwork!" (Psalms 19:2). Rabbi Yehudah HaLevi, in his famous work *The Kuzari*, writes:

> Heaven forbid that there should be anything in the Torah to contradict that which is manifest or proved!

> *Kuzari 1:67*

Likewise, Heaven forbid that there should be anything manifest or proven which would contradict anything in the Torah. As the Midrash states:

> God created everything in His universe except for the trait of falsehood.

> *Tanna D'vei Eliyahu Zuta 3*

The physical evidence contained in the world must reflect truth. Since God wrote the book of nature, everything in it must conform with the Torah; if it initially seems not to do so, we must check that both our understanding of the world and our understanding of Torah is correct. [1]

Originally Omphalos

The claim that God created the universe with a built-in history is sometimes called the Omphalos argument. This is due to it being first expounded in a book entitled *Omphalos*, written by the Christian preacher Phillip Henry Gosse and published in 1857. [2] The word *Omphalos* is Greek for "navel." It alludes to the earlier Christian debate over whether Adam possessed a navel, which is unneccessary for someone who is not born from a mother with an umbilical cord. Gosse developed his argument in considerable detail, and his articulation of this approach is much more well-reasoned than one might assume.

---

1 Some might raise a counter-objection to our argument that God does not create things that refute the truths of the Torah, in that the Torah itself tells us there may be false prophets who successfully perform wonders and try to lead us away from the proper service of God. However, this is not a comparable case. There is nothing in the miracles of a false prophet that actually refutes any of the truths of the Torah. It is merely a power that he possesses, just as Bilaam possessed the power of prophecy.

2 For a fascinating discussion, see Ron Roizen, "The rejection of *Omphalos*: a note on shifts in the intellectual hierarchy of mid-nineteenth century Britain," *Journal for the Scientific Study of Religion*, 21 (1982) pp. 365-369.

Gosse took it as a given that each animal species was created *ex nihilo* rather than having evolved. Based on that premise, he pointed out that there is no such thing as creating something at the "first stage" in an animal's existence. A cow begins life as a calf; but before that, it is a fetus, and earlier than being a fetus, it was an ovum, part of its mother. Every species is an endless cycle of life:

> It is evident that there is no one point in the history of any single creature, which is a legitimate beginning of existence.... Creation, the sovereign fiat of Almighty Power, gives us the commencing point, which we in vain seek in nature.... But the whole organization of the creature thus newly called into existence, looks back to the course of an endless circle in the past.
>
> *Omphalos*, pp. 122-124

Gosse then illustrated that no matter at which point in this cirle an organism is created, its form necessarily indicates a past history. For example, a tree has rings, which are signs of previous seasons that it lived through. Many animals can only function with teeth that are worn through use, and would have to be created with pre-worn teeth. It is therefore not at all strange that a created man would have a navel. Gosse coined the term *prochronic* to describe such creative processes that included a built-in history:

> ...A cyclical character does attach to, and is inseparable from, the history of all organic essences... we cannot avoid the conclusion that each organism was from the first marked with the records of a previous being. But since creation and previous history are inconsistent with each other; as the very idea of the creation of an organism excludes the idea of pre-existence of that organism, or of any part of it; it follows, that such records are *false*, so far as they testify to time; that the developments and processes thus recorded have been produced without time, or what I have called *prochronic*.
>
> Ibid. p. 336

Given his presumption of creatures being created, Gosse satisfactorily argued that they must include features of their non-existent history. But Gosse then addressed the question of fossils. Rather than dismiss the question as the Lubavitcher Rebbe later did, he attempted to provide an approach, that we shall now explore.

Fossils and Previous Eras

Creating a fully authentic adult creature does indeed require creating a navel. But how does it require creating fossils of prehistoric creatures? Gosse suggested that fossils could be accounted for if one could show that, like individual animals, the natural history of animal life in general also necessarily indicated previous stages. But he acknowledged that he had no way to prove this:

> In order to perfect the analogy between an organism and the world, so as to show that the law which prevails in the one obtains also in the other, it would be necessary to prove that the development of the physical history of the world is circular, like that already shown to characterise the course of organic nature. And this I cannot prove. But neither, as I think, can the contrary be proved.
>
> Ibid. pp. 342-343

In other words, while it can be demonstrated that an adult human necessarily includes a belly-button in order to appear fully-formed, it is not so simple to explain why live animals also require evidence of dead animals.

> …If we could take a sufficiently large view of the whole plan of nature, should we discern that the existence of species x necessarily involved the pre-existence of species y, and must inevitably be followed by species z?... I dare not say, we should; though I think it highly probable. But I think you will not dare to say, we should *not*.
>
> It is certain that, when the Omnipotent God proposed to create a given organism, the course of that organism was present to his idea, as an ever revolving circle, without beginning and without end. He created it at some point in the circle, and gave it thus an arbitrary beginning; but one which involved all previous rotations of the circle, though only as ideal, or, in other phrase, prochronic. Is it not possible—I do not ask for more—that, in like manner, the natural course of the world was projected in his idea as a perfect whole, and that He determined to create it at some point of that course, which act, however, should involve previous stages, though only ideal or prochronic?
>
> Ibid. pp. 343-345

Gosse had no explanation as to why the natural world as a whole would require previous stages. He merely argued that it is reasonable to suppose that some such theory may exist:

> Who will say that the suggestion, that the strata of the surface of the earth with their fossil floras and faunas, may possibly belong to a prochronic development of the mighty plan of the life-history of this world,—who will dare to say that such a suggestion is a self-evident absurdity?
>
> Ibid. p. 347

The irony is that evolution would help fill this gap. Evolution explains why the existence of species x would indeed necessarily involve the pre-existence of species y. Yet Gosse rejected evolution so as to account for why organisms had to be created at some point of their lives. Still, one could find other cause for explaining why they had to be created at some such point, such as due to the Talmud's statement that all the creatures were created in their full form. The concept of evolution would then explain why there is a prehistory of all the previous stages, if one argues that God chooses to give the appearance of working within natural law and would want the world's history to demonstrate evolution. Nevertheless, one cannot help but suspect that most adherents of prochronism are very uncomfortable with the idea of evolution, even when it is merely a false history of evolution!

A more serious problem is that although evolution would account for fossils of creatures that are directly ancestral to today's creatures, it may not suffice to account for fossils of evolutionary branches that led in completely different directions. It is difficult to argue that the entire age of the dinosaurs was a necessary prerequisite to the creatures that presently exist, unless one is very much constraining the creative process to follow the vagaries of nature.

The history of the earth includes many previous eras, such as that of the dinosaurs. To say that plants and animals were made in their final, adult form is one thing, but to say that the entire world was created with a ready-made history of previous fictional eras is far more difficult to comprehend. To put it another way: if God had wanted to create a universe that was in an "adult" state, He could have made one that was several hundred million years younger than ours. What purpose would there be to a creating a world that had advanced through previous eras? There is no doubt that creative minds will come up with a reason. But it is certainly a very different type of creation. The sole basis for stating that God made the world in a complete form was the Talmud's statement, and that statement does not mention anything about previous unnecessary eras.

The Impossibility of Complete Prochronology

There is a further basic difficulty with the prochronic approach. Gosse convincingly argued that given the premise that creatures were created at some stage in their lives, then they must show evidence of earlier stages; a tree must necessarily have had rings and man a navel. The Omphalos approach of explaining the history of the world is based on the idea of carrying this through fully.

But let us truly carry this through. Would Adam have had *memories* of his non-existent childhood? Surely not—he knew that God had made him and that he lacked human parents! Would he have possessed mementos from his non-existent childhood? Likewise, surely not. Would he have had scars from his non-existent childhood mishaps? Well, since he knew that had never experienced any such mishaps, then he surely would not have possessed scars either. But, by the same token, there is no reason why he should have had a scar from the umbilical cord being removed. Thus, it is true that working back from the perspective of man being created as a complete adult, one is led to conclude that he had a navel; but working in the other direction, from the presumption that he did not have memories of his childhood or scars, then he surely would have likewise also lacked a navel.

In other words, Gosse argued that creating an adult human necessarily implies creating a full past history. But careful consideration shows that the false history was most certainly *not* complete. Since it must have necessarily been incomplete, it is difficult to argue that God should have created any false history at all.

Returning to the Talmud's statement, this would mean that it requires a clarification. Does it mean that God created everything in a "full-size" state, or in a "matured" state? Since Adam had no childhood memories, mementos or scars, then it surely only means that he was created at full size, not as though he had lived a full lifetime. Thus, there is no Talmudic support for the idea that the world was created as though it had experienced previous stages of growth or eras of life.

Carrying it All the Way

Another problem with prochronic theory is that when it is fleshed out in all its necessary details, it becomes increasingly unreasonable. It begins with creating man with a navel. The next stage is creating fake skeletons, which stretches credulity. But there are other aspects of history that would have to be falsified.

When we look at the stars at night, we are actually not seeing them as they are today, but rather as they were a long time ago. As fast as light travels, stars are very, very far away and it takes a long time for their light to reach us. We see light coming from stars that died millions of years ago; has God created an image of something that never actually existed?[1]

There are many relics of ancient human civilization which date far earlier than six thousand years ago. God would have had to create fake cave paintings in France and fake buildings that were never built by people or inhabited. One cannot help but notice that Genesis speaks about God creating live animals and man, and makes no mention of God creating fake fossils and phony relics of ancient human civilization. This does not disprove the possibility, but it stretches credulity very far indeed.[2]

A cave painting dated to 10,000 years ago. Was it made by Neolothic man, or by God?

---

1 Actually, the Lubavitcher Rebbe argues precisely this (*Mind Over Matter*, p. 52). He suggests that the statement "Let there be light" refers to star-light that was created before stars. Still, many will find this exceedingly far-fetched.

2 Berel Dov Lerner, "Omphalos Revisited," *Jewish Bible Quarterly* XXIII:3(91) July-September 1995, pp. 162-7.

The difficulties do not stop there. Records of several ancient civilizations show them *continuing* though the period of six thousand years ago, through to five thousand years ago and later. This means that God continued to create fake evidence even after He created man! It means that when Adam's descendants reached Egypt and were the first humans to do so (according to this school of thought), they found a fake Egyptian civilization into which they neatly inserted themselves!

People who present prochronic theory as an adequate explanation of the apparent age of the universe do not generally work it through in all its details. When one does so, it becomes increasingly unreasonable.

Logical Problems and Alternative Tests

There is a commonly cited logical difficulty with the prochronic approach. If one is going to posit that the universe was made a few thousand years ago with a ready-made history, why not say that it was made five minutes ago?

Some offer a rejoinder to this. If the figure of several thousand years were to be an arbitrarily chosen figure with no other basis, then this objection would indeed be valid. However, the figure of several thousand years is no mere whim; it is the age of the world as determined by a simple reading of the Torah. Now, people find many reasons to believe that the Torah is a factual document. While there may be grounds for understanding that the six days of the creation-week are not to be taken as six days in the sense of the six days of a normal week, there are certainly also grounds for taking it literally. Thus, since there are authoritative grounds for believing that the universe was created several thousand years ago, there is a qualitative advantage to saying that it was made at that time with a ready-made history rather than saying it was made five minutes ago with a ready-made history.[1]

Still, this reveals a basic problem with the view of God that the prochronic approach presents. If one is going to posit that God might deliberately create false evidence to mislead us, this raises some serious questions. According to this approach, God created two conflicting

---

1 Rabbi Dovid Gottlieb, "The Age of the Universe."

accounts of Creation: one in nature, and one in the Torah. How can it be determined which is the real story, and which is a fake designed to mislead us? One could equally propose that it is nature which presents the real story, and that the Torah was devised by God to test us with a fake history!

The idea that God deliberately creates false testimony has disturbing implications. The Biblical commentators are quick to point out that when God instructed Abraham to bring up Isaac as an offering, He did not tell him to actually sacrifice Isaac, only to bring him up. Had God genuinely told Abraham to sacrifice Isaac, it would have been impossible for that to not have been His will. Otherwise, perhaps every commandment from Him is a test to be doubted—perhaps He does not actually want people to destroy the tribe of Amalek, and that is just a test!

One has to be able to rely on God's truthfulness if religion is to function. Or, to put it another way—if God went to enormous lengths to convince us that the world is billions of years old, who are we to disagree?

Conclusion

The statement of the Talmud concerning everything having been created in its final form is not neccessarily supporting the prochronic approach. Rabbi Menachem Mendel Kasher (1895-1983), author of the encyclopedic *Torah Sheleimah*, points out that there are also numerous Talmudic and Midrashic sources explicitly stating that man was *not* created from the outset in his final form.[1] We see that the statement about his being created in a finished form is either disputed or may turn out to have a different meaning than a superficial reading would indicate. As we shall discuss elsewhere, the diversity of views regarding creation shows that they are all individual opinions, none of which are universally binding. Thus, there is no unequivocal proof from the Talmud that the world was created to appear aged.

While the prochronic approach to the antiquity of the universe might appear foolproof, we have seen several serious difficulties with it. First, it

---

1   Rabbi Menachem Mendel Kasher, *Toras HaBeriah uMishnas HaHispaschus BeMidrashei Chazal.*

presupposes that God acts in such a way that many feel to be theologically problematic in the extreme. Second, the universe was not merely made in a "complete" state; it includes records of previous self-contained eras. Third, such a mode of creation is necessarily flawed, as there was certainly not a complete prochronology (Adam did not possess memories or mementos of his childhood). Fourth, when prochronology is fleshed out in all its details, it becomes increasingly far-fetched and ultimately extremely unreasonable. Fifth, it raises some difficult theological problems concerning when we are able to trust God.

Fortunately, there are alternative approaches to understanding the antiquity of the universe.

Chapter Twelve

The Prior-Worlds Approach

Destroying and Creating Worlds

Many accept the physical evidence for an ancient universe, and also accept that it progressed as indicated by the evidence, rather than being made in its final form with only an apparent history. There are approaches that we shall discuss which revolve around showing how the six days of creation were eras rather than regular days. However, there are also classical sources which state that although the six days were of ordinary length, there is space to insert billions of years at the beginning of the six days of creation. The earliest source for this idea is found in the Midrash:

> Rabbi Yehudah bar Simon said: It is not written here (at the end of the first day of creation), "Let there be evening," but rather, "And there was evening" (implying an already existing concept); we see from here that there was an order of time beforehand. Rabbi Avahu said: This teaches that God was building worlds and destroying them, until He created this one, saying, "This pleases Me; those did not please Me."
>
> *Midrash Bereishis Rabbah* 3:7

Various explanations of this Midrash have been given. According to Rabbeinu Bachya ben Asher, this relates to the concept presented in the Midrash that the Torah preceded the world by two thousand years.[1]

---

1 *Midrash Bereishis Rabbah* 8:2; *Midrash Tehillim* 90:4.

Accordingly, this Midrash is telling us that two thousand years are to be inserted immediately preceding the events of the first day:

> Understand that the period of the Torah preceding the world was from "In the beginning" until "Let there be light," as alluded to in the word *Bereishis* (by way of an acronym); there are two millennia (*beis*) that were foremost (*reishis*). Similarly we find in the Midrash, in *Bereishis Rabbah*: "It does not say 'Let there be evening' but 'And there was evening'; we see from here that there was a system of time beforehand." Even though time is a creation, and before creation there was no time, it refers to time in regard to those two thousand years. For those days were not as human days, but rather a day from those years was of the days about which there is no comprehension. This is as it is written, "(Job 36:26)" "Are Your years as those of men?" (Ibid. 10:5), and "Your years are not finished" (Psalms 102:28).
>
> Rabbeinu Bachya, Commentary to Genesis 1:3

This view is seen by some as providing room to account for the billions of years of the universe's history recorded by science. These years occurred during the period alluded to in the description of the first day of creation following a previous period, in which "those days were not as human days."[1]

Sabbatical Cycles

A similar explanation is based on a statement in the Talmud:

> Rabbi Katina said: The world will exist for six thousand years, and for one [millennium] will be destroyed.
>
> Talmud, *Sanhedrin* 97a

The *Sefer Ha-Temunah*, a Kabbalistic work attributed to the first-century Talmudic sage, Rabbi Nechunya ben ha-Kanah, states that this seven-thousand-year cycle is merely one Sabbatical cycle amidst a larger cycle of seven Sabbatical cycles and a Jubilee.[2] Hence, the total duration

---

1 See Rabbi Menachem Kasher, *Torah Sheleimah*, *Bereishis* vol. I section 422, for extensive discussion of Rabbeinu Bachya's view.

2 It should be noted that the entire concept of such Sabbatical cycles was disputed by two of the greatest later Kabbalists, Rabbi Yitzchak Luria (Arizal) and Rabbi Moshe Cordovero.

of the universe is forty-nine thousand years (seven times seven thousand). Some authorities state that we are currently in the second Sabbatical cycle,[1] whereas others maintain that we are in the seventh.[2] Still others understand that the world is in its sixth Sabbatical cycle, which would mean that the world is 42,000 years old.[3]

Rabbi Yitzchak ben Shmuel of Akko (1250-1350), a student of Ramban and one of the foremost Kabbalists of his time, states that since these cycles existed before Adam, their chronology must be measured in divine rather than human years. He gives the length of a divine year:

> I, the insignificant Yitzchak of Akko, have seen fit to write a great mystery that should be kept very well hidden. One of God's days is a thousand years, as it says, "For a thousand years are in Your eyes as a fleeting yesterday." Since one of our years is 365¼ days, a year on High is 365,250 of our years.

Otzar HaChaim, pp. 86b-87b

Rabbi Aryeh Kaplan (1934-1983), a dynamic teacher who synthesized his expertise in physics with his knowledge of kabbalah, states that since, according to some interpretations of *Sefer HaTemunah*, the world is in its sixth Sabbatical cycle and is 42,000 years old, then explaining these years as divine years produces a most interesting result:

> Thus, according to Rabbi Isaac of Akko, the universe would be 42,000 x 365,250 years old. This comes out to be 15,340,500,000 years, a highly significant figure. From calculations based on the expanding universe and other cosmological observations, modern science has concluded that the Big Bang occurred approximately 15 billion years ago. But here we see the same figure presented in a Torah source written over seven hundred years ago!
>
> I am sure that many will find this highly controversial. However, it is important to know that this opinion exists in our classical literature; moreover, that one of the most important Kabbalists of seven centuries

---

1 See *Derush Ohr HaChaim* cited above.

2 See *Livnat Ha-Sapir.*

3 For further discussion, see Israel Weinstock: *Be-ma'aglei Ha-nigleh Ve-ha-nistar* ("Studies in Jewish Philosophy and Mysticism") pp. 190-206.

ago calculated the age of the universe and came to the same conclusion as modern science.

Rabbi Aryeh Kaplan, Immortality, Resurrection and the
Age of the Universe: A Kabbalistic View pp. 9-10

However, a contemporary author, Rabbi Ari Kahn, contends that Rabbi Kaplan misunderstood Rabbi Yitzchak ben Shmuel:

> There are a number of problems with this approach. Rabbi Yitzchak, whose system multiplies one day by 1000 years, does not say we are in the sixth cycle, but rather that we are in Din, which would seem to be the second cycle. *Livnat HaSapir*, who says we are in the sixth cycle, does not multiply a day by 1000 years.

Rabbi Ari Kahn, Explorations, p. 291

According to Rabbi Kahn, there is no centuries-old opinion giving the age of the universe as fifteen billion years.[1] But it is still significant that these Kabbalistic sources see the world as being much more than several thousand years old, and they were not constrained by the simple reading of Genesis.

Rabbi Yisrael Lipschitz and the Megalosaurus

A lengthy explanation about the time before our era, as well as a fascinating discussion about dinosaurs, was presented in the nineteenth century by Rabbi Yisrael Lipschitz (1782-1860), author of the *Tiferes Yisrael* commentary on the Mishnah. He delivered it as a sermon, and it was subsequently committed to writing and printed in the back of most comprehensive editions of the Mishnah:

> ...As regards the past, Rabbi Avahu states at the beginning of *Bereishis Rabbah* that the words "and it was evening, and it was morning" indicate that there was a series of epochs before then; the Holy One created worlds and destroyed them, approving some and not others. The Kabbalists expanded upon this statement and revealed that this process is repeated seven times, each Sabbatical cycle achieving greater perfection than the last... They also tell us that we are now in the midst of the fourth of these great cycles of perfection...

---

1   Rabbi Kaplan reportedly later admitted to misunderstanding Rabbi Yitzchak of Akko.

We are enabled to appreciate to the full the wonderful accuracy of our Holy Torah when we see that this secret doctrine, handed down by word of mouth for so long, and revealed to us by the Sages of the Kabbalah many centuries ago, has been borne out in the clearest possible way by the science of our generation.

Rabbi Yisrael Lipschitz, *Derush Ohr HaChaim*,
found in *Mishnayos Nezikin* after *Maseches Sanhedrin*[1]

Rabbi Lipschitz proceeds to describe some of the findings of the scientists of his era:

The questing spirit of man, probing and delving into the recesses of the earth, in the Pyrenees, the Carpathians, the Rocky Mountains in America, and the Himalayas, has found them to be formed of mighty layers of rock lying upon one another in amazing and chaotic formations, explicable only in terms of revolutionary transformations of the earth's surface. Probing still further below the earth's surface, geologists have found four distinct layers of rock, and between the layers fossilized remains of creatures. Those in the lower layers are of monstrous size and structure, while those in the higher layers are progressively smaller in size but incomparably more refined in structure and form.

Furthermore, they found in Siberia in 1807, under the eternal ice of those regions, a monstrous type of elephant, some three or four times larger than those found today...

Similarly, fossilized remains of sea creatures have been found within the recesses of the highest mountains, and one natural scientist, Cuvier, has calculated that of every 78 species found in the earth, 48 are no longer found in our present epoch.

We also know of the remains of an enormous creature found deep in the earth near Baltimore, seventeen feet long, eleven feet high from the forelegs to the shoulder, and nine feet from the hind legs to its back. Bones of this creature have been found in Europe, and in the Harz Mountains. This species has been given the name "mammoth." Another gigantic creature whose fossilized remains have been found is that which is called "iguanodon," which stood fifteen feet high and

---

1 Rabbi Lipschitz's essay was translated and annotated by Yaakov Elman and printed in Rabbi Aryeh Kaplan, *Immortality, Resurrection, and the Age of the Universe.*

measured thirty feet in length; from its internal structure, scientists have determined that it was herbivorous. Another creature is that which is called "megalosaurus," which was slightly smaller than the iguanodon, but which was meat-eating.

From all this, we can see that all that the Kabbalists have told us for so many years about the repeated destruction and renewal of the earth has found clear confirmation in our time.

Ibid.

In 1878, a few years after Rabbi Lipschitz described the Iguanodon, thirty almost complete fossilized Iguanodon skeletons were discovered in a coal mine in Bernissart. Some of these are now on display at the Museum of Natural Sciences in Brussels.

Rabbi Lipschitz's explanation was endorsed by some prominent authorities, including Rabbi Shalom Mordechai Schwadron (known as Maharsham) at the turn of the twentieth century.[1] The basic approach was also suggested by Rabbi Samson Raphael Hirsch:

---

1 *Techeles Mordechai* vol. I to Bereishis, section 2. Rabbi Menachem Kasher (*Torah Sheleimah, Bereishis* vol. I section 422) states that it is a mitzvah to publicize explanations such as those of the *Tiferes Yisrael* so as to defend Judaism from science.

> Judaism is not frightened even by the hundreds of thousands and millions of years which the geological theory of the earth's development bandies about so freely… Our Rabbis, the Sages of Judaism, discuss (*Midrash Rabbah* 9; Talmud *Chagigah* 16a) the possibility that earlier worlds were brought into existence and subsequently destroyed by the Creator before He made our own earth in its present form and order.
>
> Rabbi Samson Raphael Hirsch, "The Educational Value of Judaism,"
> in *Collected Writings*, vol. VII, p. 265

It was also presented and elaborated upon by the Polish Talmudist and Kabbalist Rabbi Yehudah Yudel Rosenberg (1859-1935), author of the popular Talmudic work *Yados Nedarim* who later became Chief Rabbi of Montreal:

> Since it has become revealed and publicized that the world has existed for much longer than the time that we thought to be the time of creation, one should understand that this does not present any contradiction whatsoever to the words of our Holy Torah. For that is also the opinion of the Sages… as the Midrash has it: "Rabbi Yehudah bar Simon said, It is not written here, 'Let there be evening,' but rather, 'And there was evening'; we see from here that there was an order of time beforehand." And it is clear from that which it states "beforehand" that it refers to the inhabitation of the earth in previous Sabbatical cycles… As an aside, I should mention that I saw the great author of the *Tiferes Yisrael* commentary on the Mishnah, in his *Derush Ohr HaChaim*, write similarly to that which I have written.
>
> Rabbi Yudel Rosenberg, *Pri Yehudah*, pp. 6-9

Some authorities, however, were less than enthusiastic about *Derush Ohr HaChaim*. The Rebbe of Munkatch in the early twentieth century, Rabbi Chaim Eliezer Shapira, wrote that the essay includes "damaging views that tend towards heresy."[1] He suggested that since its purported author Rabbi Lipschitz was known as a great man, perhaps the essay was forged by his son in his name. Rabbi Shapira further attested that he removed the entire commentary of *Tiferes Yisrael* from his home, and borrows it when the rare need arises.

---

1 Responsa *Minchas Elazar* vol. I 64:2.

The Lubavitcher Rebbe claimed that Rabbi Lipschitz himself did not fully believe his approach and wrote it as apologetics to enhance the status of Judaism in the eyes of the secular world.[1] Rabbi Yaakov Yisrael Kanievsky (1899-1985) claimed that Rabbi Lipschitz wrote this essay for the sake of people who were distanced from Judaism, and added that it was a problematic essay and that the idea of destroying worlds is explained differently in Kabbalah.[2] He stated that the previous worlds may be entirely spiritual in nature,[3] and even if they were physical, there would not be a remnant in our universe. Netziv likewise argued that dinosaur fossils could not be remnants of such prior worlds:

> ...The diggers of the earth find the bones of creatures that do not exist in the world today. From this, many have determined that there was another world before this creation where there were other creatures; and in truth there is such an explanation in *Bereishis Rabbah* on the verse "and behold it was very good"—"this teaches that God created world and destroyed them, saying, This pleases Me and this does not please Me." ...Nevertheless to my mind it is difficult to say this, for it is explained in *Shemos Rabbah* (1:2)... that He created worlds and looked at them, and they were not endearing to him, and He returned them to chaos and emptiness. And if so, no vestige or trace remained from them.
>
> Netziv, *Haamek Davar*, Genesis 7:23

Placing the Six Days

Aside from the objections with the prior-worlds approach discussed above, Rabbi Dovid Tzvi Hoffman points out another difficulty with any explanation involving previous cycles of the world to explain the evidence.[4] Such explanations mean that the additional years of the history of the universe took place *before* the creation events of the six days in the Genesis account.[5] This means that *after* fourteen billion years of the world's history,

---

1 *Letters*, vol. 7, letter 996. This is very difficult explanation to accept.

2 *Kraina De-Igresa* vol. 1 section 46.

3 But compare Rambam, *Guide For The Perplexed* 2:30.

4 Rabbi Dovid Tzvi Hoffman, Commentary to Genesis, p. 49.

5 According to *Ma'areches Elokus*, the additional time is fitted into the period of

there were cataclysmic events spanning six days just a few thousand years ago, involving the placement of the sun and moon, the emergence of dry land, and the creation of plant, animal and human life from scratch. But this is entirely inconsistent with the evidence that has emerged, which reveal that no such cataclysmic events occurred in that period. The sun and moon, and plant and animal life, all continued uninterrupted during that period. Thus, while the approach of fitting in the billions of years into previous eras superficially appears to solve the conflict between Genesis and science, it actually does not solve it at all. We shall have to seek a different solution.

"astonishing void" on the first day of creation.

Chapter Thirteen

The Day-Age Approach

The Length of a Day

Contrary to popular belief, the Jewish calendar does not begin with the creation of the world. Instead, it begins with the creation of man. The first Rosh HaShanah (new year) was a Friday, not a Sunday. Thus, the Jewish calendar dates the world as having existed for 5,766 years from the Rosh HaShanah preceding this book's publication, *plus* the six days of creation.[1]

But how long is a "day"? It is clear that the word can have several different meanings. In the Torah, we find two very different definitions of the word "day" given in the same verse!

> And God called the light "day," and He called the darkness "night"; and it was evening, and it was morning, one day.
>
> Genesis 1:5

Here we have the term "day" first being ascribed to the hours of light, and then to one full period of both light and darkness. This already tells us that the word "day" is not as singular in definition as one might assume.

---

1 This is the system widely used following Talmudic times; previously, events were usually dated according to the reigning monarch or based on the time elapsed since the destruction of the Temple. The calculation of the number of years since creation is given in the Tannaic work *Seder Olam Rabbah*. It is not necessarily intended to be absolutely precise; for example, Rabbi Shimon Schwab (*Selected Speeches*, chapter 21, pp. 260-284) controversially suggested that the prophet Daniel concealed 168 years from Jewish history. Additionally, *Tosafos* to *Rosh HaShanah* 27a states that the world was only physically created in the month of Nissan, whereas the calendar begins six months earlier in Tishrei, which *Tosafos* explains to refer to the creation in God's "thoughts."

Later, another verse is understood by some to give yet another definition of the word "day":

> These are the developments of the heavens and the earth when they were created, on the day that the Lord God made the earth and the heavens.
>
> Genesis 2:4

What is the "day" on which God made the earth and the heavens? Some explain it to refer to the first day of creation;[1] others to the day following the six days of creation, when the ordinary cycle of nature commenced. But Rambam's son Rabbeinu Avraham explains the word "day" here to refer to the six days of creation:

> When it says "on the day," it means to say, in the time encompassing the six days of the beginning, not on the first day alone... Amongst the powerful attestations that a "day" can refer to a very extensive time, is that it says in the Torah: "All the commandments that I am commanding you on this day" (Deuteronomy 8:1), and it did not intend by this to refer to commandments that He commanded them on one particular day, but rather to the entirety of commandments which He commanded them at whichever time He did so, which was over many days, months, and years.
>
> Commentary to Genesis 2:4

Thus, we see that the term "day" can theoretically refer to more than one quantity of time. But what is its meaning in the context of the six days of creation? Simply speaking, the definition given in the Torah of one full period of light and darkness would mean a conventional day of twenty-four hours. Yet twenty-four hours is not really a definition, merely a different unit. The usual correct definition is that a day (and twenty-four hours) is the time it takes for the earth to complete one revolution upon its axis, relative to the sun. The term's significance therefore requires the existence of the sun. But the sun was only created on the fourth day! Rabbi Dr. Eli Munk, one of the last of the distinguished scholars of pre-war German Jewry, notes the significance of this point:

> The sun and stars began their function as ray-senders, observable on the earth, certainly not before the Fourth *Day*. The word "*yom*" in verse 5 cannot indicate a period of time determined by the effect of the sun on

---

1 Rashi and Chizkuni, commentaries ad loc.

the rotating earth… Since there is no consensus of traditional opinions about the definition of *yom* in the Seven *Days* of the Beginning, we put the word *Day* in italics.

Rabbi Eli Munk, The Seven Days of the Beginning, pp. 49-50

One might still consider that although the absence of the sun at the beginning mandates that the word "day" be interpreted non-literally, this only applies as long as the sun was not in existence; as soon as the sun was made on the fourth day, a normal system of counting days should take over. However, there are sources that indicate differently:

> God said, "Let there be luminaries in the firmament of the heaven to separate between the day and the night…"
>
> Genesis 1:14

> "…to separate between the day and the night…"—from when the Primordial Light was concealed. But for the seven days of the Beginning, the Primordial Light and Darkness served by day and night.
>
> Rashi (see Midrash Bereishis Rabbah 3:6, Pesachim 2a, Chagigah 12a)

Only at the end of creation did our system of time begin:

> Until this point (the sixth day) the counting is done relative to the universe; from this point on, a different system of counting commenced…
>
> Midrash Bereishis Rabbah 9:14

In another place, the Midrash explicitly states that the days of Creation were not ordinary days:

> "And there was evening, and there was morning, one day." This is a thousand years, which is the day of God, as it says: "For a thousand years are in Your eyes as a day" (Psalms 90:4).
>
> Midrash Pesikta Rabbasi, Hosafah 2:1[1]

Rabbi Dovid Tzvi Hoffman notes that this does not mean that the days of Creation were precisely one thousand years long:

> In many places, and especially in the book of the Zohar, it is proven that the expression "day," as it appears in the account of Creation, is not to be understood as an ordinary human day of 24 hours, but rather

---

1 Also *Midrash Bereishis Rabbasi* of Rabbi Moshe HaDarshan, cited by Rabbi Menachem Kasher, *Torah Sheleimah* vol. I p. 94 section 448. See his footnote for further discussion.

the intent is to the day of God, which lasts 1000 years-that is to say, a day that lasts for an undefined length of time.

Rabbi Dovid Tzvi Hoffman, Commentary to Genesis, p. 48

All this presents strong support for explaining the six days of creation as referring to six extended periods of time. The calendar begins less than six thousand years ago, but preceding it were six "days" of Creation that lasted for billions of years. The legitimacy of using this approach to resolve the conflict between science and the Jewish calendar is widely (albeit not universally) accepted. Even Rabbi Mordecai Plaut, editor of the highly conservative Bnei Brak edition of *Yated Ne'eman*, presents this view:

> ...We are forced to revise an unstated hypothesis, namely, that "day" is always an accurate translation for "*yom*," as it occurs in those Biblical sentences... To point out that 5763 counts only from the beginning of human activity rather than the entire physical world would seem an alternate and independent way to resolve the discrepancies between our traditional dating and that assigned by the general scientific method... Our suggestion here is that "*yom*" is applied primarily as a measure of qualitative change... Without the presence of man, when natural processes are of a completely material nature, a much larger amount of change is necessary for it to be spoken of as a qualitative equal to a human day.

Rabbi Mordecai Plaut, At the Center of the Universe:
Essays on Western Intellectual Space

The Issue of Shabbos

One objection raised against reinterpreting the six days as six eons is that it undermines Shabbos. This was stated by Rabbi Shimon Schwab:

> Since the observance of the seventh day was commanded in order to commemorate the creation of heaven and earth in six days, it seems almost self-evident that six days of Bereishit were six normal days in the accepted sense and nothing else.

"How Old Is The Universe?" Challenge, p. 165

The same argument was stated by the Lubavitcher Rebbe:

> ...The attempt to "reinterpret" the text of the first section of Bereishis to the effect that it speaks of periods or eons, rather than ordinary days... is not only uncalled for, but it means tampering with the Mitzvah of Shabbos itself, which "balances" all the Torah. For, if one takes the words, "one day" out of their context and plain meaning, one

ipso facto abrogates the whole idea of Shabbos as the "Seventh day" stated in the same context. The whole idea of Shabbos observance is based on the clear and unequivocal statement in the Torah: "For in six *days* God made heaven and earth, and on the seventh *day* He ceased from work and rested"—*days*, not periods.

Rabbi Menachem Scheerson, Mind Over Matter, p. 110

Yet this argument can and has been countered:

> …Others however do not feel that there is any force in this argument. The true nature of God's creative activity during the six days and the sense in which He can be said to have "rested on the seventh day" must remain forever beyond our comprehension, whether the days are taken literally or metaphorically. It is reasonably clear that the Torah wishes to convey that the six weekdays and Shabbat correspond to some basic structures of reality, and it can make no difference to the concept of Shabbat whether God's "activity" or "inactivity" is expressed in relation to days, *sephirot*, or other spiritual constructs.
>
> Rabbi Aryeh Carmell, Challenge p. 259

As a parable, consider the custom on Passover night to dip one's finger in wine and spill ten drops on the table. This serves to allude to "the finger of God" that smote the Egyptians,[1] and yet Judaism defines this as an allegorical "finger" rather than a physical finger.

A similar argument is made by others for different reasons. In the Jewish calendar, Shabbos begins and ends at nightfall. On the other hand, the simple meaning of the verses in Genesis is that each started at dawn and was concluded at the *end* of the following night – "and there was evening, and there was morning, day x." This would indicate that Shabbos ought to begin and end at dawn. While many interpret the verses differently, authorities such as Rashbam maintained the simple meaning; and yet Rashbam clearly did not believe that our observance of Shabbos begins in the morning. Rather, he held that the Shabbos of today need not correlate precisely with the Shabbos of the creation week:

> (According to Rashbam,) during the days of creation, the days are counted differently from how they are counted after that.
>
> Rabbi Dovid Tzvi Hoffman, Commentary to Genesis, p. 27

---

1 *Darchei Moshe*, cited in *Mishnah Berurah* 473:74.

That is to say, even though the first Shabbos began in the morning and ended at the next morning, we commemorate it weekly beginning in the evening and ending at the next evening. Here, too, we see that the significance of Shabbos is not lost even if it is not exactly the same sort of day as was the first Shabbos that it commemorates.

Objections and Difficulties

There are other objections to interpreting the six days as six eons. Some object that this explanation has no traditional basis, in that there are no classical Torah commentaries that actually explained each day to refer to billions of years.[1] We have demonstrated earlier that this does not necessarily give reason to object to an explanation. Furthermore, while there are no traditional commentaries that explain the six days to refer to precisely 15 billion years, there are certainly traditional sources that explain the days to be much longer periods than ordinary days. Still, some counter this objection by explaining that six days can simultaneously refer to six twenty-four hour periods and also to many billions of years. This is done via ingenious and controversial scientific explanations concerning the flow of time.[2]

But a substantial difficulty with any explanation that the six days are not six ordinary days is that the Torah does not only say that there were six days. Rather, the Torah also states that with each day "there was evening, and there was morning." It is difficult to imagine how this phrase could be interpreted if this does not refer to 24-hour periods on planet Earth. One could perhaps argue that it refers to the "dusk" and "dawn" of eras. Yet the Torah describes the dawn of the era as occurring at the *end* of the day, not at the beginning.

A more devastating problem with these approaches is that they simply do not solve the contradictions with science. While many people are satisfied with the approach of each of the six days lasting billions of years, whether with or without the explanation of how a day can still literally be a twenty-four hour period, careful scrutiny reveals this approach to involve

---

1 Rabbi Aryeh Kaplan, *Immortality, Resurrection and the Age of the Universe*, p. 4.

2 Prof. Cyril Domb, *B'Or HaTorah* 4, Summer 1984, pp. 66-67; Dr. Gerald Schroeder, *Genesis and the Big Bang* and *The Science of God*.

overwhelming problems. This is because although this approach reconciles the difference between a time span of six days and a time span of fourteen billion years, the *events* of those six days cannot be correlated with the scientific account of what took place during the fourteen billion years.

This problem involves two aspects. One is that some of the creations described in Genesis do not easily correlate with any known phenomena. This is the case with the description of the creations of the second day:

> And God made the firmament, and He divided between the waters that were below the firmament and the waters that were above the firmament, and it was so. And God called the firmament Heaven.
>
> Genesis 1:7-8

It is difficult to correlate the description of the "firmament" with any known aspects of our world. It was traditionally understood to refer to a firm covering encompassing the world, but as Malbim points out, we now know that no such covering exists. Malbim claims instead that the firmament refers to the atmosphere, and others explain it to refer to outer space. But Rabbi Samson Raphael Hirsch points out that etymologically, the word for firmament, *rakia*, refers to firm matter that has been flattened out into a layer.[1] The description of the "waters above the firmament" is likewise difficult to interpret.[2]

The second aspect of this problem is that the sequence of events described in Genesis does not correlate with the sequence discovered by science. For example, in Genesis, the earth and water are already present on the first and second days, before the creation of the luminaries, whereas the scientific picture is that they did not appear until long after the creation of the universe, and *after* the formation of the sun and stars.[3] In Genesis, the

---

1 Commentary to Genesis 1:6. Furthermore, Genesis 1:14 states that the luminaries were placed *in* the firmament.

2 Dr. Nathan Aviezer (*In The Beginning*, pp. 21-23) claims that it refers to the ice that exists on comets and certain planets. Yet the idea that Genesis would discuss ice in remote parts of the universe, unknown until recently, is extremely unreasonable.

3 Even according to the view that the word "earth" refers to the entire physical universe, it certainly *includes* planet Earth. Furthermore, to claim that it does not include planet Earth leads to the unreasonable result that the creation of our world, one of the most important parts of the universe, is not mentioned anywhere in the Torah.

sun, moon and stars are described as being created a day after plant life,[1] whereas the scientific evidence shows that they existed billions of years *before* plant life.[2] Genesis describes the birds as having been created on the fifth day, before the terrestrial animals that were created on the sixth; and yet the fossil record shows that birds only appeared *after* terrestrial animals.[3] The following chart illustrates the disparities in the sequence:

The Order of Genesis Chapter One	The Order Given by Science
Day One: Heavens, earth (including water), light	14 billion years ago: Universe begins
Day Two: Firmament separating waters	4.5 billion years ago: Formation of the earth (Day One) and of the moon and sun (Day Four)
Day Three: Dry land appears; vegetation, fruit trees (Talmud: Plant life remained under the soil until the arrival of man)	500 million years ago: First fish (Day Five)
	438 m.y.a.: First land plants (Day Three)
	434 m.y.a.: First terrestrial insects (Day Six)
Day Four: Creation of sun, moon and stars (Talmud: Created on the first day and set in place on the fourth)	400 m.y.a.: First flying insects (Day Five)
	360 m.y.a.: First trees (Day Three)
Day Five: Fish and aquatic life; birds, flying insects	300 m.y.a.: First terrestrial reptiles (Day Six)
	200 m.y.a.: First terrestrial mammals (Day Six)
Day Six: Terrestrial mammals, terrestrial insects and reptiles	150 m.y.a.: First birds (Day Five)

1 According to the Talmud (*Chagigah* 12a), they were created on the first day and suspended in place on the fourth, which likewise does not concord with the scientific picture.

2 Dr. Gerald Schroeder (*The Science of God*, pp. 67, 69, 204-205) cites Ramban (to Genesis 1:12) as stating that "there was no special day assigned for the command of creating vegetation," explaining him to mean that the creation of plant life "occurred over an extended period not limited to that day." Yet a careful study of the full text of Ramban reveals that he means something quite different; not that there was no *single* day when it happened, but rather, that there was no day assigned that was *distinct* from the appearance of the earth.

3 Aviezer (*In The Beginning*, pp. 84-85) and Schroeder (*The Science of God*, p. 67) claim that Genesis is speaking of flying insects, not birds. However, the text speaks of *kol ohf kanaf*, "*every* winged flying creature"; although this can *include* winged insects, it certainly does not *exclusively* refer to them. Flying insects, when referred to in exclusion to birds, are called *sheretz ha-ohf*. In any case, explaining that the verse refers to flying insects simply raises a further problem: terrestrial insects are described in the Torah as being created later, on the sixth day, and yet science maintains that they preceded the winged insects.

There have been various ingenious attempts to make the content and sequence of Genesis concord with that of science, an approach known as "concordism." Such efforts are, however, beset with serious difficulties, and do not maintain a viable interpretation of the text from an etymological, contextual and philological standpoint.[1]

A more general objection to the current efforts at concordism, which involve the insights of twentieth-century science, is that they render the true meaning of Genesis as something only comprehensible to modern man. And yet we see that, although the Torah is binding for all generations, God presented it in a form that would be meaningful to the generation that received it. The laws of damages refer to donkeys falling in pits, not trucks ramming into cars. It is unreasonable to believe that God gave an account of Creation that mankind was completely incapable of understanding for thousands of years.

If Genesis can only be reconciled with science via obscure theories, reference to irrelevant phenomena, drastic and very difficult textual reinterpretation, and ingenious intellectual gymnastics, then it is not a very impressive scientific account. The most reasonable conclusion is that Genesis was never intended to be a scientific text to begin with, but rather something more profound instead. In the following chapters, we shall explore what that might be.

---

1 See the examples in the preceding footnotes. These problems were first pointed out by Thomas Henry Huxley in "The Interpreters of Genesis and the Interpreters of Nature," *The Nineteenth Century*. See too "Genesis and Geology" in Stephen Jay Gould, *Bully for Brontosaurus* pp. 402-415 and Dr. Carl Feit, "Darwin and Drash: The Interplay of Torah and Biology," *The Torah U-Madda Journal* (1990) II pp. 31-32. For a very extensive discussion of the problems with concordism, see Paul H. Seely, "The First Four Days of Genesis in Concordist Theory and in Biblical Context," *PSCF* 49 pp. 85-95. In marked contrast to Aviezer and Schroeder, who respectively make the extraordinary claims that the two sequences display "complete harmony" (*Fossils and Faith*, p. 13) and "phenomenal" correlation (*The Science of God* p. 70), Dr. Andrew Goldfinger (*Thinking About Creation*, pp. 281-283) readily admits to some of the difficulties, but considers these not to provide sufficient reason to reject the concordist approach. I beg to differ, and I suggest that the reader draws his own conclusions.

Chapter Fourteen

Departing from Concordism

Utilize and Move On

Despite all the interpretive and intellectual creativity that is harnessed in order to match the events described in the account of Creation with the physical history of the universe as we know it, the results are extremely unsatisfactory. However, these concordist approaches are nevertheless highly significant. The approach of Rabbi Lipschitz establishes that Torah authorities were willing to accept the evidence of earth's prehistory and not propose that God created a world that was artificially aged. The widespread approach of interpreting the days of creation as referring to billions of years establishes that many are willing to interpret Genesis differently from traditional understandings, in light of contemporary evidence.

> …The expression "one day" that the Torah uses, according to its literal translation, refers to one [conventional] day. Rambam and the other early authorities truly held of this view, that each of the six days of creation lasted for one [ordinary] day, because they had no reason to believe otherwise. However, for us, there are indeed such reasons.
>
> Rabbi Gedalyah Nadel, *BeToraso Shel Rav Gedalyah*, p. 91

As we shall see, Rambam was actually of the belief that the six days were not ordinary days, or even periods of time. But we shall adopt Rabbi Nadel's approach in modifying Rambam's view in light of the evidence that faces us today.

Conceptual and Chronological Sequences

Since the Torah's description of the order of Creation does not concord with the scientific evidence, this means that the sequence given is not a literal description of the physical reality of events, but rather a conceptual order instead. This is something that we find with other episodes in the Torah. There is a principle often quoted by the classical Biblical commentators that "there is no chronological order in the Torah"—not that there is *no* order, but that the order presented is not a chronological one.[1]

For example, although Yisro's uniting with the Jewish people chronologically occurred after the national revelation at Sinai (according to many opinions), it is described as taking place earlier, because the theme of Yisro's joining the Jewish people and the lessons involved conceptually precede the theme of the acceptance of the Torah. A contemporary work explaining the structure of the Torah discusses such anomalies:

> Torah's objective also accounts for the fact that the depiction of data does not necessarily conform to the actual sequence of the occurrence of events. As the subsequent analysis shows, it seems that a small fraction of events which affected the growth of the nation did not occur at the precise moment when they were slated to occur. Because Torah's aim is the documentation of the development of relationship according to a particular predetermined scheme, it chronicles events not in a strictly chronological order but in an order that follows the line of development that it seeks to project. In a small number of instances, this development did not sequentially mirror the course of history.
>
> Rabbi Yehoshua Honigwachs, *The Unity of Torah*, p. 94

Thus, the order of events as described in the Torah is not necessarily the same as that which transpired in the physical world. Instead, it is a conceptual order that teaches certain spiritual or theological truths. Such truths are of greater importance than physical history.

---

1 Although the Talmud (*Pesachim* 6b) states that this is the only the case with different *parashiyos* (sections) in the Torah, there are instances where factors cause it to be invoked regarding events within a single *parashah* (see Genesis 24:47 and *Tosafos* to *Chullin* 95b *s.v. k'Eliezer*). See too Talmud Yerushalmi, *Shekalim* 6:1.

The Non-Chronological Sequence of Creation

The idea that the six days of creation do not represent a chronological sequence goes back many centuries. Rambam, in *The Guide For The Perplexed*, wrote a cryptic chapter about creation in which many authorities have observed that he presented this idea.

Rambam begins by noting that time can only exist when the cosmic sphere of the sun is existing and rotating; this therefore raises the problem of how there could have been "days" before the sun was created on the fourth day.

> Consider the difficulty... in the existence of time before the existence of the sun!
>
> *Guide For The Perplexed* 2:30

Rambam answers by citing a Midrash which states that the phrase "In the beginning God created the Heavens and the earth" refers to the heavens and everything contained in them, and the earth and everything contained in it.[1] His conclusion from this is that everything in the universe was created in a single instant:

> Consequently, all things were created together, but are sequentially distinguished from each other.
>
> Ibid.

But what does it mean that they are "sequentially" distinguished from each other? One might think that it means that everything was created on the first day as an amorphous mass, and was separated into place on consecutive days. Yet various other statements and beliefs of Rambam reveal that this cannot be the case. The thirteenth-century Spanish philosopher, Shem Tov Falaquera ben Joseph, explained Rambam's view in his commentary to the *Guide*:

> It is in describing the hierarchy in reality (of everything in the universe) that we say Day One, Day Two—but not that they were created in a progressive sequence, as appears from the simple meaning of Scripture. Rather, they were all created simultaneously. Only as a reflection of

---

1 *Midrash Bereishis Rabbah* 1:19.

their purpose and importance does the Torah speak of the first, second, third, and the rest of the days. Understand this.

Moreh Ha-Moreh 2:30:9

Shem Tov explains that according to Rambam, the six "days" of creation therefore do not represent a period of time during which creation took place. Instead, they are a hierarchal sequence in which everything in the universe—which was all created simultaneously—is distinguished for our comprehension. The sequence is one of purpose and importance, not chronological appearance. This was one of Rambam's secret teachings regarding Creation, as Rabbi Yitzchak Arama (1420-1494) explains:

> The Rav, the Guide, gave the reason for the mention of days in the Beginning by explaining the statement of the Sages, who said that "all the products of Creation were created in their full form" (Talmud, *Chullin* 60a); in other words, everything was created at the first instant of creation in their final perfect form. Thus the mention of an order of Creation is not describing the sequence of days; rather, [but the days are simply serving] to differentiate the status of [the elements of creation] and to make known the hierarchy of nature. This was [Rambam's] major esoteric doctrine concerning Creation as those who are understanding can discern from that chapter (*Guide For The Perplexed* 2:30) which is devoted to this extraordinary account.

Akeidas Yitzchak, Bereishis, Shaar 3

Abarbanel also noted that this was Rambam's secret message, and pointed out that it was not a very well kept secret:

> The Rambam believed that there were not separate creative acts on six days, but rather everything was created on one day, in a single instant. In the work of Creation, there is mention of "six days" to indicate the different levels of created beings according to their natural hierarchy; not that there were actual days, and nor that there was a chronological sequence to that which was created in the acts of Genesis... This is the view of the Rambam which he considered as one of the major secrets of the Creation. He tried to conceal this view with ingenuity, as can be seen in his words there. But Ralbag went and tattled, revealing his secret, as did Narboni and the other commentators to his work; they uncovered his secret and publicized his view....

Abarbanel, Commentary to Genesis, p. 10

Abarbanel himself proceeded to sharply disagree with Rambam's position:

> And I say that, notwithstanding the Rambam's exaltedness in Torah, this is a clear falsehood, as is clear for internal reasons. First, that the verses in the story of creation attest six times that "there was evening, and there was morning, day so-and-so"—and how can anyone possessing Torah deny these verses, saying that there was no quantity of days, and neither evening nor morning, but rather that everything was created simultaneously? Is this not denying and falsifying Scripture?
>
> Ibid., pp. 10-11

Yet Rambam did not feel that he was falsifying Scripture. He felt that it was perfectly legitimate to interpret the notion of six days allegorically, just as with "the hand of God."

Clearly, Rambam's view does not square with contemporary science. Indeed, there is no reason why it should; Rambam was reconciling Genesis with Aristotelian philosophy, not twenty-first century science. But it is nevertheless of great significance for us. Rambam did not believe that the description of six days in the Torah presents a chronological sequence—a scientific account of physical history. Instead, he understood it as presenting a conceptual sequence. According to Rambam, Genesis does not even present a cosmogony—an account of the origin and development of the universe. Instead, it presents a cosmology—a discussion of the *structure* of the universe. The same view is found in the writings of Ralbag:

> You already know from the preceding that God's generating the universe did not occur in time, since [its generation] was from nothing to something. Likewise, our Rabbis agreed that the heavens and the earth were created simultaneously. In the chapter "One Does Not Interpret," they said, "Both were created as one, as it is said, 'My hand has laid the foundation of the earth, and My right hand has spread out the heavens; when I call to them, they stand up together' (Isaiah 48:13)." It is therefore apparent that the description of creation as being completed in six days is not in the sense that, for example, the first day was [prior] to the second as one [whole] day. Rather, they said this in order to show the priority amongst various created things.
>
> For example, the movers of the heavenly bodies are causally and by nature prior to the heavenly bodies, whereas the latter are causally and

by nature prior to the elements and to that which is generated from them. The elements are prior to that which is generated from them by way of material causality, and the compounds of the elements are also [related] to each other by this kind of priority. For example the plant is prior to the animal; and similarly the imperfect animal is prior to the perfect animal. In the same way, an aquatic animal is prior to a flying animal, and the latter is prior to a walking (terrestrial) animal while the latter is prior to the communicating being (i.e., man). For an aquatic animal produces an imperfect egg, the bird produces a perfect egg; whereas the walking animal, produces a living animal in its own body. For this reason Aristotle says in *Historia Animalium* that the bird is more perfect than the aquatic animal and the walking animal more perfect than the bird. And there is no doubt that man is the most perfect animal amongst the walking animals.

Ralbag, Milchamos HaShem 6:8

Ralbag proceeds to explain that when the Talmud states that God created the luminaries on the first day and suspended them on the fourth, this cannot be understood to mean that they were physically put into place at a later stage. Instead, it must be understood as referring to their relationship; that is to say, the assignment of the luminaries is the fourth stage in the hierarchy of creation.

Mystical Chronology

It is not only rationalists such as Rambam and Ralbag who explained that Genesis is not giving a scientific account of creation. Another explanation of the deeper meaning of the six days is given by Ramban:

> ...Know that the days mentioned in the act of Genesis were, in [relation to] the creating of the Heavens and earth, actual days, composed of hours and minutes, and they were six, as the six weekdays, in accordance with the straightforward meaning of the verse. But with the inner meaning of the matter, "days" refers to the *sefiros* (modes of divine revelation) emanating from on high, for every creative utterance of God is called a day, and there were six of them, for to God belong "greatness, power, glory and eternity" and so on (Chronicles I 29:11— referring to the *sefiros*). The explanation of the sequence of verses here

is sublime and concealed, and our understanding of it is less than a drop from the great ocean.

Ramban, Genesis 1:3[1]

Simply speaking, Ramban is saying that while creation took place in six days as we know it, there is also a deeper layer of meaning. However, Rabbi Eliyahu Dessler cites Ramban and understands his words entirely differently:

> We see from this [explanation of Ramban] that in the simple meaning of the text—that which is conveyed to us in accordance with our own conceptual capacity—we are to understand actual days made up of hours and minutes. But in its real essence, that is to say, in its inner meaning, the text has quite a different connotation. It refers to the six *sefiros*, which are modes of revelation of the divine conduct of the world. Only for our benefit does Scripture present them to us in the form of six days. As for the relevance of the six days in their allusion to the six modes of revelation—this is something sublime and concealed from us, as Ramban says.
>
> *Michtav Me-Eliyahu*, vol. II, p. 151

The deeper meaning of the verses refers to mystical concepts—the six "modes of revelation" that God used to create the universe. But what of Ramban's stress on explaining how these "days" are composed of hours and minutes? Is this only for the purposes of the simple presentation that we can grasp? The explanation may be similar to the way in which many explain the Torah's references to "the hand of God." Obviously God does not possess a hand in a straightforward literal sense. But neither is this understood to be a simple parable. Rather, God does possess a hand in the deeper mystical sense of the term. He has the spiritual equivalent of a hand, which is a way of exerting power in the world. This is not an allegorical explanation in the conventional sense of the term; instead, it explains the literal meaning to be in reference to metaphysical reality, not physical reality. In the same way, the Torah describes creation in terms of six days "in accordance with our own conceptual capacity." Yet this is simultaneously literally true in a metaphysical sense, in accordance

---

1 Cf. Talmud, *Chagigah* 12a: "The world was created with ten things..." which Maharsha explains to refer to the ten *sefiros*.

with the mystical meaning of six days—including the mystical meaning of twenty-four hours, their minutes, and so on, all of which have their parallel in the higher worlds.

According to the way in which Rabbi Dessler explains Ramban's position, the six days refer to mystical concepts rather than time-periods. The sequence of days is therefore not a chronological sequence but rather a conceptual one. We can further understand, then, why the sequence of creation given in the Torah does not correlate with that revealed by science. Rabbi Dessler explicitly spells this out elsewhere:

> "Scripture does not teach us anything about the chronological order of events"—Rashi.[1] The reason for this is that the ten utterances with which the world was created (see *Avos* 5:1) are the ten *sefiros* whose order is the order of distinguishing revelations. The Torah instructed us according to this order in the account of creation, not according to the order of physical time.
>
> *Michtav Me-Eliyahu* vol. 5 p. 348

In the earlier citation, Rabbi Dessler correlates the *sefiros* with the six days; hence, when he writes here that the order in Genesis is the conceptual order of *sefiros* rather than that of physical time, he is stating that the order of the six days is conceptual rather than chronological.

A similar explanation is presented by Rabbi Aryeh Kaplan. He notes that there is a Talmudic discussion that speaks of there having been two processes of creation; one in God's thoughts, and one in deed that occurred later.[2] The six days of creation therefore took place in God's thoughts, in the spiritual infrastructure of the universe. They were then implemented over a period of fourteen billion years in the act of the creation of the universe.[3]

Dealing With the Simple Meaning

From the outset, the idea of explaining Genesis as a scientifically inaccurate text raises a difficulty. There is a charge that we are making the

---

1 It may seem from the context that Rashi is only addressing the specific structure of the first verse. However, Rav Dessler understands/extrapolates this to the entire section.

2 See Talmud, *Rosh HaShanah* 11b-12a, and *Tosafos* to *Rosh HaShanah* 27a s.v. *ke'maan*.

3 Rabbi Aryeh Kaplan, *Immortality, Resurrection, and the Age of the Universe*, p. 11.

Torah very plastic, constantly adapting it by way of apologetics as science advances. Why wouldn't God give us a scientifically accurate account of the universe's development to begin with?

We should first note that not every legitimate meaning of Torah has always been possessed by the nation. Each and every generation discovers new understandings of the Torah's messages, as Rav Tzaddok HaKohen of Lublin (1823-1900) writes:

> The nation of Israel and the Torah are one... and just as there is a change amongst the souls of Israel from one generation to the next, so too with Torah – and that is the Oral Torah, with which new insights arise in each generation from the scholars of Israel...
>
> Rav Tzaddok HaKohen, *Tzidkas HaTzaddik* 90

But there is a further point to be made. Let us begin by considering for whom the Torah was written. The commandments of the Torah apply to all Jews at all times and in all places.[1] Yet the presentation of Torah has to take into account the sheer diversity of this group. It includes men, women and children, of all ages, in many different cultures, who would be living over a period of many thousands of years. The Torah had to convey messages to a five-year-old boy in Ancient Rome and to an elderly woman in medieval Europe. But how can one write a book that will cater to the needs of so many different types of people?

The answer is that one writes it in such a way that it contains various layers of meaning. The simplest and most superficial layer of meaning has to be one that is acceptable and meaningful for the lowest common denominator of readership. This may require the concealment of certain truths that are too sophisticated or otherwise difficult for such people to accept. As Rabbi Dessler explains:

> "Because six days did God make Heaven and earth..." The days referred to here relate to the period before the completion of creation, when the concept of time was different from that which applies now. But the Torah was given to us in accordance with our own concepts: "Moshe came and brought it down to earth." This is the meaning of the dictum, "The Torah speaks as if in human language"; it speaks to

---

1 See Rambam, *Mishneh Torah, Hilchos Yesodei HaTorah* 9:1-2.

us in accordance with our own perceptions of matter and our own concepts of space and time.

All that the Torah recounts of matters relating to the period before the completion of creation is conveyed to us by Moshe from the mouth of God in terms of concepts which we can grasp. Just as one attempts to give a blind person some idea of that which he cannot see by making use of analogies with the sense of touch and so forth, so does the Torah present to us that which is essentially spiritual in a material guise, with some points of similarity and analogy to the spiritual message, so that we may be able to grasp it to the best of our ability.

Michtav Me-Eliyahu, vol. II, p. 151

Rabbi Dessler is explaining that the literal meaning of the verse does not refer to the factual reality, but rather presents a simplified version of events that we can grasp.[1] This concept was first discussed at length by Rambam. He explains why the study of metaphysics is unsuitable and even harmful for the unsophisticated, and how the wise therefore clad their teachings in riddles and metaphors. Rambam then notes that the Torah implements the same strategy:

You must know that it is very harmful to begin with this branch of philosophy, i.e. metaphysics; or to explain [at first] the sense of the similes occurring in prophecies, and interpret the metaphors which are employed in historical accounts and which abound in the writings of the Prophets. On the contrary, it is necessary to initiate the young and to instruct the less intelligent according to their comprehension: those who appear to be talented and to have capacity for the higher method of study, i.e., that based on proof and on true logical argument, should be gradually advanced towards perfection, either by tuition or by self-instruction. But someone who begins with metaphysics will not only become confused regarding matters of religion, but will fall into complete infidelity. I compare such a person to an infant fed with

---

1   While this runs against popular understandings of the nature of *peshat* (the literal reading of the text), similar explanations are found elsewhere. See Rabbi Aviad Sar Shalom Basilia, *Emunas Chachamim*, 23 (p. 48b), cited and discussed in *Sifsei Chaim, Pirkei Emunah u'Bechirah* vol. II pp. 266-267, concerning a case where the *peshat* of the narrative about Queen Esther does not refer to the physical reality but conveys certain lessons instead.

wheaten bread, meat and wine; it will undoubtedly die, not because such food is naturally unfit for the human body, but because of the weakness of the child, who is unable to digest the food, and cannot derive benefit from it.

The same is the case with the true principles of science. They were presented in enigmas, clad in riddles, and taught by all wise men in the most mysterious way that could be devised, not because they contain some secret evil, or are contrary to the fundamental principles of the Law (as fools, who are only philosophers in their own eyes, believe), but because of the incapacity of man to comprehend them at the beginning of his studies. Only slight allusions have been made to them to serve for the guidance of those who are capable of understanding them. These sciences were, therefore, called Mysteries (*sodos*), and Secrets of the Law (*sisre torah*), as we shall explain.

This also is the reason why "the Torah speaks the language of man," as we have explained, for it is the object of the Torah to [also] serve as a guide for the instruction of the young, of women, and of the common people...

Rambam, The Guide For The Perplexed, 1:33

Explaining the intent of Genesis as solely mystical or metaphysical would render it irrelevant for the overwhelming majority of people to have studied it over the generations. While Genesis has always been understood to be primarily an esoteric text, it is also the first part of the Torah, something studied and intended to be studied by people of all ages and backgrounds. Thus, the Torah would have to present the account of creation in terms that can be grasped even by the young and simple-minded throughout the generations.

The Most Basic Audience

The superficial meaning of the Torah has to be appropriate for the most basic audience. This does not only refer to the children and unsophisticated people in every generation. The Torah had to primarily orient its presentation of concepts towards the generation that had to fulfill the initial acceptance of it. It phrases matters in a way that was suitable for the generation that left Egypt. Thus, for example, the Torah presents laws of damages in terms of a goring ox, not in terms of a drunk driver. Yet it is not only with practical examples that the Torah is primarily aimed at the generation who originally accepted the Torah. Its presentation of concepts also had to take this into account.

While we shall not commit the common error of presuming that ancient people were simple-minded, the truth is that the minds of people work differently in different cultures and in different eras. Even many great and sophisticated people of earlier generations might not have been able to accept certain concepts that are easy for modern people to grasp, just as we cannot accept certain concepts that were easy for ancients to grasp.

In addition, there was a greater inequality amongst people in earlier generations than there is today. Nowadays, most people are literate and receive schooling. But in earlier times, this was far from the case. There was a vast gap between the scholars and the masses, which meant that teachings had to be presented at a level far lower than that which was suitable for the elite.

An extreme example of this would be Rambam's explanation of the purpose of offerings. He states that they were a necessary requirement at the time God gave the Torah, because the Jewish nation was a primitive people that had to be gradually weaned away from pagan rites. This is a radical stance, and there were many apologists for Rambam who attempted to reinterpret his position in such a way as to render it non-controversial. However, Rambam himself explicitly warned that his position would be highly controversial and offered it anyway.

Fortunately for our purposes, there are less controversial instances in which we see that the Torah's presentation of its messages (as opposed to the commandments) was geared towards the generation that accepted it, and that concepts had to be adjusted for them. For example, it is clear from many medieval sources that it was difficult for even some great people of earlier generations to conceive that God had no corporeal form. The Torah could have made this very clear, but Rabbeinu Bachya ibn Pakuda explains that instead it anthropomorphized God because that would make His existence more real to the generation that accepted the Torah.[1]

---

1   *Chovos HaLevavos, Sha'ar HaBitachon* 4.

Rambam also states that the Torah would sometimes speak "necessary truths"; things that are not absolutely true but which are necessary for the Torah to state.[1]

Likewise, Rabbeinu Bachya addresses the perplexing question that the Torah did not discuss reward and punishment in the World-to-Come, surely one of the paramount features of Jewish theology. He explains that the generation which received the Torah were not spiritually mature, and that they needed to hear about reward and punishment in the here and now, not in the hereafter:

> Of reward and punishment in the next world, the prophet [Moses] has told us nothing in his book, for several reasons... one reason is that the people were in a state of ignorance and deficiency of understanding, which is not concealed in the Scriptural account. The Creator acted towards them as a sensitive father would act toward his little child, when he wants to discipline him gently and slowly, as it is written, "Israel was a child, and I loved him" (Hosea 11:1). When a father wants to teach his young son wisdom, which ultimately will enable him to ascend to the higher levels but which he cannot presently understand, if he tries to induce the child to learn by saying to him, "Endure the strain of discipline and instruction, so that you elevate yourself via them to the desirable levels," the child will be unable to bear it and will not listen to him, because he does not understand such things.
>
> But if the father promises him things that bring immediate pleasure—such as food and drink, attractive clothing, an attractive wagon, and such similar things, and warns him of immediate discomfort, such as hunger, nakedness, lashings, and suchlike— while reassuring him of what he has promised with tangible evidence and clear and truthful attestations, it will be easier for him to endure the strain of discipline and bear its difficulty. And when he reaches adolescence and his intellect matures, he will understand the goal of this discipline, and he will direct himself

---

1 *Guide to the Perplexed* 3:28. Rambam also states that a Beis Din should sometimes give a literal explanation of the episode of Reuven and Bilha (traditionally considered to be an incorrect explanation) to a suspected adulteress in order to persuade her to confess (*Yad HaChazakah, Hilchos Sotah* 3:2).

towards it, and the measures that he originally ran towards become of lesser importance to him. This approach is seen to be of great compassion to him.

And likewise, the Creator promised immediate reward and threatened immediate punishment for His people, because he knew that as soon as they were trained for his service, their ignorance of reward and punishment in the next world would fall away, and their intent in their service would be for His sake, and they would comply in drawing close to him.

Chovos HaLevavos, Shaar HaBitachon 4

As great as were the revelations that were experienced by the generation of the exodus, this was still a group of people that began life as slaves and had not been indoctrinated with Torah theology. This necessitated the adjustment of certain concepts for them. In the next chapter, we shall explain why this required creation to be explained in the specific form that it was.

A Non-Literal Approach

Earlier, we discussed the legitimacy of taking non-literal approaches to interpreting Scripture. One view in the Talmud, subsequently adopted by Rambam, is that the entire book of Job is a fiction. Rav Saadiah Gaon and others listed circumstances in which the Torah may be interpreted non-literally, and the account of creation in particular is suited to such an interpretation. Rambam and Ralbag both explained the account of creation in an entirely non-literal manner. More recent scholars have noted this basis in tradition for such an approach to Genesis:

It is well to bear in mind that already our ancient sages, to say nothing of our medieval theologians, would not seem to have insisted upon literalness in such transcendental matters as the account of Creation.

Rabbi Yitzchak Herzog, "The Talmud as a Source for the History of Ancient Science," p. 171

Rabbi Menachem Kasher noted that it was precisely this non-absolutist approach to Genesis that lay behind the numerous different interpretations of creation that have been given over the ages:

It can be established that with regard to the explanation of the account of Genesis and the order of Creation, there is no agreed upon and accepted definitive explanation. Anyone who reads a verse from the chapter of Genesis together with the Midrashic statements will see a great abundance of explanations from the Sages and the medieval scholars on every details, even relating to the simple explanation of the verse, and there are explanations that are mutually exclusive. Regarding such things they stated, "As a hammer smiting a rock," and, "There are seventy facets to Torah"; and even regarding fundamental matters we find dispute amongst the Sages themselves.

> Rabbi Menachem M. Kasher,
> *Toras HaBeriah uMishnas HaHispaschus BeMidrashei Chazal*

The same point is made by Rabbi Dr. Joseph Hertz (1872-1946), Chief Rabbi of the United Hebrew Congregations of the British Empire. Rabbi Hertz authored a popular commentary on the Bible that has since been replaced by more modern commentaries. Yet his discussion of Genesis, printed in an essay appended to the Book of Genesis, is an invaluable discussion of this chapter:

> Now, while the *fact* of creation has to this day remained the first of the articles of the Jewish creed, there is no uniform and binding belief as to the manner of creation, i.e. as to the process whereby the universe came into existence. The manner of the Divine creative activity is presented in varying forms and under differing metaphors by Prophet, Psalmist and Sage; by the Rabbis in Talmudic times, as well as by our medieval Jewish thinkers....

> J. H. Hertz, *The Pentateuch and Haftorahs*, p. 193

The result of this is that there is license for us today to present new interpretations of Genesis:

> ...With regard to matters connected to the acts of Genesis, there are many details for which we have no clear tradition from our Sages, and permission is [therefore] give to everyone to explain and expound the explanation of the verses, for there are seventy facets to Torah.

> Rabbi Menachem M. Kasher, "*Shabbos Bereishis VeShabbos Sinai,*"
> *Talpiot* II p. 385

As we saw, Rambam and Ralbag understood that the six days of creation are not six actual days or even six time-periods of any duration.

201

Instead, they present a conceptual hierarchy of the natural world. Ralbag even added (as we shall later explore) that this sequence was altered to teach certain theological truths. The hierarchy that they presented was based on an Aristotelian worldview, and their understanding of creation was that the entire universe was created instantaneously, not even taking six days. Modern science gives cause to revise both these interpretations. But we can still maintain Rambam's and Ralbag's interpretation of the six days as representing a sequence of conceptual significance rather than a chronological sequence of historical events. Based upon this understanding, let us proceed to give an interpretation of creation that will not conflict with that which has been adequately proven from science, that will provide a meaningful and reasonable explanation of the text, that will justify why the Torah did not give the scientific description, and that will not require any interpretive gymnastics in translating the text.

Chapter Fifteen

Genesis as a Theological Text

The Importance of a Young Universe

From the outset, the idea of explaining Genesis as a text that does not literally describe the creation of the world seems problematic. We can understand why Abarbanel criticized Rambam for his belief that the six days were not actually days. And now that we know the universe to be billions of years old, we can ask why God would conceal this information. The early Torah authorities did not understand the account of creation to be referring to a fourteen-billion year old universe (and nor did they understand it to be referring to evolutionary processes). Why wouldn't God find some way of presenting this idea?

As we have learned in the previous chapter, the Torah presents its messages in such a way as to be suitable for the generation that received it. Rabbi Avraham Yitzchak Kook (1865-1935), the renowned Torah scholar[1] and first Ashkenazi chief rabbi of the British Mandate of Palestine, develops this idea at length, explaining that new concepts have to be carefully introduced into man's consciousness in a gradual way:

> We count our calendar from creation according to the literal text of the
> Torah's verses which is much more meaningful than all the knowledge

---

1 His teacher Rabbi Naftali Zvi Yehuda Berlin of the legendary Volozhin Yeshivah reportedly stated that if the Yeshiva had been founded just to educate Rav Kook, it would have been worthwhile!

Rabbi Avraham Yitzchak Kook

of prehistory, which has little relevance to us. The Torah certainly obscures the [meaning of] the act of creation and speak in allegories and parables, for indeed everyone knows that the stories of Genesis are part of the hidden Torah, and if all these narratives were taken literally, what secrets would there be? …What is most important about the act of creation is what we learn in regard to the knowledge of God and the truly moral life. The Holy One, who precisely measures out even the revelation of the prophets, has determined that only through the images of the stories of Genesis would mankind, with great effort, be capable of drawing out all that is beneficial and exalted in the great matters inherent in the act of creation…

The crux of the matter is that the time of the appearance and the effects of every idea and thought is predetermined. Nothing is haphazard. For example, we can understand that if the fact of the globe's movement was made known to the masses a few thousand years ago, man would have feared to stand on his feet lest he fall from the force of the earth's movement, all the more so would he have feared building tall buildings. A general faint-heartedness and incalculably thwarted development would have resulted. The notion of a gravitational force would not have assured him, having seen with his own eyes that anything standing on a moving object can not be secured from falling. Only after mankind matured through experience was it proper to allow men to recognize the earth's movement, so that from it only good would come to man…

Rabbi Avraham Yitzchak Kook, *Igros HaRe'iyah*, letter 91

We now have to see why this necessitated the Torah presenting creation in the way that it did and not according to the scientific facts. Rabbi Kook explains that people would have had difficulty retaining the concept of the pre-eminence of mankind if he occupies so small a section of the history of the universe:

This [idea] applies to spirituality as well… It was necessary for the people of Israel to work long and hard with the various pagan sects to make them understand that despite the vastness of the universe, man is not so inconsequential that his adherence to moral directives is without value, and that the creation of man as a moral being is of great significance—incalculably greater than even the quantitatively largest creations… What would have happened if the myriad worlds of the present state of science were known then? Man would have been like a speck and his morality of no consequence, and it would have been impossible to foster within him a spirit of greatness and universal glory. Only now, after man's emergence from his struggle with an image [of a world of overwhelming immensity] is he truly no longer frightened by the vastness of creation. But all this required time and preparation.

Ibid.

This, then, could be the reason why the Torah gave no inkling of the universe being billions of years old. There are positive benefits in the description of the universe that the Torah gave in its place. Rabbi Dessler explains the Torah's account of the young age of the universe in a way that perfectly complements the explanation of Rav Kook:

Creation, by definition, is outside our world and outside our frame of thought. If time exists only as a mode of our thought, then the act of creation is necessarily non-temporal: "above time." Every non-temporal act is interpreted in our frame of thought as an infinite time-sequence.[1] This is the reason why creation is interpreted by scientists as a process of evolution extending over vast eons of time.

Since creation does not take place in time we must ask why the Torah describes it as taking six days. The answer is that the Torah wishes to teach us a lesson in *relative values*. Everything has value only in relation to its spiritual content. Vast physical masses and vast expanses of space and time are of little significance if their spiritual content is small. The whole physical universe exists as an environment for the spiritual life of the human being; this is its spiritual content. When interpreting non-temporal creation in temporal terms the Torah deliberately contracts the time-scale compared with that which presents itself to

---

1 Apparently, Rabbi Dessler was explaining the Torah's account of creation in a way that reconciled it with the then-prevalent belief that the universe appeared to be infinitely old, with no evidence for a beginning.' Evidence for the Big Bang has since discredited this belief.

the scientist, in order to convey to us the relative insignificance of the material creation compared with the spiritual stature of man.

Collected Essays and Notes no. 33, cited in *Challenge* p. 140;
also *Michtav Me-Eliyahu* vol. IV p. 113

The clear and simple message that emerges from the small time-scale of Genesis is that the universe was created for man. A few short days transpire, in which God creates the props, and the stage is set. Now man arrives on the scene, and history begins.

The Importance of an Ancient Universe

The aforementioned discussion, however, begs the question: If the knowledge of billions of years of development can lead to man considering himself insignificant and of no consequence, and the Torah therefore had to suppress any mention of it, why did God create the universe in this way? Why not actually create the universe in six days, so that scientific discovery would teach us the lesson of man's importance?

At one level, we can answer this via the concepts that we discussed in the first chapters. For a variety of reasons, God chooses to work through natural processes. Given that God desired to create the universe and man via natural processes, this is how long it takes to do it. The late Nobel Prize-winning neurophysiologist Sir John Eccles describes this beautifully:

> If the cosmos had not been so immense, if we had a Big Bang and the total mass of the Big Bang was just the weight of our own galaxy, you would think this is an enormous mass for the Big Bang, the mass of our galaxy—then it all would have gone out and been back again within one year. There would have been no time for anything. The whole creation of time, and we have to have a long, long time for the creation of the elements in the supernovas and so on—all of this had to go on for thousands of millions of years. The total time of 15 billion years is really the minimum we could have gotten for making all the elements, putting them into the dust of the cosmos, and getting it all swept up eventually in our solar system which does have all the essential elements for life. You cannot make life out of hydrogen and helium, and that was the original stuff. You have to have the time for the creation of all the extraordinary elements that are necessary for living existence, and so you will have to have, shall we say, something

like 10,000 million years from the Big Bang until the dust was swept up to create our solar system which only came 5000 million years ago and 4600 million years ago the earth was contracting down with not only the richness of metal, of elements and so on, but also water. Water is the most wonderful substance, and the entire earth has got it in superabundance compared to any of the other planets in the solar system.

So the creation of planet Earth is itself a wonderful arrangement for life. The whole cosmos can be thought of as being immense in order to give time for the creation of Planet Earth and to give time for the evolution of life and eventually the creation of us in the evolutionary process. So I look upon the whole cosmic design as not being made in sheer immensity for no purpose. The sheer immensity is there in fact to get the time for the creation of Planet Earth with its immense richness of elements and then the time for it to cool down and then the time for the evolutionary process of life which took something like 3500 million years. That's the way you have to think of the time. And so this great cosmos of ours may look very extravagant in the way of material investment of mass but in order to get the long duration of the expansion you have to have this immense momentum going out in the expansion, and all this is applied to time for the solar system to exist and for earth to exist and the planets too and the earth to go right through evolution and finally create us. So that is the Anthropic Principle as I see it.

John Eccles, "A Divine Design: Some Questions on Origins," in *Cosmos Bios Theos*, pp. 161-162

But we can propose a further explanation as to why God created our world via a fourteen billion year process. It is indeed true that some secular materialists have used this discovery to downplay the significance of man. But we have also discovered that the universe possesses great physical size, and we do not see that as presenting a problem for religion. On the contrary, we have always understood that the wonders of the cosmos are supposed to humble man—

When I behold the heavens, the work of Your fingers, the moon and the stars, which You established; what is man, that You are mindful of Him?...

Psalms 8:4-5

207

—and simultaneously to remind him of the weight of responsibility of his duties in the world:

> …Yet You have made him a little lower than the angels, and You have crowned him with glory and honor; You gave him dominion over the works of Your hands; You have put all things under his feet.

> Ibid. 6-7

The point is that we need both the vast dimensions of time and space given to us by scientific investigation and the small dimensions given in the Torah. But they had to be revealed to man in a particular order. The brief duration of creation-time relative to man's existence, as understood by ancient man, ingrained in him the idea of his fundamental importance. Then, the subsequent discovery of the vastness of time that was needed in order for man to appear has a humbling effect that also makes us realize our responsibility in perfecting creation.

The Goals of Genesis

> "In the beginning…"—Rabbi Yitzchak said, The Torah should have only had to begin with "This month shall be to you…" (Exodus 12:2) which is the first of the commandments that Israel was instructed. And why did it begin with Genesis? Because of "He has told of the strength of His deeds to His people, to grant them the heritage of nations" (Psalms 111:6); that if the nations of the world should say to Israel, "You are robbers, that you conquered the land of the seven nations," Israel shall respond to them, "All the land belongs to the Holy One; He created it, and gives it to whoever He deems appropriate. By His will, He gave it to them, and by His will, He took it from them and gave it to us."

> Rashi to Genesis 1:1, citing the Midrash

The question that Rashi addresses is astonishing. How can it be suggested that the Torah should have just begun with the first commandment mentioned in the Book of Exodus? What about the account of the deluge, of the Patriarchs, of the Exodus?

The premise of the question is that Torah is not a history book. It is *toras chaim*, a guidebook for life. It does not describe events for historical interest. The Torah is a book of moral and theological messages.

Before we open [Torah], however, let us consider how to read it. As a subject of philological or antiquarian research? As corroboration for antediluvian or geological hypotheses? In the expectation of finding revelations of esoteric mysteries? Certainly not! As *Jews* we will read this book, as a book tendered to us by God in order that we learn from it about, what we are and what we should be during our earthly existence. We will read it as Torah—literally, "instruction" —directing and guiding us within God's world and among humanity, making our inner self come alive.

Rabbi Samson Raphael Hirsch, The Nineteen Letters, Letter Two

The specific theological message of Genesis is that God is the Maker of the universe. He created the entire world—including the stars, the oceans, the trees and the birds. This is a theological message, not a scientific lesson, and as such, it is presented as a theological story, not a scientific account.

The Torah is not a book of history, science or philosophy. The Torah is a book with goals of theological instruction. From everything in the Torah, one can learn theological instruction. Together with this, when we find narratives of events in the Torah, we must understand that the Torah is speaking truth... [Yet] the Torah does not teach us an organized professional discipline. If you want to learn a professional discipline, don't expect that the Torah will teach it to you; go and learn it in a place where they teach professional disciplines. The Torah does not teach how to be a shoemaker. It teaches how to act...

...From the theological perspective—the Torah, including the acts of creation, are relevant to every person, and can be studied by every person. In contrast to this, the inner truths of the acts of Genesis are relevant only to scholars who are suited to studying them, and are in the category of "God's secret is for those who are in awe of Him."

Rabbi Gedalyah Nadel, Be Toraso Shel Rav Gedalyah, pp. 77, 82

We have shown the problems in understanding the account of Creation as a scientific or historical account. But it is also wrong and degrading to describe Genesis as a myth, as some would do. The term "myth" carries connotations of fairy-tales or the Loch Ness monster—things that intelligent people reject. It is likewise wrong to describe Genesis as an allegory or metaphor, along the lines of the book of Song of Songs. Nor is it pure fiction, like one traditional view of the Book of Job. Rather, as

Rambam and Ralbag explained, it is conceptual instead of historical. The account of creation is a Divine adaptation of the historical occurrences, presented in a form most suited to teaching the fundamental theological truths of creation.

Eradicating Idolatry

In order to assist us in understanding how to approach Genesis, let us look at an extremely mysterious verse from later in the Book of Genesis:

> The *nefilim* were in the land in those days, and also after that; those with which the sons of gods came to the daughters of man, and bore descendants to them—they were the mighty ones, who were always men of reputation.
>
> Genesis 6:4

The nineteenth-century commentator Malbim explains this verse to be targeting, and refuting, a particular ancient belief:

> It is known that amongst all the books of the early nations they tell how in days of old, there were "sons of gods" who descended from Heaven to earth, that reigned over their countries; and that took wives from the daughters of men, and from them arose heroes and mighty men, princes and rulers... and they idolized them and built statues and altars, and worshipped them by all manner of repulsive acts of service... Therefore our teacher Moses made it known to us that these *"nefilim,"* who were giants and tyrants, about which the nations said in their books that they fell from Heaven and were *"in those days, and also after that,"* and they were *"the sons of gods which came to the daughters of man,"* to the extent that even their children were rated as demigods... know that all these stories and legends, upon which the pagan priests built all their pagan rites and stories of God and mythology, is all falsehood and deception. Shall they make a man into a god when he is not a god? Rather, *"they were the mighty ones, who were always men of reputation"*; for with every mighty hero that arose in those days, or a person that made a name for himself by way of his wisdom and deeds, they would attribute divinity to him, and they would say that he fell from the heavens, and would speak wonders about him and much nonsense...
>
> Malbim, Commentary to Genesis 6:4

A very important principle in understanding Genesis can be seen in Malbim's discussion: Genesis specifically targets ancient idolatrous beliefs that were prevalent and seeks to correct them.[1] The approach of idolatry was prevalent in the ancient world:

> Through and under [the Mesopotamian person's experience of nature] he sensed a multitude of powerful individual wills, potentially divergent, potentially conflicting, fraught with a possibility of anarchy. He confronted in Nature gigantic and willful individual powers.
>
> Thorkild Jacobsen, "Mesopotamia," p. 139

Idolatry is the single most severe prohibition in the Torah. It is the second of the Ten Commandments, immediately following the requirement to accept the existence of God. This is not the forum in which to explain precisely why idolatry is so evil; suffice it to note that a primary aim of the Torah is to uproot idolatry. Many of the Torah's commandments, at least according to their simple understanding, relate to uprooting idolatry.

By and large, the Torah has succeeded in its task. The Jewish People abandoned paganism and heralded monotheism. Through Judaism's offshoots of Christianity and Islam, much of the world has come to reject paganism and polytheism, and to believe in the One God.

> Israel, alone, was able to withstand and overcome the powerfully erosive and homogenizing forces of contemporary paganism to develop a unique religio-moral civilization of universal and eternal value. This was an accomplishment of stupendous proportions, rendered all the more astonishing because it came about in an area of the world in which the burden of tradition lay very heavily on men and in which other peoples always exhibited an amazing conservatism and an obstinate resistance to change.
>
> Nahum Sarna, *Understanding Genesis*, p. xxx

This amazing success has not only been triumphed by Jews; it has also been acknowledged by non-Jews:

> The Hebrews arrived late upon the scene and settled in a country pervaded by influences from the two superior adjacent cultures (of

---

1   We also see from Malbim's discussion that familiarity with other ancient religions assists in shedding light upon the meaning of the messages of Genesis.

Egypt and Mesopotamia). One would expect the newcomers to have assimilated alien modes of thought, since these were supported by such vast prestige. Untold immigrants from deserts and mountains had done so in the past; and many individual Hebrews did, in fact, conform to the ways of the Gentiles. But assimilation was not characteristic for Hebrew thought. On the contrary, it held out with a peculiar stubbornness and insolence against the wisdom of Israel's neighbors.

Henri Frankfort, "The Emancipation of Thought from Myth,"
Before Philosophy p. 241

But this success did not come easy, and the hardest work was at the beginning. Breaking people out of the pagan mindset, ingraining the concept of monotheism that comes so naturally to us, was very difficult:

The dominant tenet of Hebrew thought is the absolute transcendence of God. God is not in nature. Neither earth nor sun nor heaven is divine; even the most potent natural phenomena are but reflections of God's greatness... In the field of material culture such a conception of God leads to iconoclasm and it needs an effort of the imagination to realize the shattering boldness of a contempt for imagery at the time, and in the particular historical setting, of the Hebrews.

Henri Frankfort, ibid.

The natural tendency is to increase the number of deities, not to decrease them:

The sheer multiplicity of divine principles available to be worshipped often leads to a perturbation of the picture. If two cultures become closely familiar with each other's religions, thanks to invasion or intense trade, people began to see yet more aspects of the world than before, aspects which their new acquaintances view as willful and hence potentially dangerous if slighted. Prudence suggests that one adopt these new divinities... If someone else is worshipping a different (Willful) aspect than you, add or graft it onto your pantheon to be safe... Deleting deities from the pantheon, on the other hand, causes far more trouble... for the same reason: fear of offending divine powers.

Elizabeth W. Barber and Paul T. Barber, *When They Severed Earth From Sky: How the Human Mind Shapes Myth*, pp. 62, 65

Thus, it was an uphill battle for the Torah to accomplish its important objective of uprooting idolatry. This was a primary goal of the Torah's account of Creation: refuting heathen ideas about the world's origin and stressing the monotheistic account. Establishing the concept of One God requires establishing the concept of a God who transcends nature; Who created everything in the natural world:

> Nowhere else do we meet this fanatical devaluation of the phenomena of nature... in view of the unique significance of the divine. It has rightly been pointed out that the monotheism of the Hebrews is a correlate of their insistence on the unconditioned nature of God. Only a God who transcends every phenomenon, who is not conditioned by any mode of manifestation—only an unqualified God can be the one and only ground of all existence.
>
> Henri Frankfort, ibid. p. 243

Genesis Today: Genesis Triumphant

If the account of creation is understood to be primarily a text aimed at uprooting pagan concepts of the world, does that mean that it is irrelevant today? In a sense, it is certainly less relevant, just as the commandments prohibiting pagan child sacrifice are less relevant. But this decline in relevance signifies the triumph of Judaism. The Torah has succeeded, via Judaism and via its offshoots of Christianity and Islam, in abolishing paganism.

Still, this does not mean that this message of Genesis is now entirely redundant. While idolatry in the simple sense has largely been eradicated, the ideology of it still remains. Many people still believe in attributing innate metaphysical power to amulets, crystals, or even holy men. It is still vital to contemplate the lessons of Genesis and to remember that there is only One power.

Another product of the success of Genesis is the very science that people with a superficial understanding of the text are using to challenge it. As we discussed extensively in the first part of this book, it was the understanding that there is an underlying unity to the cosmos which prepared the intellectual groundwork for science. And the current goal of science is to prove this essential point—that all phenomena in the universe can indeed be unified under a single set of laws:

…While it is not the object of Torah to teach us physics, astronomy, geology, zoology or biology, the cumulative effect of its account of the Creation, even when we read it "while running," is to convey to us the grandest truth towards which science, as the result of centuries of patient labor and research, is feeling its way—the organic unity and symmetry of the cosmos.

Rabbi Yitzchak Herzog, "The Talmud as a Source for the History of Ancient Science," *Judaism: Law, and Ethics*, p. 171

The Timely and the Timeless

The messages of the Torah vary in relevance with changes in culture. Some of the messages of Genesis are of great relevance in today's age of atheism; these were of less relevance a few hundred years ago, when most people accepted the existence of God. Other messages were of primary relevance in ancient times, when the challenges of the day were idolatry and paganism.

Naturally, some will feel uncomfortable with this approach to Genesis. There is a fear that it will lead people to think that the Torah is an outdated document, Heaven forbid; that its commandments are no longer binding. Such a belief is utterly incompatible with Judaism, which sees Torah as an eternal covenant. Yet we must recognize, as discussed earlier, that the fear of a slippery slope is not reason to avoid the slope entirely, just to tread with care. Sometimes there are very good reasons for entering the slope.

We must be careful to understand the nature of the Torah's commandments and the Torah's messages. The commandments are binding at all times; although their application may be qualified by external factors, such as the existence of a Temple or whether one is in the Land of Israel. Such qualifying factors are inbuilt, whether in the Written or Oral Law. But the messages of the Torah, while all true and meaningful, are of varying application depending upon the cultural milieu in which we find ourselves. Certain messages are more relevant and important for some cultures than they are for others. Many of the Torah's messages were primarily oriented for the generation that received the Torah on behalf of all of the Jewish People for all time. Their primary task was to uproot the primary evil of idolatry which was the greatest threat to that generation.

The Power of Genesis

Some have a secret fear that Genesis, if proven not to be accurate from a scientific perspective, is just a collection of old legends like those of other nations. Nothing could be further from the truth, as even a cursory survey of creation literature from other nations proves.

> Genesis… is pre-eminent in the literature of religion. No other ancient account of creation (cosmogony) will bear a second reading. Most of them not only describe the origin of the world, but begin by describing how the gods emerged out of a pre-existing chaos (theogony). In contrast with the simplicity and sublimity of Genesis I, we find all ancient cosmogonies, whether it be the Babylonian or the Phoenician, the Greek or the Roman, alike unrelievedly wild, cruel, even foul…
>
> Each religion has certain specific, teachings, dogmas. Such a dogma of Judaism is its belief that the world was called into existence at the will of the One, Almighty and All-good God. And nowhere does this fundamental conviction of Israel's Faith find clearer expression than in Genesis I. When neighboring peoples deified the sun, moon and stars, or worshipped stocks and stones and beasts, the sacred river Nile, the crocodile that swam in its waters, and the very beetles that crawled along its banks, the opening page of Scripture proclaimed in language of majestic simplicity that the universe, and all that therein is, are the product of one supreme directing Intelligence; of an eternal, spiritual Being, prior to them and independent of them.
>
> Rabbi J. H. Hertz, *The Pentateuch and Haftorahs*, p. 193

Leon Kass, an eminent University of Chicago bioethicist, published a remarkable work that documented his own encounter with Genesis at a relatively late stage in life. His Jewish education was negligible. His training as a scientist meant that he did not take Genesis seriously as a scientific account of creation. But Dr. Kass writes that he was overwhelmed by the extraordinary power of Genesis:

> How much damage does science—and modern thought generally—really do to the biblical teachings about human life and the human good? Can a thoughtful person today still accept or affirm the teachings of the Bible? The answer to these questions depends, of course, on what the Bible in fact says and means…

...Genesis is famously a book about beginnings: the beginning of the heavens and the earth; the beginning of human life on earth; the beginning of the Children of Israel, beginning with Father Abraham; and before, behind, and above all these temporal beginnings, the tireless and enduring beginning that is God—Creator of the world, maker of man in His own image, covenant maker with Abraham and with Israel...

Read philosophically, they convey a universal teaching about "human nature," an anthropology in the original meaning of the term: a *logos* (account) of *anthropos* (the human being). Without using argument or philosophical language—there is no biblical Hebrew word for "nature"—the stories of these first eleven chapters nevertheless offer (among other things) a coherent anthropology that rivals anything produced by the great philosophers.

Leon Kass, *The Beginning of Wisdom: Reading Genesis*, pp 9-10

Kass proceeds to describe in detail the various aspects of this anthropology, using the approach that we have presented in this and the following chapter. He writes about the effects of his studies upon him with words that are an astonishingly powerful testimonial to the power of this approach:

The reader may well wonder how these studies have affected my own outlook on life, morals, and religion. I wish I could give a definitive answer, but I am still in the middle of my journey. There are truths that I think I have discovered only with the Bible's help, and I know that my sympathies have shifted towards the biblical pole of the age-old tension between Athens and Jerusalem. I am no longer confident of the sufficiency of unaided human reason. I find congenial the moral sensibilities and demands of the Torah, though I must confess that my practice is still wanting. And I am frankly filled with wonder at the fact that I have been led to this spiritual point....

When I was an undergraduate at the University of Chicago in the mid-1950s... I was then inclined to think all religions were fossils... Little did I then imagine that I would later come to see the insufficiency of the scientific understanding of human life and the Enlightenment's view of the world. It would have been inconceivable to me that I would later find a most compelling kind of wisdom in the oldest of the still living religions… Who is to say that the Lord does not move in mysterious ways?

Ibid. pp. xiv-xv

Looking at Genesis, we see that it presents five fundamentally important truths:

- God created the universe.[1]
- God is the Creator of everything in the universe.
- The world is good.
- Man is the goal of the world's creation.
- Creation is consecrated by the day of Shabbos.

In the words of Rabbi Hertz:

> *God the Creator and Lord of the Universe, which is the work of His goodness and wisdom; and Man, made in His image, who is to hallow his week-day labors by the blessedness of Sabbath-rest*—such are the teachings of the Creation chapter. Its purpose is to reveal these teachings to the children of men—and not to serve as a textbook of astronomy, geology or anthropology. Its object is not to teach scientific facts; but to proclaim highest religious truths respecting God, Man, and the Universe.

Rabbi J. H. Hertz, The Pentateuch and Haftorahs, p. 195

Of course, there are subsidiary lessons too, relating to the description of each component created and the sequence in which they were created. We shall explore these in the next chapter.

---

1 The concept that He created it from nothing, *ex nihilo*, is often stated to be a fundamental. However, this is not so clear. Rambam and Kuzari state that they would not have difficulty in explaining that God created the universe from pre-existing matter, were there to be sufficient reason; it seems that Ralbag indeed held of this view. Perhaps the strong emphasis on creation *ex nihilo* that we find is a reaction to Aristotle, which related the view that the universe was eternal to a host of concepts that were genuinely antithetical to Judaism. Modern science has long since refuted Aristotle's view of the universe.

Chapter Sixteen

The Content and Sequence of Genesis

The Elements of Creation

In the previous chapters, we learned that Rambam and Ralbag saw Genesis not as a scientific text, but rather as one that teaches vital theological truths. We explained the primary goal of Genesis as teaching man that all the disparate phenomena in the world were created by the One God, rather than emerging from a maelstrom of gods. This helps us understand why the Torah describes some phenomena in a way that sounds outmoded to our ears. Rabbi Samson Raphael Hirsch notes that although there is no actual solid layer surrounding the earth that could be called a firmament, Scripture nevertheless uses that term because that is how the sky appears to man; as a dome over and around the earth.[1] The message to man living in a pagan world was that everything that he recognized in the universe—the stars, the firmament, the plants and the animals—was created by God.

The contrast between Genesis and the creation myths of pagan world is remarkable. Take, for example, the creation of the heavens and the oceans. In the prominent Babylonian creation epic Enuma Elish, the god

---

1 Commentary to Genesis 1:6. Cf. Rabbi Akiva Eiger, note to the phrase *u'vokeya chalonei rakia* in *Siddur Otzar HaTefillos* p. 672. See too Maharzav to Midrash Bereishis Rabbah 6:8.

Marduk defeats the sea-god Tiamat in battle, slices Tiamat's body in half, and uses the two halves to make the sea and sky. Here is an extract that has been condensed for ease of reading, but which we are citing at enough length to illustrate its bizarre emphasis on the clash of titanic deities:

> Then advanced Tiamat and Marduk, the counselor of the gods; To the fight they came on, to the battle they drew nigh. The lord spread out his net and caught her, And the evil wind that was behind him he let loose in her face. As Tiamat opened her mouth to its full extent, He drove in the evil wind, while as yet she had not shut her lips. The terrible winds filled her belly, And her courage was taken from her, and her mouth she opened wide. He seized the spear and burst her belly, He severed her inward parts, he pierced her heart. He overcame her and cut off her life; He cast down her body and stood upon it.
>
> When be had slain Tiamat, the leader, her might was broken, her host was scattered. And her helpers the gods, who marched by her side, trembled, and were afraid, and turned back. They took to flight to save their lives; But they were surrounded, so that they could not escape. He took them captive, he broke their weapons... And on the eleven creatures which she had filled with the power of striking terror... They and their opposition he trampled under his feet. Moreover, Kingu, who had been exalted over them, he conquered...
>
> Now after the hero Marduk had conquered and cast down his enemies... he returned to Tiamat, whom he had conquered. And the lord stood upon Tiamat's hind parts... And with his merciless club he smashed her skull... He split her up like a flat fish into two halves; One half of her he established as a covering for heaven...
>
> *Enuma Elish*

Contrast this with the simplicity and purity of Genesis:

> God said, Let there be a firmament in the midst of the waters, and let it divide the waters from the waters. And God made the firmament, and divided the waters which were under the firmament from the waters which were above the firmament; and it was so.
>
> Genesis 1:6-7

The contrast is remarkable and profound.

> Genesis... proclaims, loudly and unambiguously, the absolute subordination of all creation to the supreme Creator who thus can

make use of the forces of nature to fulfill His mighty deeds in history. It asserts unequivocally that the basic truth of all history is that the world is under the undivided and inescapable sovereignty of God. In brief, unlike Enuma Elish in Babylon, the Genesis Creation narrative is primarily the record of the event which inaugurated this historical process, and which ensures that there is a divine purpose behind creation that works itself out on the human scene.

Nahum Sarna, Understanding Genesis, p. 9

Time as an Element

Aside from the importance of Genesis stressing that the physical elements of the universe are nothing more than God's creations, there is a fundamental lesson in the very concept of this creation stretching over several days. As Rambam and Ralbag stated, the days are not truly periods of time at all, but rather present a conceptual hierarchy of the universe. But why would the Torah present this hierarchy as a sequence of time? Perhaps because it also had to teach us that sequences of time, involving transitions from day to night and back to day, are themselves nothing more than the creations of God. This might seem obvious, but only because the Torah has succeeded in removing us from the mindset of ancient pagans, who looked at the world very differently:

> Another approach is also possible, an approach not toward the sequence of phases as a while but toward the actual transition from one phase to another—the actual succession of phases. The varying length of the night, the ever-changing spectacles of sunrise and sunset, and the equinoctial storms do not suggest an automatic smooth alternation between the "elements" of mythopoeic time. They suggest a conflict, and this suggestion is strengthened by the anxiety of man himself, who is wholly dependent upon weather and seasonal changes… Each morning the sun defeats darkness and chaos… [in Egypt] the snake Apophis is the hostile darkness which the sun defeats every night on his journey through the nether world from the place of sunset in the west to the place of sunrise in the east.

> Now this "dramatic conception of nature which sees everywhere a strife between divine and demoniac, cosmic and chaotic powers" (Wensinck), does not leave man a mere spectator. He is too much involved in, his

welfare depends completely upon, the victory of the beneficial powers for him not to feel the need to participate on their side. Thus we find, in Egypt and Babylonia, that man—that is, man in society—accompanies the principal changes in nature with appropriate rituals.

Henri Frankfort, "Myth and Reality," in Before Philosophy pp. 33-34

Ancient man was tempted to worship the heavenly bodies that seemed to bring about the changes in time. The Torah presented a completely different picture.

> In Genesis… we read that God made a covenant with the living creatures, promising not only that the flood would not recur but also that "while the earth remaineth, seedtime and harvest, cold and heat, summer and winter, day and night shall not cease" (Genesis 8:22). The order of time and the order of the life of nature (which are one) are freely granted by the God of the Old Testament in the fullness of his power; and when considered in their totality, as an established order, they are elsewhere, too, thought to be founded upon the willed order of Creation.

Ibid. p. 33

Conceptual vs. Chronological History

The presentation of the order in which the different phenomena of nature were created is also one that aims for theological truths rather than a scientific account of the universe's development. It does not matter that the sequence of creation that Genesis presents does not correlate with the sequence that science tells of physical history. As we saw earlier in the writings of Rambam and Ralbag, Genesis does not intend to teach an account of the physical sequence, but rather a conceptual sequence that contains important ideas.

One might ask, couldn't the Torah have given a chronological order anyway? Wouldn't it have made life easier? Again, one must remember that Genesis is visibly not a scientific text at all. It speaks of six days rather than billions of years. There is no pretense of it being a scientific account.

In fact, Genesis overtly indicates that it is not presenting a scientific account of the sequence of events. For in the second version of the creation story, the sequence is changed! Whereas in the first chapter of Genesis, man is created after everything else, the second chapter presents a different order:

> And the Lord God said, It is not good that the man should be alone; I will make him a help to match him. And the Lord God formed every beast of the field out of the ground, and every bird of the air; and brought them to the man to see what he would call them; and whatever the man called every living creature, that was its name.

> Genesis 2:18-19

Here, the animals are made *after* man, instead of before.[1] Rabbi Joseph Soloveitchik, in his renowned work *The Lonely Man of Faith*, explains that the two sequences represent two different but complementary views of man's role in the world. The first sequence describes "majestic man," who appears as the pinnacle of nature and conquers it. The second sequence describes "lonely man" who does not subdue nature but interacts with it to achieve a personal relationship with God. According to this understanding, neither sequence is intended to be a scientific account of the development of the world; both are presenting true aspects of man's spiritual existence.

An Order of Priorities

One example of an important theological truth in the sequence of creation is in the order of priorities that it thereby imparts. We noted earlier that the Torah presents the sun as having been created after plants, whereas science tells us that it appeared several billion years earlier. But the Torah is not interested in teaching us science. Instead, there is something much more important for its purposes; downplaying the importance of the sun.

> Rabbi Pinchas ben Yair said: Why did God decree that grasses, herbs and fruit trees should sprout from the ground on the third day, and He created the luminaries on the fourth day? To make His strength known, that He can make the earth sprout vegetation without the luminaries."

> *Midrash Tadshei* 1, cited by Kasher in *Toras HaBriah*

---

1 Rashi avoids this inconsistency by explaining the verse to mean that "God *had* formed every beast." This is in accordance with Rashi's general approach of explaining the Torah such that every verse matches every other and complements the Talmud. This is not, however, the only approach possible.

Of all the features of the natural world, the sun was most of all revered and worshipped by many cultures.

> In the history of mankind no form of idolatry has been more widely practiced than that of the worship of the sun. It may well be described as universal; for there is scarcely a nation in which the worship of the sun in some form has not found a place. In Egypt, the oldest nation of historic times, under the names of Ra and Osiris, with half a dozen other forms; in Phenicia and the land of Canaan, under the names of Baal, Melkarth, Shamas, Adoni, Moloch, and many other forms; in Syria, Tammuz and Elagabalus; among the Moabites, under the names of Baal-peor and Chemosh; among the Babylonians and Assyrians, under the names of Bel and Shamas; among the Medes and Persians and other kindred nations, under the name of Ormuz and Mithra; among the ancient Indians, under the name of Mitra, Mithra, or Mithras; in Greece, under Adonis, Apollo, Bacchus, and Hercules; in Phrygia, under the term Atys; and in Rome, under Bacchus, Apollo, and Hercules; — in all these places, and under all these forms, the sun was worshiped by all these peoples.
>
> A.T. Jones, *The Two Republics*, Chapter 7

Standing in marked contrast is the Torah. God creates the sun, simply another item on the laundry-list. Furthermore, it is neither created at the beginning, which might lead one to consider it a pre-eminent being, nor at the end, which might lead one to consider it the pinnacle of creation; instead, it is created in the middle of the process, on the fourth day.

> The Bible is the document of the greatest effort ever made to deprive all heavenly bodies of all possibility of divine worship... The most striking characteristic of the biblical account of creation is its demoting or degrading of heaven and the heavenly lights.
>
> Leo Strauss, *Jewish Philosophy and the Crisis of Modernity*, pp. 293, 383

Ralbag also discusses this issue and makes a similar point:

> There are difficulties here... According to the natural scheme of things, the creation of [the luminaries] should have taken place on the third day, for the heavens and the heavenly bodies are causally and ontologically prior to the elements and that which is derived from them (and yet which the Torah describes as having been created earlier)... This is quite difficult, and yet we shall try to solve it to the extent

of our ability. Since it is the entire intention of our perfect Torah to lead its students who follow it to true happiness, as we have explained in our Commentary to the Torah, the Torah intended through this ordering of the account of creation to awaken man through his reason to the secrets of existence… It does this by making him pause…. If it included nothing that would make a person pause, he would not study the Torah carefully, and this would be the cause that prevented him from reaping its benefits. Indeed, the change in the ordering of creation in this matter was precisely for this reason. For if the creation of the heavenly bodies had been mentioned before the appearance of the dry land, it would have been possible for someone to err on this matter and think that the appearance of dry land was attributable to the influence of the heavenly bodies, as Aristotle and his followers believed. Therefore, the Torah first mentions the appearance of dry land before it mentions the creation of the heavenly bodies.

Ralbag, Milchamos Hashem, 2:6:8

Thus, Ralbag explicitly states that the sequence of Genesis does not correlate precisely with what one expect the natural sequence to be, but was instead altered from that sequence for the sake of the greater theological truth of downgrading the importance of the luminaries.

The Pattern of Genesis

The order of creation in Genesis is not merely a matter of prioritizing things. The entire sequence follows a striking pattern that reflects the fundamental theology of the Torah.

Let us begin by noting that there is an immediately obvious pattern that can be discerned in the six days of creation. If the six days are split into two groups of three days, the creations of the latter set correlate with the creations of the former set:

One: Light	Four: Luminaries
Two: Sea and Sky	Five: Fish and Birds
Three: Land and vegetation	Six: Animals and man

On each of the first three days, the primal elements were created: Light, the oceans and heavens, and land. On the latter three days that correlated to these, the bodies that make use of these elements were created: the luminaries making use of light, fish and birds living in the oceans and heavens, and animals and man living on the land and living off vegetation.[1] This pattern, noted by many diverse authorities,[2] already lends support to the position of Rambam and Ralbag that the sequence of Genesis is not intended to be chronologically linear.

The same pattern, of seeing a sequence not as a single linear progression but as two twinned series, is also seen in the Ten Commandments. The Ten Commandments were given as two tablets, each of which contained five commandments. Placed side by side, each commandment has a corresponding commandment on the other tablet:

1. I am God	6. Do not murder
2. You shall not have other gods	7. Do not commit adultery
3. Do not take God's Name in vain	8. Do not steal (kidnap)
4. Sanctify the Sabbath	9. Do not bear false witness
5. Honor your parents	10. Do not covet

Rather than being a series of ten laws, they can be viewed as a single series of five laws that has two manifestations. The series of five laws serves to take one from being an egotistical taker to becoming a selfless giver who fully unites both with God and man. These five stages of growth are manifest in their application to achieving unity with God on one tablet, and in their application to achieving unity with man on the other, as depicted in the following chart:[3]

---

1 The plants created on the third day can be seen either as another element required for animals to operate, and/or as an outgrowth of the land. With the latter explanation, the obvious parallel is that man is an outgrowth of the animal kingdom, a concept that we shall later discuss at length.

2 Vilna Gaon, *Biurei Aggados, Bava Kama* 32b; Rabbi Samson Raphael Hirsch, *The Pentateuch*, Genesis 1:20; Rabbi Dovid Tzvi Hoffman, Commentary to Genesis 1:20, p. 36; Umberto Cassuto, *From Adam to Noah*, p. 17. Cf. *Midrash Bereishis Rabbah* 11:8.

3 This idea is taken from Rabbi Yehoshua Honigwachs, *The Unity of Torah*.

Beginning with: Selfishness; Isolation; Focus on the Individual

TABLET #1 *Manifestation between* *Man and God*	DEVELOPMENT	TABLET #2 *Manifestation between* *Man and Man*
Accepting God *Acceptance of God's existence*	STAGE ONE *Acceptance of others' existence*	Do Not Murder *Other people's right to exist;* *Value of life*
Do Not Worship Idols *Accepting God's ownership* *of the entire universe*	STAGE TWO *Acceptance of their domain*	Do Not Commit Adultery *Accepting the other* *person's domain*
Don't Take God's Name in Vain *No unlawful use of God's Name*	STAGE THREE *No unlawful use of property* *(lawful coexistence)*	Do Not Steal (Kidnap) *No unlawful use of another's* *being, person or property*
Observing Shabbos *Testifying to God's authority*	STAGE FOUR *Readiness to cooperate* *(particularly through speech)*	Do Not Testify Falsely *No destructive talk;* *hence, cooperate*
Honoring Parents *Unity with one's source*	STAGE FIVE *Total unity*	Do Not Covet *No resentment of others*

Cumulating in: Selflessness; Unity with God and man;
Integration into the Community

The Ten Commandments are a twin five-stage pattern that develops a process of growth, taking man from the extremes of egotism, in which society is an anarchy of selfish elements, towards a state of unity between all men and God. In the same way, the six days are a twin three-stage pattern, but which do the reverse—they take the universe from the unity of God towards the multiple elements of the universe, as we shall now explain.

The Separation from Unity

The Torah begins with *Bereishis*, "In the beginning," which begins with the letter *beis*. Every letter in the Torah is of great significance; especially the very first letter, and in a Torah scroll, this *beis* is traditionally written enlarged. *Beis* is the second letter of the Hebrew alphabet, and in the system of *gematria*—ascribing numerical values to letters—it carries the value of two.

> *Beis*, with its *gematria* of two, symbolizes our world, since everything earthly is embedded in plurality. Absolute Oneness prevails only with the Divine.
>
> Rabbi Michael L. Munk, *The Wisdom in the Hebrew Alphabet*, p. 58

Creating something means producing something that is distinct from oneself. When God created the universe, His unity gave forth distinct phenomena. The process of creation is that of Unity producing multiplicity. It is a process of one becoming two; of division and separation. It is essential for creation to be presented in this way so that one can work back and see that it all comes from the One God, not from the bevy of lesser gods and demigods of the pagan cults. This process of division and separation, from unity to multiplicity, is beautifully expressed in the six days of creation.[1]

On the first day, God created light. Light was created via a process that is explicitly described as separation—"And God separated the light from the darkness"—and it is the means by which time itself is separated into distinct units—"And God called the light Day, and the darkness He called Night." Light is also the means by which one can discern and distinguish things; by which one can perceive the process of separation. Thus, light is the most basic element of separation.

On the second day, the physical world becomes two distinct parts, sea and sky, again in a process that is explicitly described as separation: "And God said, Let there be a firmament in the midst of the waters, and it shall separate the waters from the waters."

On the third day, God separated the land from the sea. He then drew out the vegetation from the land. Vegetation is a new level of separation in that the process of vegetative growth is one in which it continually separates itself from its source.

---

1 This explanation is adapted from Leo Strauss, *On the Interpretation of Genesis*, and Leon Kass, *The Beginning of Wisdom: Reading Genesis*. The latter has an extremely detailed discussion of this sequence.

We then move to the next series of three days. These are collectively in a different realm from the first three days, in that all the elements of them are animate. The luminaries move across the sky, and the animal kingdom and man are all capable of locomotion. Movement is itself a process of separation, in that one separates oneself from one's location.

On the fourth day, and first in the second set of three days, are the luminaries. These possess the most basic form of motion, in that while they can move, they are restricted to following set paths.

On the fifth day God created the first animal life—aquatic creatures and flying creatures. These possess a greater form of motion than the luminaries in that not only can they separate themselves from their place, but they can also separate themselves from whatever path they are on and move in a different direction. In fact, animal life is defined most fundamentally by being animate. One way in which we see this is that the lowest and most basic level of life—creeping, swarming creatures—are called *sheretz* in the Torah, which is explained by some to refer to their being the first class of created things to possess independent movement.[1] The first life that was created, aquatic life, is described with the phrase, *Yishretzu hamayim sheretz*—"Let the waters swarm with moving things." This movement represented a new form of separation.

On the sixth day, God created terrestrial animal life and man. Terrestrial animals may initially appear to belong with birds and fish on the fifth day, in possessing the same degree of motion. But since they are affiliated with the land, which was created a day later than the sky and sea from which it was separated, they are created on the day that correlates with the land.[2]

---

1 Rabbi Samson Raphael Hirsch; Cf. Ramban, commentary to Genesis 1:20, who explains it as referring to the constancy of movement amongst small animals, as opposed to their being the most basic class of creatures to possess the capacity of motion.

2 Umberto Cassuto, *From Adam to Noah*, p. 53. An alternate explanation is that birds are conceptually similar to fish and therefore precede animals in the account of creation. One indication that fish and birds are conceptually similar is seen in the Mishnah (*Chullin* 49a), which uses the word *poreyach*, "flying," to describe the motion of fish through water. The Torah, in classifying animals, considers their posture and methods of locomotion to be the fundamentally important characteristics. The Torah classifies the animal kingdom in terms of groups such as aquatic animals—including fish and

The final stage in creation is man. Man is a degree of separation beyond animal life, in that he possesses a Divine soul. This enables him to separate himself from whatever path he is on—not only in terms of his physical path, but also his spiritual path. He can change his direction in life, either for the good or bad.

> The creatures of the first three days cannot change their places; the heavenly bodies change their places but not their courses; the living beings change their courses but not their "ways"; men alone can change their "ways."
>
> Leo Strauss, "Jerusalem and Athens,"
> in *Jewish Philosophy and the Crisis of Modernity* p. 383

A Pattern for Life

The overall pattern of the six days can be summarized as follows:

	Element:	Actualized by:
↓ *Increasing Separation* ↓	Day 1: Light	Day 4: Luminaries
	Day 2: Sea and Sky	Day 5: Fish and Birds
	Day 3: Land and plants	Day 6: Animals and man
	Inanimate World → *Increasing Separation* →	Animate World

The sequence presented is a conceptual one that illustrates the essence of creation—a progression from unity to separation.[1]

---

marine mammals; aerial creatures—including birds, insects and bats; animals that walk on paws; and crawling animals (see Leviticus chapter 11). The posture and method of locomotion fundamentally defines the creature. Thus, the fact of fish and birds both "flying" through their medium relates to their basic essence. Motion in water and air, although complex in terms of the actions required, is smoother than motion on land, and therefore appears more fluid and simpler. In the unfolding pattern of creation, where the universe unfolds from unity into the complex multiplicity of the physical, both fish and birds are conceptually one stage earlier in the process than terrestrial animals.

1 Cf. Dr. Carl Feit, "Darwin and Drash: The Interplay of Torah and Biology": "The

Earlier, we discussed how the twinned pattern of Creation is similar to the twinned pattern of the Ten Commandments, in which there is a five-stage process that takes society from a mass of individuals towards unity with God and man. Creation is also a series of ten, in that there were ten creative utterances involved, as the Mishnah states:

> With ten utterances the world was created. What does this come to teach us—surely it could have been created with one utterance? Rather, it was to exact punishment from the wicked who destroy the world that was created with ten utterances, and to bestow goodly reward upon the righteous who sustain the world that was created with ten utterances.
>
> Mishnah, *Avos* 5:1

> If the Torah teaches us about the creation of the world in ten utterances—this is as the Tanna said: "With ten utterances the world was created…" That is to say: See what a beautiful and sophisticated world was created and prepared for you; you, man, the pinnacle of the acts of Genesis; and take care that you do not destroy it. "Take care that you do not damage and destroy my world" (*Midrash Koheles Rabbah* 7). How do we destroy the world or build it up—the Torah proceeds to tell us. This is the entire Torah.
>
> Rabbi Gedalyah Nadel, *BeToraso Shel Rav Gedalyah* p. 82

We thus see that there is an underlying connection between Creation and Commandment. The ten creative utterances of Genesis signify a process of division from unity to diverse multiplicity. Man, the final stage of the process, is someone who can sink to being the most selfish of creatures. But he also possesses a divine spark which can enable him to move towards unity with God and man. The Ten Commandments return him through the ten utterances of creation back to unity.

---

description, then, is not an attempt to give a linear, chronological sequence but rather a presentation of the process of refinement and differentiation; God acts more like a sculptor than a carpenter. He created by revealing and unfolding potentiality rather than by adding pre-formed parts. Detail is drawn out of chaos in a continuous process of refinement, making finer and finer distinctions, one after another."

Chapter Seventeen

Dinosaurs and Sea Monsters

Dinosaurs in the Torah

We have proposed a successful reconciliation of the billions of years of the world's history with the Torah account, based on the approach of Rambam and Ralbag that the Torah was not interested in providing a scientific account of the world's development. We have even explained why there was both a need and a benefit in the existence of these billions of years: a need in terms of providing the conditions required for man (in a naturalistic way), and a benefit in terms of the realization of man's responsibility in this world.

Still, one can ask why the earth had to be populated during these billions of years. Specifically, it is the reign of the dinosaurs that perplexes many people. What is the significance of dinosaurs?

In seeking to find the significance of dinosaurs from a Jewish perspective, some people—generally those who wish to understand Genesis as a scientific text—search for where they are mentioned in the Torah. Some think that they have found such a mention:

> And God created the great *taninim*...

Genesis 1:21

What are the "great *taninim*" ? There are places in the Torah where the word *tanin* (the singular form of *taninim*) refers to snakes.[1] There

---

1 Deuteronomy 32:33.

are also places in Scripture where it refers to crocodiles.[1] It is therefore argued that *tanin* refers to the general category of these animals—reptiles. Thus, it is claimed that the great *taninim* of Genesis are the great reptiles: dinosaurs.[2]

The idea that the Torah would mention dinosaurs is sensational and immensely appealing for many people. Unfortunately, appealing ideas are often not subject to careful examination. In fact, this is a highly problematic proposal, for numerous reasons.

First of all, while the word *tanin* can refer to snakes and crocodiles, it does not refer to the general category of reptiles in the zoological sense. For example, there is no reason to believe that it would refer to lizards or turtles. Furthermore, while *tanin* can refer to reptiles such as snakes and crocodiles, it can also refer to non-reptiles such as whales.[3] In any case, dinosaurs were more closely related to birds than reptiles. It seems that the name *tanin* refers to serpentine creatures, not reptiles; and the majority of dinosaurs were not serpentine (aside from not being reptiles). They stood high from the ground on long legs. The Torah does not classify animals based on internal anatomy but rather based on gross external form. Dinosaurs would mostly be rated as types of *chayos*, wild animals, rather than *taninim*.

Second, the description of the "great" *taninim* does not mean that the *taninim* of Genesis were any larger than those of today, since the same phrase is used elsewhere in Scripture to describe the crocodile.[4] Thus, there is no reason why it should not carry the same meaning.

Third, if we look at the entire verse and its context in Genesis, we see that it is referring to aquatic creatures:

> And God said, Let the waters be filled with many kinds of living creatures, and birds that may fly above the earth in the open firmament

---

1 Ezekiel 29:3.

2 Gerald Schroeder, *The Science of God*, p. 193.

3 This seems to be the meaning of Psalms 148:7, which indicates that the *taninim* live at great depths. Radak in *Sefer HaShorashim* states that *tanin* refers to both terrestrial snakes and large aquatic serpentine creatures (i.e. crocodiles and perhaps whales).

4 Ezekiel 29:3.

of heaven. And God created the great *taninim* and every kind of living creeping creature that swarms in the water, and every kind of winged bird, and God saw that it was good.

Genesis 1:20-21

The overwhelming majority of dinosaurs were terrestrial rather than aquatic creatures, and would thus surely be created with the same powers used to create the terrestrial animals of the sixth day rather than the aquatic creatures of the fifth day.

Finally, the entire question is based upon a flawed premise. There is no reason to expect to find dinosaurs in the Torah any more than we would expect to find ammonites or mammoths. There have been countless varieties of creatures that have long gone extinct, and the Torah does not mention them. The Torah does not mention kangaroos or penguins, since they did not live in same part of the world as the Jewish People and would therefore have been unfamiliar to them. Nor does it mention bacteria, which ancient man was not able to see or know about. By the same token, it does not mention creatures that became extinct millions of years ago. We should not be trying to understand Torah as *National Geographic*.

Other Proposed Contenders

There have nevertheless been efforts to find dinosaurs elsewhere in Scripture. One popular candidate is the behemoth described by God in his speech to Job:

> Behold now behemoth, which I made with you; he eats grass like an ox. Behold now, the strength of his loins, and the power in his belly. He thrusts his tail like a cedar; his testicles are bound by twisted cords. His bones are like tubes of bronze; his limbs are like bars of iron. He is the head of the works of God; let Him who made him bring near His sword to him. The mountains bring him forth food, where all the beasts of the field play. He lies under the shady trees, in the cover of the reeds and swamp. The shady trees cover him with their shadow; the willows of the brook surround him. Behold, he plunders a river without hurry; he trusts that he can draw the Jordan into his mouth. He takes in the river with his eyes, his nostrils are as though pierced by hooks.
>
> Job 40:15-24

233

A myriad of creationist websites present this as a description of a sauropod dinosaur such as Apatosaurus (formerly known as Brontosaurus). Their reasoning is that no other creature matches the description given of the behemoth: a mighty yet herbivorous creature, living in the swamp. In particular, the description of it thrashing its tail like a cedar is argued to only match a dinosaur—there is no large herbivore today that possesses such a tail.

A sauropod dinosaur

Such a theory is, however, untenable. No dinosaur lived at the same time as Job. Instead, the verses are describing a hippopotamus.[1] The description of it "thrusting its tail like a cedar" can refer euphemistically to a different part of its anatomy, as the commentaries deduce from the subsequent words in the verse.[2]

Another creature that is proposed to be a dinosaur is the leviathan. This creature is described alongside the behemoth as a giant scaly beast. Yet there is no reason not to assume that the term refers to aquatic monsters such as whales and crocodiles.

There is another creature from the Jurassic era that is proposed to be in the Torah. Dr. Gerald Schroeder, a physicist who attempts to correlate Genesis with modern science, argues that the Torah speaks of archaeopteryx.[3] This is a strange dinosaur-like creature that looked very much like a bird, possessing wings, a wishbone for anchoring wing muscles, and feathers. But it also possessed jaws with teeth rather than a beak, a long bony tail, and reptilian claws on its wings. It is considered to be a transitional form in the evolution of birds from dinosaurs.

---

1   See *Mysterious Creatures* by this author for further discussion.

2   Malbim ad loc.; see too Rashi, Ibn Ezra, Ralbag, and *Metzudas Tziyon* to Job 40:17 and Deuteronomy 25:18 with the commentaries of Rashi citing *Midrash Tanchuma*, *Rabbeinu Bechaya*, and *Daas Zekeinim* ad loc.

3   Gerald Schroeder, *The Science of God*, pp. 95-96.

Schroeder claims that when the Torah lists a creature called the *tinshemeth* in its list of non-kosher birds, and a creature called the *tinshemeth* in its list of impure *sheratzim* (reptiles), this must refer to the same creature: archaeopteryx. Only the archaeopteryx would be listed amongst the birds because of its avian features, and listed amongst the reptiles because of its reptilian features.

Archaeopteryx

However, closer investigation reveals that this proposition, while sounding attractive, involves serious difficulties. First of all, categories such as "bird" and "reptile" are modern zoological definitions based upon anatomy and have no bearing on the Torah's system of classification. The Torah classifies animals based on their size, mode of locomotion and other factors unrelated to anatomy. An *ohf* is not a bird, but rather a flying creature. Likewise, *sheratzim* are not reptiles, but rather are vermin, including certain reptiles and also certain mammals. Thus, even assuming that both mentions of the *tinshemeth* refer to the same creature, all we know is that it is a vermin-like creature that flies, a description which is most obviously met by the bat. But they need not refer to the same creature to begin with; none of the classical commentaries take this to be the case. Instead, they refer to creatures that possess similar characteristics that relate the etymology of their name. *Tinshemeth* means "breathing" or "hissing"; thus, the flying *tinshemeth* is a type of owl,[1] and the creeping *tinshemeth* is probably the chameleon, which hisses and puffs itself full of air.

Furthermore, the term *sheretz* only refers to small, ignoble, prolific creatures that creep on the surface of the ground, as the commentators explain based on the anatomy of the term. The list of *sheratzim* thus does not include large reptiles such as crocodilians. It would likewise also not include archaeopteryx, which stood high from the ground on two legs and would fundamentally not meet the definition of *sheretz*.

---

1 Rashi to Talmud, *Chullin* 63a; Radak, *Sherashim*; Ralbag

Finally, and most simply, it is bizarre to suppose that the Torah would discuss the non-kosher status of a creature that has been extinct for a hundred million years. The Torah does not teach us about the non-kosher status of pterodactyls and neither does it need to teach us about the non-kosher status of archaeopteryx.

The Designation of *Taninim*

Although the *taninim* are aquatic monsters such as whales and crocodiles rather than dinosaurs, the verse does raise questions:

> And God created the great sea-monsters and every kind of living creeping creature that swarms in the water, and every kind of winged bird, and God saw that it was good.

Genesis 1:21

Why are the *taninim* the only creatures in creation to be singled out by name, and furthermore to have the phrase "And God created" attached to them? It is significant not just that God's Name is mentioned, but also that the phrase "created" rather than "formed" is used. What is the significance of this?

Ramban explains that due to the great size of the monsters of the sea, the Torah attributes their creation to God. His intent may be that man might have been tempted to attribute inherent power to them, and the Torah therefore stresses that they were created by God; alternatively, that it is enhancing the glory of God by emphasizing that even such wondrous creatures as these were created by God.

Malbim explains that the phrase "And God created," is not referring specifically to the sea-monsters, but rather to the entire contents of the verse, i.e. all aquatic life. These were the first creatures to be made, and they required an extra "ingredient"—life itself. This qualitatively new phenomena is thus described with the word "created."

Earlier, we saw how Malbim explained aspects of Genesis as serving to demythologize ancient man's perception of the world. The account of the sea monsters is explained in the same way by Rabbi Professor Umberto Cassuto (1883-1951). Umberto (Moshe David) Cassuto was Chief Rabbi of Florence, Italy and later became Professor of Bible Studies at the

Hebrew University of Jerusalem. While some of his views were at odds with Orthodoxy, he fought an impressive campaign against Bible critics in defending the unity of the Biblical text and demonstrating its power. His expertise in ancient religions enabled him to show how the Torah successfully weaned people away from paganism, as demonstrated by his explanation of the account of the creation of sea monsters:

> In Egypt, in Mesopotamia, in the land of Canaan and in the countries of the East generally, all sorts of legends used to be recounted about the battles of the great gods against the sea dragon and similar monsters… The Torah is entirely opposed to these myths. It voices its protests in a quiet manner, relating: *So God created the great sea monsters.* It is as though the Torah said, in effect: Far be it from any one to suppose that the sea monsters were mythological beings opposed to God or in revolt against him; they were as natural as the rest of the creatures, and were formed in their proper time and in their proper place by word of the Creator, in order that they might fulfill His will like the other created beings.

> Umberto Cassuto, *From Adam to Noah*, pp. 49-51

Just as Malbim explained the Torah as demythologizing the "sons of God," so too the Torah demythologizes the monsters of the deep. In Ugaritic creation legends, the god Ba'al overcomes a dragon of the sea named *Tannin* in battle. But in the Torah, instead of the *taninim* being dragons of the deep that are on the level of gods, they are now merely the large aquatic creatures that are another of God's creations, along with "every kind of living creeping creature that swarms in the water."

Whichever explanation one adopts regarding the significance of the *taninim* of Genesis, there is no reason to believe that they are dinosaurs. As intriguing as dinosaurs are, they play no role in God's description to the Jewish People of cosmology and cosmogony. But the monsters of the deep, on the other hand, play a very significant role indeed.

Part Three:

EVOLUTION

Chapter Eighteen

Untangling Evolution

Jewish Responses to Evolution

Even more than the age of the universe, evolution is an issue that has been of great concern to religion—or at least, to many religious people. While this is best known in its manifestation of disputes between scientists and the Christian community, there has also been a long history of widely differing attitudes to evolution within the Jewish community. In general, however, the Jewish community has displayed less antagonism towards evolution than has the Christian community, as one comprehensive study of attitudes to evolution concludes:

> Relative to the ongoing uproar that Darwinism has generated in the Christian world, the responses to Darwinism by Jewish thinkers seem to have been proportionately fewer, less focused and more conciliatory.
>
> Michael Shai Cherry, *Creation, Evolution and Jewish Thought*, p. 351

In many cases these responses were surprising in their diversity and unpredictability. The nineteenth century saw great hostility towards evolution from leading rabbis in the Reform movement, such as Abraham Geiger and Isaac Mayer Wise, as well as from traditionalist Jewish communities in the United States. This subsequently reversed itself in the Reform movement, however.[1] Meanwhile, the Italian kabbalist Rabbi

---

1 Marc Swetlitz, "American Jewish responses to Darwin and evolutionary theory, 1860-

Eliyahu Benamozegh (1822-1900) wrote that were evolution to ever be proven, it would not contradict the Torah as long as one understands it as having been guided by God.[1]

Naftali Levy (1840-1894), a Polish Orthodox scholar, went further and embraced evolution. He wrote *Toldos Ha-Adam*, "The Generations of Man," a work extolling evolution as greatly enhancing the Torah, and sent it to Charles Darwin along with a letter of praise that Darwin greatly appreciated![2] Yet Levy was on the border between Orthodoxy and the *haskalah* movement,[3] and faced opposition for his support of evolution.[4] Another work, by Yosef Yehudah Leib Sossnitz (1837-1910) was entitled *Achen Yesh Hashem*, "Rather, There Is God," a reference to the Biblical verse, "Rather, there is God in this place, and I had not known it," (Genesis 28:16). The subtitle explained that its goal was to refute secular materialism—"to protect religion against those that deny God and any metaphysical force."[5] But it argued that guided evolution was compatible with Judaism.

1890," in *Disseminating Darwinism*. Geoffrey Cantor, in *Quakers, Jews and Science*, documents the diverse responses of the British Jewish community to evolution in the nineteenth century. See too Naomi Cohen, "The challenges of Darwinism and biblical criticism to American Judaism," and Lois Dubin, "*Pe'er Ha-adam* of Vittorio Hayim Castiglioni: an Italian chapter in the history of the Jewish response to Darwin."

1 *Em LeMikra* (Leghorn 1863), commentary to Deuteronomy 22:10, p. 87a-88b. See Jose Faur, "The Hebrew Species Concept and the Origin of Evolution: R. Benamozegh's Response to Darwin," *La Ressegna Mensile di Israel* 63, no. 3 (1997): 42-66.

2 The letter was published by Francis Darwin in *More Letters of Charles Darwin* vol. I, letter 277. See Edward O. Dodson, "*Toldot Adam*: A Little-Known Chapter in the History of Darwinism," and Ralph Colp Jr. and David Kohn, "A Real Curiosity: Charles Darwin Reflects on a Communication from Rabbi Naphtali Levy."

3 He was a disciple of Rabbi Meir Auerbach who later became rabbi of the Jerusalem Orthodox community, and his *halachic* works received approbations from rabbis in Poland and Russia. But *Toldos Ha-Adam* was also published in *Ha-Shachar*, a journal of the *Haskalah* movement.

4 When Levy moved to England and attained prominence, acting as a *shochet* for the London Board of *Shechitah*, Rabbi Joseph Kohn-Tzedek of London asked the rabbis who had written approbations to Levy's work to retract them.

5 The author was associated with the *haskalah*, but used the same arguments that would later be used by Orthodox figures.

Yet, with a few prominent exceptions that we shall discuss, the overall attitude to evolution by the Orthodox Jewish community has been hostile. At a meeting of rabbis in Kovno in 1885, the suggestion was even raised that the community ostracize anyone who studied Darwinian evolution. Rabbi Yitzchak Elchonon Spector and Rabbi Alexander Moshe Lapidus opposed the measure, but only due to the wise foresight that it would inevitably result in people being more attracted to it and rebelling against rabbinic authority.[1]

Our aim here is to show how some prominent Torah authorities have constructed a path in Genesis, supported by traditional teachings, that is not only consistent with most aspects of evolution but in some cases shows them to actually enhance our understanding of the Torah. These authorities include Rabbi Samson Raphael Hirsch, Rabbi Avraham Yitzchak Kook, Rabbi Joseph Soloveitchik, and Rabbi Gedalyah Nadel. We shall discuss all their approaches, as well as performing our own more detailed analysis of the topic, for the sake of those who have studied the evidence for evolution and find it convincing, and might be under the mistaken impression that it poses a challenge to Judaism. As we shall see, it decidedly does not.

The Importance of Definitions

A large part of the controversy concerning whether evolution is "proven" stems from confusion regarding the terminology being used. The word "evolution" is extraordinarily ambiguous, something which is taken advantage of by both evolutionists and creationists.[2] Evolutionists advance proof for one type of evolution as proof for all types of evolution; creationists do the reverse. 90% of all arguments between people about the validity of evolution could probably be solved by simply defining the term "evolution."

---

1 Rabbi Ahron Soloveitchik, *Logic of the Heart, Logic of the Mind*, p. 55.

2 The term "creationist" is used here in the colloquial sense, which has the primary connotation of a Biblical literalist who believes that God instantaneously formed every creature from the earth a few thousand years ago. It is not intended to include everyone who believes that God created the world, many of whom are also evolutionists.

In this section, therefore, we shall distinguish between a number of different aspects that are commonly grouped under the term "evolution," and then we shall explore the status of each. First of all, a brief review of the evolution of evolutionary theory is in order, which will also enable us to define some of the terms that we shall be using.

Charles Darwin, in *On The Origin Of Species*, presented two main propositions. The first was that all the diverse new species that have appeared in the world originated from a very small number of common ancestors, perhaps a single microscopic ancestor, via an extremely gradual process that he called "descent with modification." The second proposition was that these transformations occurred by way of natural selection, also known as "survival of the fittest." This means that every so often, a creature's offspring will possess a favorable characteristic, one that slightly enhances its survival ability. As a result, proportionately more of creatures with such characteristics will survive to pass on this trait to the next generation. Eventually, this characteristic will be found in a large part of the population, and the accumulation of changes such as these will ultimately result in the formation of complex organs and new species.

Darwin himself was unsure how these favorable characteristics, which he called "variations," would come about. Later research into the concept of genes explained it in terms of genetic mutation, and the combination of this concept with Darwin's theory became known as "neo-Darwinian evolution" or "the modern synthesis."

In the 1970s, Stephen Jay Gould and Niles Eldredge proposed a variation on this called punctuated equilibrium. This posited that evolution, rather than being a very gradual process, occurred in relatively brief spurts of only a few hundred thousand years, separated by long periods of stasis in which there was no change. The reasons for this theory, and the extent to which it differs from orthodox Darwinism, will be discussed later.

A relatively new entry in evolutionary theory is that of emergent complexity and self-organization. This is a highly speculative field of science that attempts to explain how significantly helpful mutations can occur, even though these have always been considered statistically unlikely.

We shall now explore several different aspects of evolution, clearly distinguishing between them, and later surveying the extent of evidence for each. As with the topic of the age of the universe, we shall work with the premise that God is not out to deceive us; we shall draw reasonable conclusions from that which the physical world shows us.

(A) The Origin of Life

Strictly speaking, all theories of evolution deal only with the development of new species from previous ones. The starting point is that there are organisms which are alive and reproduce, and the theories of evolution take off from that point. But many people (on both sides of the debate) also consider the term "evolution" to include the explanation for the original formation of life from inanimate matter. The reason for this appears to be that the evolution-creation debate largely (albeit mistakenly) revolves around the existence or non-existence of a purely naturalistic explanation for everything. Most evolutionists seek to find a naturalistic explanation for everything; hence, they are not satisfied with merely finding an explanation for how creatures developed from the first life-form, but rather they also want to find an explanation for how the first life-form itself developed. Thus, Douglas Futuyma, author of a leading book defending evolution, explains the "evolution" of bacteria from the presumed primordial soup, and describes it as one of the "claims of evolutionists."[1]

Likewise, most creationists seek to uphold the literal meaning of Genesis and also want to preserve God's open hand in affairs. They are aware that most evolutionists are opposed to this, and therefore infer that evolutionists are also opposed to the idea of the first life-form coming about through supernatural means. This happens to be a correct assumption in the vast majority of cases, but it is not always the case. It is important to make this distinction because many creationists would accept the theory of evolution provided that they can still attribute the formation of the first life-form to God's direct intervention.

---

1 *Science on Trial*, pp. 94, 95.

(B) Change

Although not often used in this sense today, the term "evolution" has been used in the past to mean simply that the creatures found on Earth today are not the same as the creatures that used to exist (without necessarily saying that the current creatures are descended from the former ones). Nowadays, this concept is so widely accepted that it isn't seen as needing discussion. But it used to be universally held that God created all the creatures at once and there have been no changes since then—nothing ever became extinct, and no new species ever appeared.[1] When the paleontological evidence began to show that the current inhabitants of the earth are not the same as the earlier inhabitants, this caused considerable controversy. But the evidence quickly became overwhelming.

Certain people still dispute this point, and contend that there was indeed only one act of creation in which all species were created, some of which have since become extinct. In light of the paleontological and geological evidence, however, this is untenable. There are distinct strata of rock that reflect different periods of the earth's history, and different fossils are found in each layer. No fossils of large mammals have ever been found in the same strata as the dinosaurs. It is clear that there was an age of dinosaurs, then an age of saber-toothed cats and woolly mammoths, and now the age of the animals that we see. It is undeniable that new types of creatures have continually come into existence over the history of the earth—the only question is as to *how* this happened.

(C) Common Ancestry

Evolution at its most basic definition means that all the different present-day species developed from a single earlier organism (this is sometimes referred to as "the fact of evolution"), without defining *how* this could have happened. For example, it means that both whales and bats are descended from terrestrial mammals, along with lions and elephants. All mammals, in turn, are descended from reptiles, which in turn evolved from amphibians, which evolved from fish, which evolved from simple organisms.

---

1 See, for example, *Sefer HaChinnuch* mitzvah 545, which states that no creature ever becomes extinct.

As we shall see, there are excellent reasons to accept this assertion, on both scientific and theological grounds. It is accepted as fact by the overwhelming majority of the scientific community. Contrary to popular belief, it is even accepted by most leading figures in the "Intelligent Design" movement.

(D) Mechanisms of Evolution

"Common ancestry" merely states that current creatures are descended from earlier creatures; it does not explain how that could have happened, which is an entirely separate issue. In the scientific community, the primary theory to explain evolutionary change is neo-Darwinian theory. There are other mechanisms that are considered to play a role too, and there is some debate over the degree to which each is involved.

Many biologists use the title "the theory of evolution" to refer to such explanations of evolutionary mechanisms. This leads some laymen to dismiss evolution as being "just a theory." In doing so, they are making two errors. First of all, the appellation "theory" is only being used with regard to the mechanisms of evolution, not with regard to common ancestry, which is regarded as being as sufficiently proven as any fact in nature. Second, "theory" as a scientific term does not mean the same as "theory" in colloquial English. A theory is any explanation of a mechanism behind a phenomenon. We have the theory of gravity and the theory of thermodynamics; it is clearly absurd to dismiss these on the grounds that they are "just a theory."

(E) The Darwinian Mechanism

Neo-Darwinian evolution theorizes that changes in a species happen by way of very small random genetic mutations that gradually accumulate by way of natural selection. Just how probable such things are is the subject of considerable dispute. Creationists and Intelligent Design advocates claim that they are far too improbable to have occurred by chance; most evolutionists dispute such charges. However, recently some scientists have argued that complexity theory, which proposes that there is an innate drive for self-organization in the universe, lies behind the evolution of new characteristics and creatures in a way that accounts for the previously assumed wild improbability of such things evolving by chance.[1]

The Results of Disentanglement

Disentangling the evolution controversy clears up much of the confusion and argument. Of particular importance is distinguishing between common ancestry and evolutionary mechanisms. Many religious people believe that "anti-evolutionists," such as Intelligent Design advocate Michael Behe, endorse the traditional view of Biblical creation. Nothing could be further from the truth, as Behe himself admits:

> "I'm an 'evolutionist' in the sense that I do think natural selection explains some things... But from what I see, the evidence only shows natural selection explaining rather small changes, and I see profound difficulties in thinking that it explains much more than trivial changes. It is fine by me if common descent is indeed true, and there is some sort of designed program to power changes over time (i.e., evolution). And I think things like pseudogenes are strong arguments for common descent..."

> Michael Behe, cited by Michael Ruse,
> *The Evolution-Creation Struggle*, p. 256

The other famous proponents of "Intelligent Design" likewise accept that all animals evolved from a single bacterium. Law professor Phillip

---

1 Although unproven, this is significant in that it shows that sometimes, as soon as scientists think they have found a naturalistic explanation for events, they are willing to concede that the phenomena would otherwise appear impossible to happen without God; yet as long as such a naturalistic explanation was lacking, they scoffed at anyone who pointed out the difficulties. Thus, by way of example, in response to Phillip Johnson's statement that "the possibility that such a complex entity [a DNA or RNA macromolecule] could assemble itself by chance is fantastically unlikely," Stephen Jay Gould wrote that "no scientist has used that argument for 20 years, now that we understand so much more about the self-organizing properties of molecules and other physical systems" ("Impeaching a Self-Appointed Judge," *Scientific American* 267). The truth is that we know very little about such self-organizing properties, and evolutionists can be divided into two groups: those who accept the improbability of such a thing occurring by chance but counter that the theory of self-organization is true and accounts for it, and those who do not accept that the theory of self-organization has any substance and (therefore) deny that chance formation of complex macromolecules is overly improbable.

Johnson, considered the leader of the Intelligent Design movement, makes a rare admission:

> At a more general level, the pattern of relationships among plants and animals suggests that they may have been produced by some process of development from some common source.
>
> Phillip Johnson, *Darwin on Trial*, p. 158

And theologian William Dembski, author of numerous books advocating Intelligent Design, frankly states that he accepts common ancestry:

> "Right now I'm inclined toward a preprogrammed form of evolution in which life evolves teleologically (human being the end of the evolutionary process."
>
> William Dembski, cited by Michael Ruse, *The Evolution-Creation Struggle*, p. 256

While these people oppose the idea of fully naturalistic explanations of how one species changes into another, they accept that species have indeed, somehow, changed from one to another. Most of the time, citations from evolutionists about "flaws" in evolution are referring to neo-Darwinian explanations of evolutionary mechanisms, not to whether all animals evolved from a common ancestor. This distinction is usually lost upon the person using such citations.

Another aspect of disentangling evolution is realizing that the scientific validity of any aspect of evolution has nothing to do with the social implications. While the Nazis and others have claimed evolution as a basis for their evil beliefs, this has nothing to do with the issue of whether or not evolution is true, just as the claims of some as the Bible being the basis for their evil actions has nothing to do with whether the Bible is true.

Untangling the Conflict with Religion

Not only is much of the debate over evolution based on ambiguities and vagueness as to the term "evolution," but there is also a considerable lack of clarity as to how exactly evolution is supposed to contradict religion. This is an extremely important matter to clarify.

In the last section, we saw that a large part of the controversy concerning whether evolution is "proven" stems from confusion regarding the terminology being used. The word "evolution" is extraordinarily ambiguous, something which is taken advantage of by both evolutionists and creationists. Evolutionists advance evidence for one aspect of evolution as proof for all aspects of evolution; creationists take difficulties with one aspect of evolution and use it to reject all aspects of evolution.

But it is also confusion regarding the definition of religion which feeds a large part of the conflict between evolution and religion. The parameters of religious belief are not widely understood or agreed upon, which is also taken advantage of by both evolutionists and creationists. Secular evolutionists consider that evolution disproves religious belief according to their own definition of religious belief, but it may well not disprove the religious belief of others. Conversely, some creationists feel that *their* understanding of religious belief means that evolution must be incompatible with religion, but do so without realizing that religious belief may be more sophisticated than they assume.

The reasons for which evolution is thought to contradict Torah can be divided into five categories:

(A) The conflict between the view that life originated by God's overt intervention and naturalistic explanations of how life began;

(B) The conflict between evolution at its most basic meaning of gradual descent by modification (common ancestry) with the simple meaning of the Torah;

(C) The conflict between theological views of God's role as Creator with naturalistic explanations of evolutionary mechanisms via which creatures evolved into different species;

(D) Conflicts between aspects of Darwinian evolutionary mechanisms (such as "bad design," the bitter struggle and destructiveness of it) and God's running of the world;

(E) The conflicts (conceptual and textual) between the idea of man being created from dust in the image of God with the idea of man evolving from an apelike ancestor.

We shall explore these five categories over the course of the next five chapters. It is important to remember that these categories are distinct from each other. For example, someone who considers human evolution (E) to be an unacceptable proposition can still accept the evolution of other animals (A-D); and someone who rejects Darwinian mechanisms of evolutionary change (C-D) can still accept evolution via other mechanisms (B).

Chapter Nineteen

The Origin of Life

A Great Unsolved Mystery

As noted earlier, the topic of the *origin* of life is entirely different from that of the *development* of life, and strictly speaking it should not be termed "evolution." Nevertheless, we shall discuss this topic, since it is often discussed in the context of evolution-creation debates.

What of the scientific theory as to the origin of life? The famous experiment in this field was that of Stanley Miller, working in the laboratory of Harold Urey at the University of Chicago, in the early 1950s. He combined a mixture of gases thought to replicate the atmosphere of the early earth. When an electrical charge was passed through this mixture—similar to a bolt of lightning—some amino acids, the building blocks of proteins, were formed as a result.

The implications of this experiment are, of course, subject to debate between evolutionists and creationists. Evolutionists consider such experiments to prove that, in the words of one person, "such evolution is not only plausible but almost undeniable."[1] On the other hand, others argue that amino acids are a far cry from DNA and proteins. We shall

---

1 Douglas Futuyma, *Science on Trial*, p. 95.

not go into the extensive debate as to the significance of the Miller-Urey experiment; it is sufficient to note that there *is* debate.

Furthermore, this cannot be classified as a debate along the lines of that between, say, Darwinian evolutionists and the Intelligent Design movement, where the latter has little credibility in the scientific community. With the origin of life, it is widely admitted that science has yet to come up with a solid answer. The prestigious magazine *New Scientist* recently published an article about the ten biggest unanswered questions relating to life, and top of the list was the mystery of how life began.[1] Included in the list of possible explanations was that life was transported to earth from outer space—which, of course, just pushes the question elsewhere. The *New York Times* likewise described the origin of life as an enigma:

> Everything about the origin of life on earth is a mystery, and it seems the more that is known, the more acute the puzzles get... The chemistry of the first life is a nightmare to explain. No one has yet devised a plausible explanation to show how the earliest chemicals of life— thought to be RNA, or ribonucleic acid, a close relative of DNA— might have constructed themselves from the inorganic chemicals likely to have been around on the early earth. The spontaneous assembly of small RNA molecules on the primitive earth "would have been a near miracle," two experts in the subject helpfully declared last year.
>
> ...The best efforts of chemists to reconstruct molecules typical of life in the laboratory have shown only that it is a problem of fiendish difficulty. The genesis of life on earth, some time in the fiery last days of the Hadean, remains an unyielding problem.
>
> Nicholas Wade, "Genetic Analysis Yields Intimations of a Primordial Commune," *The New York Times,* June 13th, 2000

It is therefore reasonable for someone to adopt the position that there is no current viable naturalistic explanation for the origins of life, and that it should be attributed to overt Divine intervention. Yet let us explore whether those who do feel that there is a viable naturalistic explanation— or that one is likely to be discovered—face a conflict with Judaism.

---

1 Michael Brooks, "The Mysteries of Life," *New Scientist,* 4 September 2004.

Theological Perspectives

A simple reading of the Torah indicates that life came about through "special creation," i.e. by direct supernatural means from inanimate matter:

> God said, Let the earth bring forth all kinds of living creatures, domestic animals and creeping things and wild beasts of the land after their kind; and it was so.
>
> Genesis 1:24

We already explained that, according to many opinions, Genesis is a mystical, esoteric description of divine secrets, garbed in a simple form for people of all generations to understand. The literal reading of text need not be seen as an account of the physical history of the world. But it cannot be ignored either, and there is a very significant word used in this section regarding the very first life. It states that God *created* it:

> And God created the great sea monsters and every kind of living creeping creature that swarms in the water, and every kind of winged bird, and God saw that it was good.
>
> Genesis 1:21

The word *beriyah*, "creation," is usually understood to mean creation *ex nihilo*. This would signify that the original formation of life required supernatural intervention, the creation of something from nothing.[1]

As we have seen, the scientific explanations for the origins of life are highly debatable. It is certainly reasonable, therefore, for one to take the position that even if creatures developed through evolutionary means, the ultimate origin of life involved God's direct action. Such a position has strong support from the Torah and does not conflict with the scientific evidence currently available.[2]

However, even here, matters are not so straightforward. According to some, even the term *beriyah*, used here at the beginning of the creation of animal life, need not refer to creation *ex nihilo*.[3] It might refer to a

---

1 Malbim to Genesis 1:21 states this explicitly.

2 It does require arguing that the *beriyah* of the verse refers only to the very first life-form rather than to all the sea-creatures and birds, as the simplest reading of the verse indicates.

3 See Ibn Ezra and *Aderes Eliyahu* to Genesis 1:1.

qualitatively new phenomenon that God caused to exist—life—without necessarily meaning that this involved a supernatural act of creation. Thus, the Torah support for open divine action is not unequivocal. One who chooses to accept a scientific explanation for the origin of life is therefore not going against the Torah.

Chance and Necessity

It should also be noted that even within the view that the origin of life can be explained in purely naturalistic terms, there are two distinct streams of thought as to what these naturalistic terms are. One school of thought states that the first life-form came about as a freak result of unlikely circumstances, a chance event with extremely fortuitous results. This is the position advanced by Jacques Monod:

> Life appeared on earth: what, before the event, were the chances that this would occur? The present structure of the biosphere certainly does not exclude the possibility that… its a priori probability was virtually zero.
>
> Jacques Monod, *Chance and Necessity*, p. 136

The other school of thought proposes that the laws of nature are such that the evolution of life from non-life is almost inevitable.[1] Nobel Prize winning scientist Christian de Duve writes:

> Life is the product of deterministic forces… Life was bound to arise under the prevailing conditions, and it will arise similarly wherever and whenever the same conditions obtain… Life and mind emerge not as the result of freakish accidents, but as natural manifestations of matter, written into the fabric of the universe.
>
> Christian de Duve, *Vital Dust: Life as a Cosmic Imperative*, pp. xv, xviii

When synthesized with a religious perspective, these different perspectives produce two distinct themes.

The first school of thought is that life came about as a freak result of unlikely circumstances, an improbable event with extremely fortuitous results. The religious interpretation of this would be that it is along the

---

1 A practical difference between these two views is whether it is worthwhile to search for life on planets where there is water.

lines of the miracle recounted in the Book of Esther and celebrated on the holiday of Purim. In that case, a string of unlikely coincidences and seemingly chance events ultimately resulted in a conclusion so wonderful that it became clear in retrospect that the chance events were not so arbitrary after all.

The second school of thought is that the laws of nature are constructed such that the formation of life is extremely likely, perhaps even a foregone conclusion. The religious interpretation of this would be that it is along the lines of the Chanukah story, the ideological victory of which was that the laws of nature are seen to be programmed by God. Likewise, if the laws of nature are such that the remarkable phenomenon of life is the result, it clearly points to their having been contrived by a Designer. Even scientists are well aware of the theological implications of this model of life's origins:

> If it transpires that life emerged more or less on cue as part of the deep lawfulness of the cosmos—if it is scripted into the great cosmic drama in a basic manner—it hints at a universe with purpose. In short, the origin of life is the key to the meaning of life... if life is somehow inevitable, accidents of fate notwithstanding, a particular end is certain to be achieved; it is built into the laws. And "end" sounds suspiciously like "goal" or "purpose"—taboo words in science for the last century, redolent as they are of a bygone religious age.
>
> Paul Davies, *The Fifth Miracle*, pp. 27, 247

These two types of scientific explanations, one based on happenstance and the other based on underlying laws, and the two matching religious interpretations, one along the lines of Purim and the other resembling Chanukah, also apply to the evolutionary development of life. Darwinian theory, involving random mutations and chance circumstance, is the former; other, newer forms of evolutionary theory, which are based on the idea of inherent laws in nature resulting in emergent complexity, resemble the latter. We shall discuss this in greater detail later.

Chapter Twenty

Common Ancestry

The Case for Common Ancestry

The notion that different but similar species descend from common ancestors has widespread support, not only from evolutionists but even from many Biblical literalists. Just as it is universally accepted that all breeds of dog, from the Chihuahua to the Great Dane, originated from a single breed—after all, this occurred in recent history—it is likewise widely acknowledged that similar species originated from one type (although there are differences of opinion as to the mechanism that caused this). As we shall later see, in classical Jewish sources there is considerable mention of this.

Common ancestry of species in dissimilar groups and the ultimate common ancestry of all species, on the other hand, is not quite as straightforward. We shall discuss these two categories together, as evidence for the former would be taken by almost everyone as adequate evidence for the latter.

The evidence for common ancestry is considered to be very strong indeed. Because of this, and also since it is a description of events that are presumed to have happened as opposed to an explanation of the cause of what happened, many describe common ancestry as the "fact of evolution," vis-à-vis explanations of evolutionary mechanisms, which are termed the "theory of evolution." The evidence for common ancestry can be grouped into four categories which we shall discuss in turn.

I. Homologous Similarities

One of the first ideas to discuss is the concept of analogous and homologous body parts. Analogous body parts are those that perform a similar purpose, but are very different in terms of their internal structure. A good example would be the fin of a shark and the flipper of a whale. Although both serve to direct the creature's motion in water, they are anatomically very different; the former is comprised of flesh and cartilage, while the latter is made of jointed bones. Homologous body parts, on the other hand, might not be similar in external appearance or purpose, but are similar in their underlying structure. The flipper of a whale, the hand of a monkey, and the wing of a bat all serve very different functions, but they are all formed of a five-fingered hand (the pentadactyl limb). The indication is that they were all formed from the same original structure, the five-fingered paw of a terrestrial mammal.

An objection to the concept of homologous similarities being used as evidence for common ancestry is that it has to be considered in light of alternative possibilities, such as that each species was separately created by God. It is argued that with this scenario, homologous similarities also make sense. Since the pentadactyl limb is a good component for a body-plan, why shouldn't God use it for all sorts of different functions? Indeed, such similarities were understood well before Darwin, and were explained in precisely this way. Rabbi Bachya ibn Pakuda, discussing the unity of God, writes:

> The second [argument for God's unity] is drawn from the signs of wisdom which are manifest throughout this world, in its upper and lower regions, in its minerals, vegetation, and animals. When we study the world, it shows us that it is entirely the plan of a Designer, the work of a single Creator. For we find that, with all the differences in its substances and elements, it shows uniformity in its effects and parts. The signs of the Creator's wisdom, manifest in the smallest as in the largest creatures, testify that they all have one wise Creator. If the world really had more than one Creator, diverse forms of wisdom would be manifest in its different parts and in its species and individuals.
>
> *Chovos HaLevavos, Shaar HaYichud* 7

Yet it is nevertheless the case that homologous similarities are *suggestive* of common ancestry. Although one can claim that there are reasons for making a whale's flipper in the design of a pentadactyl limb, the fact that fish are designed completely differently makes it more reasonable to conclude that whales are built like land mammals because they descend from the same ancestors. Similarly, the fact that all

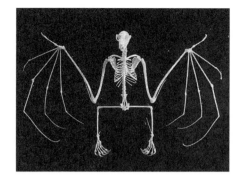

The structure of a bat skeleton is so similar to that of other mammals that it suggests common ancestry

mammals in Australia are marsupials makes it more reasonable to conclude that they share a common marsupial ancestor than that there was some unknown reason for Australian animals to all be created with the same unusual method of giving birth.

II. *The Fossil Record*

Fossils can never categorically prove common ancestry, no matter how perfect the sequence. But they are extremely suggestive of it if they can show that older forms are simpler than modern forms, and especially if there is a gradual sequence from a few ancient species to a multitude of modern species.

In terms of the first requirement, that ancient forms should be more primitive, the fossil record would certainly seem satisfactory. For example, there are no extremely ancient fossils of specialized mammals such as whales amongst the ancient fossils of the first mammals. But we do find fossils of early terrestrial mammals with some whale-like characteristics, and we also find some later fossils of primitive whales that possess rudimentary legs. This does not categorically prove that whales are descended from earlier creatures, but it is extremely suggestive of it.

The second expectation, that there should be a gradual sequence of fossils from ancient to modern forms, is more controversial. Evolutionists will claim that it is as good as can be expected, if not better, and point to some extraordinary specimens that have been discovered in recent years. Creationists claim that it is woefully inadequate.

It was largely the paucity of the fossil record that led to paleontologists Stephen Jay Gould and Niles Eldredge formulating their theory of "punctuated equilibrium." As Gould writes, the fossil record does not show the predicted gradual sequence of transitions:

> The history of most fossil species includes two features particularly inconsistent with gradualism:
>
> 1. Stasis. Most species exhibit no directional change during their tenure on earth. They appear in the fossil record looking much the same as when they disappear; morphological change is usually limited and directionless.
>
> 2. Sudden appearance. In any local area, a species does not arise gradually by the steady transformation of its ancestors; it appears all at once and "fully formed."
>
> Stephen Jay Gould, "The Episodic Nature of Evolutionary Change,"
in The Panda's Thumb, p. 180

Gould and Eldredge therefore theorized that evolution occurs too fast to leave a trace in the fossil record. (It should be noted that "fast" in their terms does not mean over a few years; it means over a few thousand years rather than over a few million years.) This has been distorted into a flawed argument by some evolutionists. Douglas Futuyma, in his book *Science on Trial: The Case For Evolution*, states:

> Undeniably, the fossil record has provided disappointingly few gradual series. The origins of many groups are still not documented at all. But in view of the rapid pace that evolution can take, and the extreme incompleteness of fossil deposits, we are fortunate to have as many transitions as we do.
>
> Douglas Futuyma, Science on Trial, p. 190-191

Futuyma claims that because we know evolution progresses rapidly, it is to be expected that the fossil record will show few transitional forms! Whereas the truth is the reverse: *Because* there are so few transitional forms, it was *therefore* theorized that evolution progresses rapidly. Punctuated equilibrium is a result of the fossil record, not a prediction of it.

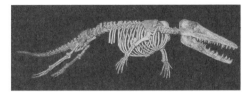

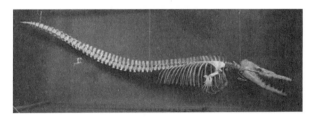

This sequence of fossils shows a progression from terrestrial mammals to primitive whales. First is Pakicetus, 52 million years old, which possesses a unique whale-like skull. Second is Ambulocetus, 49 million years old, which possessed an even more whale-like skull and whose vertebrae showed that it undulated its body when swimming like a whale. Third is Basilosaurus, 35 million years old, which was entirely aquatic but with tiny, fully-formed rear legs.

Yet many anti-evolutionists entirely misunderstand punctuated equilibrium, and quote people such as Gould in support of the claim that there are no fossil sequences at all. This is simply not the case. There *are* transitional forms, even though they are fewer and farther between than evolutionists had hoped for. Their scarcity has more implications for certain theories of evolutionary mechanisms and rates of evolution than for common ancestry. The fact that such transitional forms exist at all is indeed suggestive of common ancestry.

In summary: We see an overall trend in the fossil record from simpler earlier creatures to more complex later ones. We see that such sequences within groups occur in particular regions of the world. We also find that the earliest fossils found in each group possess primitive characteristics. This strongly suggests an ancestral family relationship.

III. Vestigial Structures and Embryology

The strongest direct evidence for common ancestry comes from vestigial structures and embryonic development of species. Vestigial structures are rudimentary body parts, such as organs and limbs, which seem to serve no function, but would make sense if they are leftovers from an earlier version of the creature. There are countless examples of vestigial body parts—the extra toes of sheep and cows that don't reach the ground, the tiny and useless wings of flightless beetles, the human appendix and wisdom teeth, and so on.

One of the most popular examples has always been the hipbones of whales. Whales have no legs, of course, but the presence of hipbones in certain species, attached to no limb, indicates that they used to have legs. At least, this had always been one of the most popular examples, until it was recently discovered that these bones may serve as an attachment point for the muscles that control the reproductive organs. This shows the potential flaw in describing a limb as merely vestigial; it may be entirely functional in a way that we don't know about. Nevertheless, it appears that even though the whale's hipbones may serve a function, they are still evidence of the hindlimbs that whales used to possess; mutant whales are sometimes born with limbs protruding from their hindquarters, revealing the genetic potential that still remains in their DNA.

Furthermore, to say that all apparently vestigial parts can be explained as possessing a function would really be going out on a limb. There are vast numbers of such organs, in creatures whose anatomy is well understood. The most reasonable conclusion to draw is that these creatures descended from creatures in which these parts are functional, which in turn indicates that most (or indeed all) creatures descended from common ancestors.

A similar line of argument for common ancestry is advanced from embryology. For example, the embryos of whales, anteaters and birds develop teeth and then absorb them again before birth. This indicates that these species evolved from creatures that possessed teeth.

One could perhaps account for vestigial structures and embryonic similarities in a similar way to homologous structures; maybe they are just part of God's basic body-plan for animals that is not fully implemented in this particular model. Still, such an argument is certainly weak; once the features are going to be functionless, why not omit them entirely rather than keeping them at an embryonic stage or as rudimentary parts? Vestigial structures certainly present a strong argument for common ancestry.

IV. The Lack of Reasonable Alternatives

A different line of argument for common ancestry is that there is no reasonable alternative as to where new life-forms come from. Considering the previously discussed facts that the species that exist presently are different from the species that used to live on earth, one has to wonder where the new species came from.

Is it reasonable to state that the new species came directly from the earth? As we discussed extensively at the beginning of this book, there is a strong trend within Judaism of rationalists such as Rambam who felt that it is better to understand God as working via natural processes than via miracles. But if the universe is only a few thousand years old, then creation clearly did not follow any natural laws and it could only have been miraculous. It is for this reason that Rambam and others did not seek to explain the development of animal life in terms of natural laws. However, since we now possess evidence that the universe developed over a period of billions of years, then this both allows the possibility for creation taking place via natural laws and also indicates that such was the case. The fossil evidence shows many different eras of creatures living their lives normally, which indicates that the system of natural law was in effect during that time. This in turn suggests that animal species also developed via natural laws, rather than being zapped into existence. The rationalist approach tells us that new creatures most likely developed by some process of *derech eretz*, natural law, rather than through an open miracle. This indicates that new creatures came from existing creatures, rather than directly from the earth.

Thus, if one accepts the evidence that many thousands of new species continually came into existence over the course of millions of years, one must wonder where they came from. It is not only from a secular materialist point of view that it is most reasonable to assume that they developed—somehow—from the already existing creatures. Even from a religious perspective, there are strong grounds for arguing that it is most reasonable that God formed new creatures—somehow—from the already existing creatures, rather than miraculously created them from dirt. Making new creatures from existing creatures is much more within the realm of natural law. God chooses to work within a system of natural law; not because He has to, but because He wants to. As Rabbi Hirsch states:

...Judaism considers it vitally important for its adherents to become aware that their entire universe is governed by well-defined laws, that every creature on earth becomes what it is only within the framework of fixed laws, and that every force in nature can operate only within specified limits... Man himself, then, can exercise power only if he, in turn, obeys the laws set down for him and for his world

The Educational Value of Judaism, in *Collected Writings* vol. VII p. 263

The rationalist approach in Jewish thought leads to the conclusion that God formed new creatures from existing creatures, using some ordered mechanism, rather than miraculously intervening to make each species pop out of the ground.

V. Conclusion

Although much of the evidence for common ancestry isn't as strong as is commonly thought—being suggestive rather than decisive—and none of it conclusively rules out the alternative, there is nevertheless plenty of extremely persuasive evidence for common ancestry, as well as the powerful argument of where else the new creatures would have come from. Someone who denies common ancestry would have to believe that God popped millions of species into existence over a period of hundreds of millions of years, with each species possessing physical characteristics and appearing at a time and place that would falsely give the overwhelming impression that they descended from earlier creatures.

It must be stressed again that common ancestry says nothing about *how* one species changed into another. Nevertheless, the mere concept of common ancestry is of great significance to the evolution-creation debate. The disagreement between a creationist and an evolutionist is far smaller if the creationist accepts the concept of common ancestry.

Conceptual Support for Evolution

Although there is no explicit mention of the common ancestry of animal life in traditional Torah commentaries, there is certainly a good deal of conceptual and suggestive support for it. In other words, there are classical views about the nature of existence which lend themselves well to an evolutionary model. One is that which we have discussed above, the idea that God works through natural means wherever possible. According to this, it makes sense that God would have used a system of natural law to develop later creatures from earlier ones, rather than using special creation in each case.

But there are also classical views about the very nature of the creation process itself which fit well with the concept of evolution. There are two concepts which, especially when taken together, are strongly suggestive of evolution:

1) Gradualism—the idea that different categories of living things are not separated by large gaps but rather there is a gradual range of intermediate forms.

2) Transformation—the idea that successive stages of creation involved the transformation of previous stages.

Let us explore each of these concepts in turn.

I. Gradualism

The fifteenth-century philosopher Rabbi Yosef Albo states that the four basic levels within the physical world—inanimate matter, plants, animals, and man—are not as distinct as is commonly assumed:

> Coral is intermediate between inanimate matter and plants. We also find the sea sponge which only has the sense of touch, and is an intermediate between plant and animal stages. We also find the monkey to be intermediate between animals and man.
>
> Rabbi Yosef Albo, *Sefer Ha-Ikkarim* 3:1

Malbim discusses this idea, which is similar to the notion of the "great chain of being" that was popular for many centuries,[1] in more detail:

> Creation progressed from level to level; inanimate matter, plants, animals, and man. Everything that came earlier was a preparation for that which came later. After God established the luminaries—without which life could not survive—He gave instruction for the creation of animal life. It is known that also in rising up through the ladder of stages, creation did not proceed in discontinuous leaps, but rather through intermediate stages. Thus, coral is intermediate between

---

1 See Arthur O. Lovejoy, *The Great Chain Of Being*.

inanimate matter and plants, polyps are intermediate between plants and animals, and monkeys are intermediate between animals and man. Similarly, every level rose in an order of lower to higher, as we have written with the formation of plant life, where it rose from herbage to grasses to trees. So too did it proceed with the formation of animal life, where the scholars of natural history have divided animals into six levels: (a) worms, (b) flying or creeping insects, (c) fish, (d) aquatic animals—amphibians—which live both in water and on land, (e) birds, (f) animals.

Commentary to Genesis 1:20

While this is not presenting the idea of each stage evolving from the preceding stage, the concept of a gradual progression does downplay the boundaries between groups. It shows that, contrary to the popular notion that there must be distinct and significant gaps between the groups, this is not the case at all.

Furthermore, if we find that classical Jewish sources seek to stress the importance of smooth gradations and gradual progressions, then it is reasonable to suggest that this would also be case with the development of each species. That is to say, if we are seeking to avoid discontinuities, then each species should also come into existence by way of gradual development rather than appearing directly from the earth in a single leap. If the concept of gradual progressions is found in the *array* of species, it is reasonable to say that it is also found in the *development* of species.

We further find discussion of the notion of spiritual evolution as being indicative of an underlying pattern of development in the world. Rambam explains the commandments concerning the bringing of sacrifices as a gradual attempt to lead the Jewish people away from paganism. He states that this reflects the pattern of gradual development that is part of the fundamental nature of the universe:

> On considering the divine acts, or the processes of nature, we obtain an insight into the prudence and wisdom of God as displayed in the creation of animals, with the gradual development of the movements of their limbs and the relative positions of the latter, and we perceive also His wisdom and plan in the successive and gradual development of the whole condition of each individual... Many concepts in the Torah come from similar guidance by the Controller of the universe,

and we thus find that it is impossible to go suddenly from one extreme to the other.

Guide For The Perplexed 3:32

It would certainly make sense that the pattern of gradual development, which Rambam states to be an underlying theme of God's plan for both the spiritual evolution of mankind and the physical development of individual creatures, also describes the development of species. Rabbi Avraham Kook, in an essay entitled *On Evolution*, explicitly applies this concept of spiritual gradualism to the evolution of animal life:

> The evolutionary way of thinking, so popular as a result of recent scientific studies, has caused considerable upheaval among many people whose thought had been wont to run in certain regular, well-defined paths. Not so, however, for the select, hard-thinking few who have always seen a gradual, evolutionary development in the world's most intimate spiritual essence. For them it is not difficult to apply, by analogy, the same principle to the physical development of the visible world. It is indeed fitting that the emergence of the latter should parallel the spiritual development of all being, where no step in the gradually unfolding pattern is ever left vacant. Ordinary people, on the other hand, find it very hard to embrace a complete and comprehensive evolutionary view and are unable to reconcile such a view with a spiritual outlook on life... People find difficulty in holding within one spiritual context two apparently conflicting approaches to creation. On the one hand there are their previous simpler, and in a sense less demanding, thought-patterns, in which creation is characterized by sudden discontinuities. On the other there is the unfamiliar but increasingly popular conception of the gradual unfolding of all things within an evolutionary context.

> To bridge this gap we need to turn on a great searchlight of educative power so that the illumination gradually penetrates all strata of our community, so that a well-ordered and well-articulated unified outlook wins general acceptance... The essential need of the hour is therefore an educational effort to propagate the broader view, the grander and more refined conception that we have alluded to above. The coarser-textured faith, in the unrefined form in which it is so often presented, can no longer maintain its position.

> Rabbi Avraham Yitzchak Kook, *Orot HaKodesh* p. 559

Rabbi Kook explains that although for many people, it is easier to see the world in terms of black-and-white, the reality is often different. For those who have always understood the spiritual realm as progressing via gradual developments, it is easy to embrace the idea of that happening in the physical world too.

II. Transformation

Another aspect of classical Jewish thought in which we see conceptual support for common ancestry is in the trend of reducing the *ex nihilo* aspects of creation. Rabbi Nissim ben Reuven (1320-1380) states that the only act of creation *ex nihilo* took place at the first moment of creation:

> "In the beginning, God created the heavens and the earth, and the earth was desolate..." All the true commentaries agreed in explaining these verses that their intent is to say that at the beginning of creation, a unified substance was created for everything under the lunar sphere... this was because the Will of God was to continue the nature of existence according to the possibilities, and not to create many things *ex nihilo*, since it is possible to make one substance that includes everything.... the creation of two substances in the lower world *ex nihilo* would be without benefit; it suffices to have this wondrous and necessary origin.
>
> *Derashos HaRan* 1

Abarbanel cites this view and further explains how God sought to minimize the acts of creation *ex nihilo*:

> The first day was distinguished from the six days of creation via two distinctions. One was that the creative work of the first day was entirely *ex nihilo*, where the creative work of the other days was formed from pre-existing matter. Second is that on the first day the sources (lit. "fathers") and beginning were created, whereas on the other days the results that exude from them were created. The sources and beginnings that were created on the first day, were created with their forms, and the power was given to them to make the descendants from them that Scripture recounts on the subsequent days.
>
> Abarbanel, Commentary to Genesis 1:6, p. 39

The concept of creating matter *ex nihilo* is being restricted to the first instant of creation. Subsequent to that moment, creation did not involve the genesis of physical entities *ex nihilo* but rather transformed them from previously existing matter. It would sit well with this concept that the *forms* of physical entities were also not created *ex nihilo* but rather involved the transformation of previously existing forms.

Further conceptual support for transformation is seen in a discussion by Malbim:

> More advanced creations incorporate in a perfected form those things that had appeared earlier. Thus the plant includes both the specific features that identify vegetative life and the inorganic elements; the animal comprises the processes of the plant—nourishment, growth— in addition to possessing the animate soul; man does not lack the capacities of the animal, even as he is imbued with the intellectual soul... Everything formed on a given day was incorporated into the things formed on the next day.
>
> Malbim, Commentary to Genesis 1:25

While Malbim is only applying this concept between successive days of creation, it eases the application of it to different creations within the same day. More advanced creations incorporate in a perfected form those things that had appeared earlier.

In summary, although there is no explicit traditional position supporting the gradual descent of all animal life from common ancestors, there is certainly a wealth of conceptual support from classical Torah perspectives. There is the concept of God working through a system of *derech eretz*, natural law; the concept of there being a smooth progression in the natural world; and the concept of minimizing the *ex nihilo* aspect of creation.

Evolution and Progression

The idea of life progressing from simple origins to ever more sophisticated forms was one aspect of evolution that was welcomed by some in the Jewish community.[1] Although Rabbi Menachem Mendel Kasher personally denied evolution altogether, he noted that those who

---

1   See Rabbi Dovid Cohen, *"Torat HaHitpachtut beChochmat haKodesh,"* *Sinai*, Nissan 5706, vol. 19, pp. 34-40.

accepted it saw this idea of an upwards progression as being complimentary to the Torah's outlook:

> One can understand why the idea of evolution conquered the hearts of many of those who believe in the Torah and observe it. The reason is that the broader concept of evolution includes not only the concept that the world develops from lower to higher, but also (in its view) explains all the questions and problems of the world, such as social evolution, interpersonal relationships, and international relationships, etc. The essence of this idea does have a foundation in Judaism, and that is the belief in our righteous Messiah and in the perfection of the world in the kingship of God, and in the wickedness evaporating like smoke, and all the land being filled with wisdom, and so on, just as all the prophets foresaw.
>
> Rabbi Menachem Kasher,
> *Torat HaBriah uMishnat HaHitpachtut beMidrashei Chazal*

It is interesting to note that secular evolutionists generally do not speak of evolution as progressing upwards. This is mainly because they refuse to accept that man possesses inherent superiority over animals; instead, he is merely another kind of animal with different aptitudes. Thus, eagles posses acute vision, cheetahs can run fast, and man has a powerful brain. Yet from a religious perspective, man's capacity for free will, consciousness and intellect do indeed place him as being a more advanced being than animals. In any case, evolution undeniably involves the idea of increased sophistication—from bacteria to fish to amphibian to reptile to mammal to man. In an essay entitled *Evolution and Providence*, Rabbi Kook wrote of the significance of this pattern of movement:

> "Wherever heretics have gone astray, the true answer lies at hand." This applies not only to the text of the Torah but also to emotional trends and intellectual movements. The selfsame arguments and lines of thought which lead to the ways of God-denial, lead in their essence, if we search out their true origin, to a higher form of faith than the simple conceptions we entertained before the apparent breakdown.
>
> Formative evolution, to which all who follow a sense-based intellect now tend, seems at first to block off the light of faith with its consciousness of the limitless power of God… However once a thought-form of this kind makes its appearance in the intellect, though at first it may raise doubts and superficially drive the divine light from the mind, at a

deeper level it forms a most sublime basis on which to rest the concept of divine providence.

For evolution itself, moving upwards coordinately and undeviatingly from the lowest to the highest, demonstrates most clearly a pre-vision from afar—a pre-set purpose for all existence. Divine greatness is thereby enhanced and all the goals of faith confirmed, and trust in and service of the divine is all the more justified... Since all strives upwards and man has it in his power to improve and perfect himself and his world, he is manifestly thereby doing the will of his creator. Spiritual perfection is thus seen to be in the center of all existence....

Rabbi Avraham Yitzchak Kook, *Orot Ha-Kodesh* p. 565[1]

The Torah's Account of the Origins of Species

Although we have seen there to be much conceptual support in Judaism for the idea of a single ancestor giving rise to all animal life, there appears to be a blatant contradiction to this concept from Scripture. The Torah seems to present an entirely different view: that of "special creation," a direct supernatural act of creating an animal from earth or water.

And God said, Let the waters be filled with many kinds of living creatures, and birds that may fly above the earth in the open firmament of heaven. God created the great sea-monsters, and every kind of creature that lives in the waters, and every kind of winged bird, and God saw that it was good. God blessed them, saying, Be fruitful, and multiply, and fill the waters in the seas, and let the birds multiply in the earth. And there was evening and there was morning, the fifth day.

God said, Let the earth bring forth all kinds of living creatures, cattle, and creeping things, and beasts of the earth after their kind; and it was so. God made the beasts of the earth after their kind, and cattle after their kind, and every thing that creeps upon the earth after its kind; and God saw that it was good.

Genesis 1:20-25

If many kinds of creatures were made by way of special creation, then this stands in contradiction to the concept of all creatures sharing common

---

1 For further discussion of Rabbi Kook's views, see Michael Shai Cherry, "Three Twentieth-Century Jewish Responses to Evolutionary Theory."

ancestry. However, it does not necessarily contradict the common ancestry of similar creatures. There are some authorities who take the view that there was progressive special creation. This means that God created a certain range of basic types, and the current multitude of types originated from the basic types by way of limited evolution.

Rabbi Naftali Tzvi Yehudah Berlin (Netziv) saw this as implicit in the repeated use of the phrase "after their *min* (kind)" in the description of the creation of animal life. In Jewish law, the category of *min* is far broader than the classification of species employed by modern zoology. Netziv explains this verse to mean that God created only one general type of each animal, from which a multitude of species subsequently evolved.[1] Rabbi Nissim ben Reuven uses this concept to explain how Noah managed to fit all the animals into the Ark; he states that there were simply far fewer types of animals in existence back then, and the diverse range of species that we see today evolved from the earlier types.[2]

Thus, important Torah commentaries state that it is possible for one species to evolve into another over a very short period of time. This is an interesting inversion of the evolution-religion conflict in that it is a case where religious authorities were more pro-evolution than evolutionists; no evolutionist would accept that such a rapid rate of evolution is possible.

---

1   In a different explanation of this verse, Rabbi Samson Raphael Hirsch, discussing the laws against interbreeding and the theory of evolution, writes: "This would be nothing else but the actualization of the law of *le-mino*, the 'law of species' with which God began His work of creation. The principle of heredity set forth in this theory is only a paraphrase of the ancient Jewish law of *le-mino*, according to which, normally, each member of a species transmits its distinguishing traits to its descendants." ("The Educational Value of Judaism," in *Collected Writings*, vol. VII, p. 264.)

2   Ran, Commentary to Genesis 6:14-15. Ramban (commentary to Genesis 6:19) answers that a miracle was involved; but for reasons discussed earlier, we can understand why other commentators preferred not to resort to invoking miracles and did not adopt Ramban's answer. Aside from Ran's explanation, others explained that the deluge did not cover the entire earth, hence not every species of animal had to be taken on board; see Rabbi Dovid Tzvi Hoffman, commentary to Genesis, pp. 140-141; Rabbi Azriel Leib Rakovsky (disciple of Rav Yaakov Karliner, author of *Mishkenos Yaakov*), *Shelemah Mishnaso* to *Berachos* 56b, and Rabbi Gedalyah Nadel, *BeToraso Shel Rabbi Gedalyah* pp. 116-119. For further discussion of various approaches to the topic of the deluge, see Rabbi J. Hertz's "Additional Notes to Genesis" at the back of *The Pentateuch*.

What is interesting is that many religious people today who claim that it is scientifically impossible for one species to evolve into another, would nevertheless be hesitant to dismiss Ran and Netziv as being mistaken. [1]

Still, even interpreting the Torah to be speaking of progressive special creation does not allow for the common ancestry of dissimilar creatures. The Torah seems to clearly state that the different types of animals were created separately from the earth.[2] Yet as we discussed earlier, both the physical evidence and the rationalist approach leads many to conclude that all animals descended from a single common ancestor. Can this be reconciled with the Torah?

Common Ancestry and the Text of the Torah

How are we to reconcile common ancestry with the literal reading of the text of the Torah? Naftali Levy, in his nineteenth-century reconciliation of evolution entitled *Toldos Ha-Adam*, argued that the Scriptural term used for the creation of animal life, *yatzar*, "He formed," as opposed to *bara*, "He created," indicated that animals transformed from one species into another. Rabbi Aryeh Kaplan also considered there to be textual support for evolutionary origins of life:

> Another interesting wording is found in the fifth and sixth days of creation when the Bible describes the creation of fish and animals. The Bible does not state that God said, "Let there be creatures in the water" or "Let there be animals." Rather, the Bible says "Let the water bring forth living creatures" and "Let the earth bring forth living animals." This suggests that God did not actually create life at this time, but merely imparted to matter those unique properties that would make

---

1 An even more extreme example of "evolution" is proposed by many Torah authorities to resolve contradictions between statements in the Talmud about biology and contemporary science. The answer of *nishtaneh hateva*, "nature has changed," is in many cases a far more radical theory of evolution than biologists would deem viable.

2 The Talmud likewise appears to state that animals were individually created from the ground: "The ox which Adam brought as an offering, had its horns precede its hooves" (Talmud, *Chullin* 60a). Rashi explains this to mean that when the first ox was created, it emerged from the ground head first. However, Rabbi Chaim of Volozhin (*Nefesh HaChaim* 1:20) explains it instead to mean that when Adam sacrificed the ox, he sacrificed its horns before its hooves.

evolution take place, first to lower, and then to higher forms of life, and eventually to man himself.

"Creative Evolution," in *Faces and Facets*, pp. 83-84

Still, such explanations appear to be more wishful reading into the text than drawing meaning out of it. But our earlier discussion regarding literalism and the development of the universe is applicable here. As Rambam and others stated, Genesis is not a scientific account of the physical history of the universe. Instead, it is a conceptual presentation that teaches important theological truths, but presented in a simplified form that is also suitable for an unsophisticated audience. Rabbi Joseph Hertz notes that the evolutionary account of life's development is entirely inappropriate to the Torah's purposes:

> There is much force in the view expressed by a modern thinker: "(The Bible) neither provides, nor, in the nature of things, could provide, faultless anticipations of sciences still unborn. If by a miracle it had provided them, without a miracle they could not have been understood" (Balfour). And fully to grasp the eternal power and infinite beauty of these words—'And God created man in His own image'—we need but compare them with the genealogy of man, condensed from the pages of one of the leading biologists of the age (Haeckel):—

> "Monera begat Amoeba, Amoeba begat Synamoebae, Synamoebae begat Ciliated Larva, Ciliated Larva begat Primeval Stomach Animals, Primeval Stomach Animals begat Gliding Worms, Gliding Worms begat Skull-less Animals, Skull-less Animals begat Single-nostrilled Animals, Single-nostrilled Animals begat Primeval Fish, Primeval Fish begat Mud-fish, Mud-fish begat Gilled Amphibians, Gilled Amphibians begat Tailed Amphibians, Tailed Amphibians begat Primary Mammals, Primary Mammals begat Pouched Animals, Pouched Animals begat Semi-Apes, Semi-Apes begat Tailed Apes, Tailed Apes begat Man-like Apes, Man-like Apes begat Ape-like Men, Ape-like Men begat Men."

> Let anyone who is disturbed by the fact that Scripture does not include the latest scientific doctrine, try to imagine such information provided in a Biblical chapter.

Rabbi J. Hertz, *The Pentateuch*, Additional Notes to Genesis

Rabbi Kook likewise pointed out that of all the potential regions of conflict between evolution and religion that may exist, that of the conflict between evolution and the literal reading of Genesis is the least difficult:

> These hesitations (in accepting the idea that all living things descended gradually from a common ancestor) have nothing to do with any difficulty in reconciling the verses of the Torah or other traditional texts with an evolutionary standpoint. Nothing is easier than this. Everyone knows that here, if anywhere, is the realm of parable, allegory and allusion. In these most profound matters people are willing to accept that the true meaning lies on the mystical plane, far above what is apparent to the superficial eye. Their ears are attuned to the concept *sitrey Torah* ("secrets of the Torah") and when told that this verse or the other belongs to that realm they are satisfied. Here they are at one with the more sophisticated thinker who senses the inner meaning of the sublime poem which lies hidden within these ancient phrases.
>
> Rabbi Avraham Yitzchak Kook, *Orot HaKodesh* p. 559

In conclusion: The concept of common ancestry is well-supported by evidence; it is preferable from the perspective that God works within His laws of nature wherever possible; there is much conceptual support for it from classical Jewish thought; and one need not be concerned that the literal reading of Genesis indicates otherwise, since Rambam and others explained that Genesis is not a literal account of creation. Several recent Torah scholars have explicitly noted that evolution (in terms of gradual descent with modification) does not contradict the Torah, and others, such as Rabbi Kook, saw it as supportive of the deeper patterns in Torah thought that had always been known.

> What is striking is the extent to which the theological elements in these responses to Darwinism and evolutionary theory were previously embedded in traditional Jewish thought. To borrow an image, the traditional Jewish notions of divine immanence, the unity of creation and lawful, progressive unfolding of Torah and natural history are all adaptive elements for Judaism in the emergence of the new evolutionary environment of the late-nineteenth century.
>
> Michael Shai Cherry, *Creation, Evolution and Jewish Thought*, p. 153

Chapter Twenty-One

Evolutionary Mechanisms and Intelligent Design

The What and the How

In the previous chapter, we discussed common ancestry—the concept that all living things are, somehow, related to each other on one gigantic family tree. We must now turn to the issue of *how* one species is proposed to change into another—the mechanism via which evolution takes place. Descent with modification describes *what* happened; now we shall discuss mechanisms which explain *how* it happened. Thus, one can simply choose to reject current explanations of evolutionary mechanisms, and still to accept that all life-forms descended from a single ancestor through some unknown process. However, we shall explore whether the currently accepted explanations are necessarily contradicting the religious viewpoint.

The primary explanation for this mechanism today is that which is known as the "neo-Darwinian synthesis"—random genetic mutations in combination with natural selection. There is heated debate as to whether this is an adequate explanation to account for the diverse animals of the world and their characteristics. We shall not discuss the scientific arguments for and against the neo-Darwinian mechanism of evolution. Instead, we shall explore whether it is of any consequence for theology.

The neo-Darwinian explanation of evolutionary mechanisms involves several unique theological issues, which we shall explore in the next chapter. In this chapter, we will focus primarily on issues that are raised by there being *any* sort of naturalistic mechanism that would explain how one species changes into another. One of the primary religious objections to evolution is that "Scientists say that they can explain the natural world with evolution, but we know that God did it."

> Had the neo-Darwinians succeeded in establishing their case, the Torah believer would have had two choices: (1) he could simple reject the theory… or (2) he could engage in apologetics to show how the Creator and creation could be accommodated by smuggling Divine control into randomness… The second choice would be unsatisfying to any but the most committed accommodationist. If the theory works well, then a creationist explanation is superfluous… Although there are defensive positions the religious believer could have taken against the neo-Darwinian Theory, the theory *does* deny creation.
>
> Lee Spetner, "Evolution, Randomness and *Hashkafa*,"
> *BDD* vol. 4 p. 48; *Not By Chance!* p. 210

In other words, people feel that science, in giving a naturalistic explanation for how bacteria turned into the diverse creatures of the world—and one based on randomness, no less—is painting God out of the picture. But is it indeed doing so?

Astronomy and Biology

In order to understand God's role in biology, let us first consider astronomy. Judaism considers that the celestial phenomena are a primary means of perceiving God as a Creator:

> Lift up your eyes upon high, and perceive Who created these!
>
> Isaiah 40:26

> The heavens speak of God's glory, and the sky tells of His handiwork!
>
> Psalms 19:2

In the daily liturgy, we speak of how God Himself arranged the stars in their place:

In His wisdom, He changes the times and alters the seasons, and arranges the stars in their watches in the firmament according to His will.

Evening prayers

As we saw in the first chapter, one of the foremost Jewish philosophers cites the celestial bodies in particular as presenting an argument for a Designer:

There are men who say that the world came into existence by chance, without a Creator Who caused it and formed it. I find this astonishing. How could any rational human being, in his right mind, entertain such a notion? If one who held such a view were to hear someone make a similar claim about a revolving water wheel—that it came about without the design of a craftsman who invested effort in putting it together, constructing it, and supplying all its parts so that it perform its intended function—he would be amazed by such a statement, speak slightingly of the one who made it, consider him a total ignoramus, and be quick to expose him and reject his claim.

Now, if such a claim is rejected when it is made about a petty and insignificant little water wheel, which can be made with limited skill and serves a small plot of land, how can one allow himself to make the same claim about the great celestial "wheel" which encompasses the entire earth and all of its creatures; which reflects such an intelligence that its essence is beyond the grasp of all human understanding; which serves the well-being of the entire earth and everything in it? How can one say that it came into being without the intent of a Designer, without the planning of an omnipotent Intelligence?

Rabbeinu Bachya ibn Pakuda, *Chovos HaLevavos, Shaar HaYichud* 6

And yet today, the science of astronomy is highly advanced. We have built up a comprehensive picture of the universe. We understand how stars form. We understand the laws of gravity that govern their motion. So should we oppose the science of astronomy? Does it profess to tell us that Rabbeinu Bachya's argument was meaningless? Does it contradict the prayers that speak of God arranging the stars? Does it mean that the prophet Isaiah and King David were speaking out of ignorance when they told us to look up at the cosmos and perceive God?

The answer is that of course it doesn't. As we explained at length at the beginning of this book, a natural, scientific explanation of things in no way contradicts the concept of God as a Designer. Instead, it provides a new tapestry for Him to have designed. The laws of science are an exquisite description of the mechanism that God uses in creating and operating the world. As Rabbi Chaim Friedlander writes:

> We see that the sun shines upon the world, but we nevertheless praise God and say about Him in the morning prayers that "He illuminates the world and its inhabitants"; only, He does this via a conduit that is called the sun.
>
> *Sifsei Chaim, Emunah VeHashgachah* vol. 1 p. 16

Why, then, should biology be any different from astronomy? Certainly there is no basis in classical Judaism for saying that God is perceived only in the animal kingdom and not elsewhere in the universe. On the contrary; as we have quoted, astronomy was always seen as a primary area in which to perceive God as Creator and Designer. In the same way as we do not see the science of astronomy as negating this, the science of evolutionary biology does not paint God out of the picture of the development of life.

Operation and Design

The point that we are making is so critical as to be worth considering another example—an especially important and relevant one. In the day-to-day activities of the natural world, Judaism perceives God's operations:

> My soul shall bless God; O God my Lord, You are very great; You are clothed with glory and majesty... He sends the springs into the valleys, they flow between the mountains... He makes the grass grow for the cattle... The trees of the Lord have their fill; the cedars of Lebanon, which He has planted... May the glory of God endure for ever; may God rejoice in His works.
>
> Psalms 104:1-34

And yet we know that melting snow causes springs to flow down the mountains. We know that photosynthesis makes the grass grow. And we know that the cedars of Lebanon were planted by the natural forces operating in Lebanon. So is there none of God's glory in nature? Of course there is! We perceive God in the constant running of nature notwithstanding the natural explanations. Rambam notes that Scripture will even describe such processes as being directly controlled by God even though there are indeed natural causes:

> It is clear that everything produced must have an immediate cause which produced it; that cause again a cause, and so on, till the First Cause, i.e. the will and decree of God, is reached. The prophets therefore sometime omit the intermediate causes, and ascribe the production of an individual thing directly to God, saying that God has made it... I will give you examples, and they will guide you in the interpretation of passages which I do not mention: As regards phenomena produced regularly by natural causes, such as the melting of the snow when the atmosphere becomes warm, the roaring of the sea when a storm rages: "He sends His word and melts them" (Psalms 147:18); And He spoke, and a storm-wind rose up and lifted up its waves (Psalms 107:25)...
>
> *Guide For The Perplexed* 2:48

Another example: Jewish law requires a blessing to be pronounced upon food. "Consider the blessing upon fruit: Blessed are You... Creator of the fruit of the tree." This does not refer to the first fruit in history, but to the fruit that you have in your hand and are about to eat. And we know that the tree made this fruit! We also possess a thorough understanding of exactly how trees make fruit. But this does not prevent us from blessing God for having created it.

As Rabbi Samson Raphael Hirsch puts it:

> All the laws of mechanics, physics, chemistry and physiology can no more do without the One Who governs and guides the course of the universe (and, according to Jewish teaching, also the life of the individual in accordance with His purposes) than a living body, breathing in accordance with the laws of physiology, can do without the unfettered guidance of a human intelligence, or than a steamship, operating in accordance with the laws of mechanics, can do without the helmsman who guides it in accordance with his own free will.
>
> *The Educational Value of Judaism*, in *Collected Writings* vol. VII pp. 261-262

To be sure, with the daily functioning of the world, there is the question of where exactly God operates to guide events (as opposed to "merely" sustaining everything). As we discussed earlier, there are a variety of possible explanations—minute tweaking here and there, intervention at a quantum level, or control in a way that defies human understanding. Whichever explanation one adopts to understand God's involvement with the guidance of the human world, the same explanation can be adopted with regard to its design. The chance genetic mutations that are proposed to form the basis of evolutionary change may be linked to the quantum phenomena that we discussed earlier in the book as a possible method for God's control of the world. Thus, some propose that quantum effects, as well as being the solution to the problematic concept of determinism, also explain how God can influence the evolution of life without disturbing the laws of nature.

However, this explanation would not necessarily be required. It is far easier to explain God's involvement with regard to the design of the natural world than with regard to the daily operation of the world. His daily operation of the world needs to be dynamically responsive to man's free will (which makes it more challenging to understand how it can still not openly defy natural law). But His design of the world can be a simple matter of designing laws of nature which produce the world that He wanted. The development of animal life would be something that is set in advance and would not be subject to change based on man's deeds. God can set up the natural world and program its laws such that seemingly blind processes would produce life as we see it.

We all appreciate that science is very good at explaining the daily functioning and operation of the world. And yet we see God's hand in the day-to-day running of the world notwithstanding the scientific explanation. Since science does not prevent us from perceiving God in the operation of the world, it should certainly not prevent us from perceiving God in its design.

The Riddle of Rejection

In light of the above, any scientific problems with Darwinian mechanisms of evolution are irrelevant. As we have noted several times, our understanding is that God chooses to operate the world through natural law. Even if Darwinian theory turns out to be inadequate to explain the development of life, it seems that there is likely to be *some* sort of natural explanation, as that is how God generally runs the world. Certainly natural explanations do not rule out a role for God.

The obviousness of this point raises an interesting question. Why do evolutionists consider that, as Futuyma writes, "if the world and its creatures developed purely by material, physical forces, it could not have been designed and has no purpose or goal"? Such a conclusion is not reached in any other field of science. All agree as to how the sun was formed—and it was through material, physical forces. Yet few have ever argued either that this shows that it has no design or that it has no purpose or goal. It is well understood that God can easily use precisely these material, physical forces to fulfill His design for a sun, and also to accomplish His goal of providing light and heat for the earth. In the daily prayers, we say that God "causes the wind to blow and the rains to fall," even though we have an excellent understanding of the meteorological processes involved. Why is it proposed to be any different with evolution?

There are actually two separate questions to be discussed here. One is the question of why religious people, who well understand that astronomy does not rule out praising God as the Mover of the cosmos, do not feel the same way about evolution. The second is why atheists who understand that astronomy does not score points for them against religion nevertheless feel differently about evolution. We shall have to address these points separately.

The Atheistic Opposition to Theistic Evolution

Why are Darwinian evolutionists more prone than other types of scientists to thinking that naturalistic explanations rule out God? One intriguing possibility is indicated by Intelligent Design advocate Phillip Johnson:

> Naturalism is not something about which Darwinists can afford to be tentative, because their science is based upon it. As we have seen, the positive evidence that Darwinian evolution either can produce or has produced important biological innovations is nonexistent. Darwinists know that the mutation-selection mechanism can produce wings, eyes and brains not because the mechanism can be observed to do anything of the kind, but because their guiding philosophy assures them that no

other power is available to do the job. The absence from the cosmos of any Creator is therefore the essential starting point for Darwinism.

Phillip Johnson, *Darwin on Trial*, p. 117

In other words, states Johnson, statements about God are only made as conclusions by evolutionists because they are really preconditions for them. A physicist has strong grounds for saying that he knows how the sun was formed, he has theories that can be tested in a laboratory, and so he can easily admit that this does not rule out an underlying divine purpose. But, claims Johnson, a Darwinian evolutionist has few grounds for his theory other than how-else-could-it-happen,[1] and therefore it is inextricably linked with saying that there is no God.

> Metaphysics and science are inseparably entangled in the blind watchmaker thesis… the metaphysical statement is no mere embellishment but the essential foundation for the scientific claim. This is because the creative power of mutation and selection is never demonstrated directly; rather, it is thought to exist by necessity, because of the absence of a more satisfactory alternative. If God exists, on the other hand, and has the power to create, there is no need for a blind watchmaker mechanism to exist—and the lack of evidence that one does exist becomes worthy of notice.
>
> Ibid., p.168

Some will disagree with Johnson's argument. But the important point is that, at the end of the day, just as our understanding of astronomy does not prevent us from saying that God makes the sun shine, so too an explanation for the development of life based on "random" mutations and natural selection would not prevent us from saying that God designed animal life. Darwin himself, in later editions of his book, pointed this out:

> I see no good reason why the views given in this volume should shock the religious feelings of any one. It is satisfactory, as showing how transient such impressions are, to remember that the greatest discovery ever made by man, namely, the law of the attraction of gravity, was also attacked by Leibnitz, "as subversive of natural, and inferentially of

---

1 Obviously, many evolutionists dispute this assessment.

revealed, religion." A celebrated author and divine[1] has written to me that "he has gradually learned to see that it is just as noble a conception of the Deity to believe that He created a few original forms capable of self-development into other and needful forms, as to believe that He required a fresh act of creation to supply the voids caused by the action of His laws."

Charles Darwin, *On The Origin Of Species*, second ed., ch. XIV

Religious Opposition to Naturalistic Evolution

To a large extent, the opposition by religious people to the naturalistic explanation of biology but not astronomy, of evolution but not gravity, may not have any genuine basis at all. It may simply be the case that evolution is a newer "threat" than astronomy, or that it is easier to make a simple argument for the existence of a Creator from the animal kingdom than from the distant stars, or that evolution has some associated issues (e.g. regarding man's origins) that make people more suspicious of it. It can well be that the idea of a scientific explanation not ruling out God's role is simply hard for even intelligent people to grasp. Rambam notes that even some of those renowned as great sages have difficulty in appreciating this point:

> How bad and injurious is the blindness of ignorance! Take a person who is believed to belong to the wise men of Israel, and tell him that God sends His angel to enter the womb of a woman and to form the fetus there, and he will be satisfied with the account. He will believe it, and even find in it a description of the greatness of God's might and wisdom; although he believes that the angel consists of burning fire, and is a third the size of the universe, yet he considers it possible as a divine miracle. But tell him that God gave the seed a formative power which produces and shapes the limbs, and that this power is called an "angel," or that all forms are the result of the influence of the Active Intellect, and that the latter is the angel, the Prince of the world, frequently mentioned by our Sages, and he will turn away; because he cannot comprehend the true greatness and power of creating forces that act in a body without being perceived by our senses. Our Sages

---

1 Charles Kingsley, in a letter dated 18th November 1859.

have already stated—for him who has understanding—that all forces that reside in a body are angels, much more the forces that are active in the Universe.

Guide For The Perplexed Part II, Ch. 6

Fortunately, there have been great Torah scholars who did appreciate this point. An early explicit reference to evolution by a Torah authority came in 1873, just fourteen years after the publication of Darwin's *Origin of Species*, by Rabbi Samson Raphael Hirsch. Although he considered at that time that evolution was "a vague hypothesis still unsupported by fact," he declared that while certain stated implications of the theory were wrong, the essence of it is by no means incompatible with Judaism:

> Even if this notion were ever to gain complete acceptance by the scientific world, Jewish thought, unlike the reasoning of the high priest of that nation (probably a reference to Thomas Huxley, who advocated Darwinism with missionary fervor—N.S.), would nonetheless never summon us to revere a still extant representative of this primal form (an ape—N.S.) as the supposed ancestor of us all. Rather, Judaism in that case would call upon its adherents to give even greater reverence than ever before to the one, sole God Who, in His boundless creative wisdom and eternal omnipotence, needed to bring into existence no more than one single, amorphous nucleus, and one single law of "adaptation and heredity" in order to bring forth, from what seemed chaos but was in fact a very definite order, the infinite variety of species we know today, each with its unique characteristics that sets it apart from all other creatures.
>
> *The Educational Value of Judaism*, in *Collected Writings*, vol. VII, p. 264[1]

Rabbi Hirsch makes it clear that a naturalistic explanation does not paint God out of the picture. On the contrary—in this case, it testifies all the more to the genius of the Creator, to His "creative wisdom."

---

1 It is interesting to note that even Darwin himself (but certainly not all of his supporters) was receptive to this viewpoint. In later editions of the *Origin of Species*, he complimented those who had drawn positive inferences about design from evolution, who had "gradually learnt to see that it is just as noble a conception of the Deity to believe that he created a few original forms capable of self-development into other and needful forms…"

Defining the Intelligent Design Movement

The Intelligent Design movement began as an opposition to Darwinism that did not identify with the Bible (or at least, not openly). Rather, they criticized Darwinist explanations of evolution on scientific grounds. Some, notably the lawyer Phillip Johnson, also criticized it as being inextricably linked with naturalism, the view that everything must be explicable in terms of natural processes. The main purpose of the movement is to prove that life contains evidence of being intelligently designed.

William Dembski, a primary figure in the Intelligent Design movement, introduces us to its philosophy as follows:

> ...Intelligent Design begins with the observation that intelligent causes can do things which undirected natural causes cannot. Undirected natural causes can place scrabble pieces on a board, but cannot arrange the pieces as meaningful words or sentences. To obtain a meaningful arrangement requires an intelligent cause. This intuition, that there is a fundamental distinction between undirected natural causes on the one hand and intelligent causes on the other, has underlain the design arguments of past centuries.

> ...What has emerged is a new program for scientific research known as Intelligent Design. Within biology, Intelligent Design is a theory of biological origins and development. Its fundamental claim is that intelligent causes are necessary to explain the complex, information-rich structures of biology, and that these causes are empirically detectable.

> "The Intelligent Design Movement," in *Cosmic Pursuit*, Spring 1998

The point of the theory is that even if there is common ancestry and all life forms developed from earlier forms, this cannot be explained in purely naturalistic terms. Intelligent Design advocates state that it is apparent from nature that there is an intelligent Designer Who made the world with a certain end goal.

> ...Where does this leave special creation and theistic evolution? Logically speaking, Intelligent Design is compatible with everything from the starkest creationism (i.e., God intervening at every point to create new species) to the most subtle and far-ranging evolution (i.e., God seamlessly melding all organisms together in a great tree of life). For Intelligent Design the first question is not how organisms came to

be (though this is a research question that needs to be addressed), but whether they demonstrate clear, empirically detectable marks of being intelligently caused. In principle, an evolutionary process can exhibit such "marks of intelligence" as much as any act of special creation.

Ibid.

In practice, however, ID does not refer to either of the extremes described by Dembski. Although some religious people trumpet various statements by ID spokesmen in order to attack evolution and implicitly support special creation, these ID spokesmen generally accept that all life-forms did indeed develop from a common ancestor over billions of years. And, at the other extreme, although some ID advocates may speak of perceiving God within a fully naturalistic framework, this is not at all what the ID movement presents.

> In any discussion of the question of "Intelligent Design," it is absolutely essential to determine what is meant by the term itself. If, for example, the advocates of design wish to suggest that the intricacies of nature, life, and the universe reveal a world of meaning and purpose consistent with an overarching, possibly divine, intelligence, then their point is philosophical, not scientific. It is a philosophical point of view, incidentally, that I share, along with many scientists…. This, however, is not what is meant by "Intelligent Design" in the parlance of the new anti-evolutionists… Their view requires that behind each and every novelty of life we find the direct and active involvement of an outside Designer whose work violates the very laws of nature that He had fashioned….

Kenneth Miller, "The Flagellum Unspun," in Debating Design p. 94

The Intelligent Design movement presents certain things in particular that are considered to show evidence of intelligent design. One of the spokesmen for ID, biochemist Michael Behe, wrote a book called *Darwin's Black Box* which was a flagship work for the ID movement. Behe claims that certain features of biological organisms exhibit what he calls "irreducible complexity." This means that such organisms require various components to work in unison and would not work if any of these components were faulty. The claim is that such organisms could not have evolved without guidance, since there is no intermediate stage which is functional. The prime examples offered are the bacterial flagellum—a tiny whip-like structure that some bacteria use to swim—and the structure of proteins in the human blood-clotting system. Whether these things do indeed demonstrate irreducible complexity is debated.[1] These scientific debates are beyond the scope of this work and are not especially relevant to us. Of concern here is that the ID movement involves some extremely problematic theological aspects which escape the attention of many people.

The Theological Problems of "Intelligent Design"

Many well-meaning people assume that the ID movement is a friend of religion and their cause should be supported. But this is not the case at all. In fact, the ID movement presents a view of God that is theologically problematic and is a great danger to religion.

The ID movement claims that we should look for signs of intelligent design in biological phenomena, and that schools should teach this perspective in their biology classes. But nobody claims that we should do that in a class studying (secular) history, or physics, or geology! A bizarre aspect of ID is the place that it allocates for God showing His hand in nature. It tells us that while God's hand is not to be looked for in the movement of the planets, in the formation of the world, or in the harmony of nature, it can be seen in the bacterial flagellum and the blood-clotting system. These are odd choices of places for God to show Himself.

The ID movement effectively tells us that the prophets of Scripture who perceived God in the cosmos and the natural world were all speaking out of ignorance. ID claims that, since we have scientific explanations for these things, God cannot be seen there. Instead, God is to be found in the bacterial flagellum and the blood-clotting system!

Aside from the theological absurdity of such a belief, the danger of intelligent design theory is that it risks forming a "God-of-the-gaps"—a Creator who is invoked to account for phenomena that science cannot explain, but whose existence is unnecessary if science is eventually able to explain such phenomena in naturalistic terms. Phillip Johnson admits to this peril, and presents his response:

---

1   See, for example, Kenneth Miller, "The Flagellum Unspun," in *Debating Design*.

> There is a risk in undertaking such a project, of course, as the theistic evolutionists constantly remind us by referring to the need to avoid resorting to a "God of the gaps." If the naturalistic understanding of reality is truly correct and complete, then God will have to retreat out of the cosmos altogether. I do not think the risk is very great, but in any case I do not think theists should meet it with a preemptive surrender.
>
> Phillip Johnson, *Darwin on Trial,* p. 169

Johnson's statement that "if the naturalistic understanding of reality is truly correct and complete, then God will have to retreat out of the cosmos altogether," is by no means true. A complete explanation of the celestial bodies by astronomy, or an explanation of the formation of mountains by geology, or of rain via meteorology, does not paint God out of the picture, but instead means that He works through science. But Johnson denies such a role for God.

An ID proponent might take a different position from Johnson and claim that they indeed perceive God in those aspects of organisms that can be explained by evolutionary mechanisms, but that they see Him all the more powerfully in aspects which they believe cannot be described by such processes. Yet this would appear to be a slight to God's creative abilities. Was He incapable of designing laws that could accomplish all His objectives, and therefore had to interfere to bring about the results that He wanted?

The ID movement, in its usual manifestation, is no friend to Judaism. It denies the role of God in 99% of the universe, relegating Him to being little more than the designer of bacterial flagella and blood-clotting systems; or it implies that He was only able to engineer processes that would accomplish 99% of His objectives, but not all of them. Postulating the intelligent design of organisms means postulating the unintelligent design of natural laws.

> Design does remain a possibility, but not the type of "Intelligent Design" of which they speak... I do not believe, even for an instant, that Darwin's vision has weakened or diminished the sense of wonder and awe that one should feel in confronting the magnificence and diversity of the natural world. Rather, to a person of faith it should enhance the sense of the Creator's majesty and wisdom. Against such

a backdrop, the struggles of the Intelligent Design movement are best understood as clamorous and disappointing double failures—rejected by science because they do not fit the facts, and having failed religion because they think too little of God.

Kenneth Miller, "The Flagellum Unspun," in Debating Design p. 95

Theistic Darwinian Evolution

On the other hand, some argue that Darwinian evolution is uniquely opposed to religion in a way that other sciences are not. It is true that Rabbi Hirsch and Rabbi Kook, who spoke of the compatibility of Torah with evolution in terms of gradual descent from common ancestors via naturalistic mechanisms, did not deal with the "blind watchmaker" aspect of Darwinian evolution; that which Richard Dawkins describes as "the blind, unconscious, automatic process which Darwin discovered, and which we now know is the explanation for the existence and apparent purposeful form of all life, has no purpose in mind." It is this which is regarded by some as the aspect of evolution most dangerous to religion. Proponents of ID consider this ideology to be inextricably linked to Darwinian evolution. It would certainly appear at first glance that the blind-watchmaker thesis, which is the essential feature of Darwinian evolution, is incompatible with the concept of a seeing-watchmaker. We shall have to analyze this carefully.

One point to note is that it is impossible to ever determine whether something is truly random. One could take a string of a hundred seemingly random numbers and perform every conceivable test, and discover no pattern. Yet it could be that those numbers were actually the numbers preceding the one hundred digits that appear after the millionth digit of Pi. So, they were not actually random at all.

Another point to note is that the words "blind," "chance," and "random," when used in the context of Darwinian evolution, refer to the combination of chance genetic mutation together with arbitrary deterministic forces of circumstance such as environmental change, and so on; they are only "blind" in that they are not visibly geared towards the eventual structure of the creature.

…Some are agitated by the conflict between the apparent random nature of change required by evolution and the "guided" or more gradual or organized kind of "Evolution" presented in the Bible. I consider this to be an error based on a misunderstanding of terminology. When a biologist speaks of random mutation, he does not really mean that those changes that occur are completely uncaused and arbitrary, but rather that since we do not know all the details of what occurs, we refer to it by use of the statistics of randomness… To claim that evolutionary theory suggests that evolution occurred as a result of mere accident is to misrepresent the theory of evolution.

Carl Feit, "Darwin and Drash: The Interplay of Torah and Biology,"
The Torah U-Madda Journal (1990) II p. 30

The prominent philosopher Michael Ruse, author of numerous books on the evolution/ religion controversy, points out that "chance" does not mean true randomness but rather human ignorance:

Suppose that something is put down to chance. Does this mean that law is ruled out? Surely not! If I argue that a Mendelian mutation is chance, what I mean is that with respect to that particular theory it is chance. But I may well believe (I surely will believe) that the mutation came about by normal causes and that if these were all known, then it would no longer be chance at all but necessity… Chance is a confession of ignorance, not (as one might well think the case in the quantum world) an assertion about the way things are)… One might want to say of something that it is produced by laws, is chance with respect to our knowledge or theory, and fits into an overall context of design by the great orderer or creator of things.

Michael Ruse, Darwin and Design, p. 323

Thus, while the term "chance" causes many religious people to instinctively recoil, a careful analysis of its usage in describing evolution reveals that there is no reason for this.

Chance and Randomness

It cannot be adequately stressed is that apparent "chance" is fully consistent with the classical Jewish view of how God runs the world. This is spelled out explicitly in Scripture:

> [When] the lot is cast in the lap, its entire verdict has been decided by God.
>
> Proverbs 16:33

Malbim elaborates:

> There are things that appear given to chance but are actually providentially determined by God... "the lot is cast in the lap," hidden from the eye of man, handed over to chance, but nevertheless the eye of God's providence is displayed in it, and the verdict that the lot brings up is not chance but is from God; just as with the apportioning of the land and so on, where the lot was under God's providence.
>
> Malbim, Commentary ad loc.

The example that Malbim gives is the dividing of the Land of Israel amongst the twelve tribes, which was done via a lottery:

> God spoke to Moses, saying, To these the land shall be divided for an inheritance according to the number of names. To the more numerous you shall give a larger inheritance, and to the fewer you shall give a smaller inheritance; to every one shall his inheritance be given according to those who were counted by him. However the land shall be divided by lot; according to the names of the tribes of their fathers they shall inherit. According to the lot its possession shall be divided between many and few.
>
> Numbers 26:52-56

Despite the seeming randomness of the process, Jewish tradition is emphatic that the apportionment was not truly random. Rather, each tribe received the portion of land that was predestined for it.[1] The seemingly random process of the lottery was merely a guise for the Divine decision.

The idea that God works through seemingly chance events is the fundamental message of the festival of Purim, celebrating the events recorded in the Book of Esther. The Book of Esther does not mention God's Name even once; there are no open miracles. Instead, there are a string of "happenstance" events whose importance only becomes clear at the end of the story. The entire purpose of Purim is to teach that even seemingly chance events are seen by their eventual results to have been

---

1   See Talmud, *Bava Basra* 122a.

part of a greater plan, and not as random as they superficially appeared. The randomness of Darwinian theory, which so many religious people believe has to be opposed, is no more problematic for Judaism than the "random" events of the Book of Esther.

It is abundantly clear from all this that the randomness of Darwinian evolution poses no theological problem whatsoever. Judaism has no problem with processes that *appear* to be random, and in fact it sees them as an ideal means via which God dynamically exerts His will. While the evolutionary process may well *appear* to be random from our perspective, it can simultaneously be directed from God's perspective. Later, we shall explore how so-called blind-watchmaker evolution is not only compatible with God, but can even be seen as evidence for His role as a designer for life.

Theistic Darwinian Evolution in Action

As an example of how a theistic view of evolution differs from an atheistic view, let us consider the following verse:

> The high hills [are] for the ibex, the rocks as a refuge for the hyraxes.
>
> Psalms 104:18

Ibex are a species of wild goat, spectacularly agile creatures that are found in the rough hills of the Negev in Israel. Hyraxes are small animals that live in rocky areas; when enemies approach, they quickly dart down to hide amongst the rocks. The simple creationist perspective is that the terrain was made to suit the animals. God designed the world based upon the hierarchy in creation. Man, as the goal of creation, is the most important creature. Following man come animals, and then come plants and inanimate matter. Ibex are therefore more important than terrain. God created the terrain to suit the ibex. The high hills are *for* the ibex, created specifically to suit their needs.[1]

The secular Darwinian perspective, on the other hand, is that these animals are the unplanned product of natural selection, having evolved to suit their environment. Ibex, powerfully built but with short legs, are

---

1 *Midrash Tehillim*, Rashi, Radak ad loc; *Midrash Bereishis Rabbah* 12:8.

adapted for negotiating steep hillsides, an ideal way of escaping predators. Natural selection favored those ancestors of the ibex that had random genetic mutations which rendered them better suited to this environment. Eventually, such characteristics were reinforced to produce the ibex as we see it. Likewise, natural selection favored the mutations of hyraxes that had sweat glands in their feet which assist in gripping the surface of rock, and long tactile hairs at intervals over their bodies which help them feel their way inside dark fissures and tunnels. The ibex are for the hills rather than the hills being for the ibex. Both species are the result of blind forces causing adaptation to their terrain.

The religious Darwinist perspective would be as follows. To be sure, the animals adapted to their habitat through evolutionary forces. But the habitat is the way that it is such in order that the animals would evolve in that way. A child's teeth change to fit his braces, but it would not be true to say that the final look of his teeth is unplanned. The braces are made such that the teeth will adapt to become straight. In the same way, God made the high hills so that His laws of evolution would select the ancestral goats that had shorter and more powerful legs, in order to eventually produce the ibex.

The Danger of "Sympathetic" Darwinian Evolutionists

We have seen that the mistake of many in the religious camp is to state that evolution is by definition atheistic, that God definitely cannot and did not work through evolutionary processes. This is simply wrong, as we have explained at length. Naturalistic Darwinian evolution is fully compatible with religion.

However, some Darwinian evolutionists are being deceptive when they say that they believe this to be the case. It may well be true that it *is* compatible, but *they* certainly don't really believe that to be the case. Examples of their disingenuousness are seen all too frequently. Douglas Futuyma claims that "religion is not necessarily opposed to evolution,"[1] and that "science cannot deny the existence of supernatural beings... [it]

---

1 *Science on Trial*, p. 19.

cannot prove that God didn't create the universe,"[1] yet he also presents quite a different opinion:

> ...if the world and its creatures developed purely by material, physical forces, it could not have been designed and has no purpose or goal. The fundamentalist, in contrast, believes that everything in the world, every species and every characteristic of every species, was designed by an intelligent, purposeful artificer, and that it was made for a purpose. Nowhere does this contrast apply with more force than to the human species. Some shrink from the conclusion that the human species was not designed, has no purpose, and is the product of mere material mechanisms—but this seems to be the message of evolution.
>
> Douglas Futuyma, *Science on Trial*, p.13

Again, whether or not the message of Darwinian evolution is that the universe is purposeless is subject to debate—we have argued that it is in fact *not* the message of Darwinian evolution. But the point is that many prominent evolutionists certainly consider that to be the case. One should be wary of their claims otherwise, as they are presenting a view of religion that is utterly inconsistent with Judaism.

A prime example of such disingenuousness is Chet Raymo's *Skeptics and True Believers: The Exhilarating Connection between Science and Religion*. The book's title is reinforced by a description on the book's jacket that the author, a professor of physics and astronomy, will make "a statement that science and religion can mutually reinforce the way we experience the world." However, what Raymo actually does is to assure his readers that there are no supernatural beings, and that "God" (to whom he makes frequent and passionate references) refers simply to the sense of wonder at the marvels of the universe that people feel. A sense of awe at the universe's beauty is a fine thing, and Raymo is free to define religion for himself in any way that he wants, but it is highly misleading to claim that what he is presenting has anything to do with what most people refer to as "religion."

But the worst offender in this regard must surely be the late Stephen Jay Gould. Gould wrote an entire book, *Rocks of Ages*, about how science and

---

1 Ibid. p. 169.

religion are of equal importance and operate in entirely different domains. He waxes on for chapter after chapter about how they deal with non-overlapping magisteria, which does not render either science or religion any the less important. Yet his definition of religion is nothing more than "all moral discourse on principles that might activate the ideal of universal fellowship among people."[1] He sees no problem in making metaphysical conclusions from science that man is "not the nub of universal purpose"[2] and that indeed there is no objective purpose to the world at all.[3]

Gould's problem emerged most clearly when he contested Phillip Johnson's "false and unkind accusation that scientists are being dishonest when they claim equal respect for science and religion." Yet Gould gave himself away in his defense. He stated that science and religion are separate but equal, because:

> ...science treats factual reality, while religion struggles with human morality.
>
> Stephen Jay Gould, "Impeaching a Self-Appointed Judge,"
> *Scientific American* 267:1 (July 1992) p. 120

As others have pointed out, most people who believe in God would be very horrified to be told that their belief has nothing to do with factual reality! Gould claims to grant equal importance to evolution and religion, but his definition of religion is deeply offensive.

It can indeed be stated that religion and science do not, generally speaking, overlap. Rabbi Joseph Hertz makes this very point:

> [Genesis'] object is not to teach scientific facts; but to proclaim highest religious truths respecting God, Man, and the Universe. The "conflict" between the fundamental realities of Religion and the established facts of Science is seen to be unreal as soon as Religion and Science each recognizes the true borders of its dominion.
>
> Rabbi J. H. Hertz, *The Pentateuch and Haftorahs*, p. 195

This may sound similar to Gould—but it is utterly different. We define religion as an objective reality rooted in a real God. Gould defines

---

1 *Rocks of Ages*, p. 62.

2 Ibid. p. 206.

3 Ibid. p. 200.

religion as nothing more than individual beliefs about moral direction, and sees science as providing ultimate truths about metaphysics. When evolutionists argue against the Intelligent Design movement, one of their claims is that religion has no place in a science class. But atheistic evolutionists themselves engage in this when they make metaphysical inferences from science. Both believer and evolutionist must accept the inherent limitations of what evolutionary biology can discover.

Does Darwinian Evolution Provide Evidence for God?

So far, we have only discussed the argument that the blind-watchmaker thesis need not be incompatible with the concept of God. Theistic evolution fully agrees with the Darwinists, except that it claims that God is behind the whole process. Initially, this may appear to fully conform with our thesis that God created a scientific framework in which He would work. It is certainly theoretically possible that He would cause creatures to evolve in a manner which would appear to be based on random mutation and unguided evolution, but which would in fact be guided, just as the seemingly chaotic weather patterns or random falls of a dice are guided by God.

However, Darwinian evolution would initially seem to be fundamentally incompatible with the Torah. For it is clear from Scripture that we are supposed to perceive God from the natural world. If the natural world appears to have come about by chance, then how can we perceive God from it?

> As far as design theorists are concerned, theistic evolution is an oxymoron, something like "purposeful purposelessness." If God purposely created life through the means proposed by Darwin, then God's purpose was to make it seem as though life was created without any purpose. According to the Darwinian picture, the natural world provides no clue that a purposeful God created life. For all we can tell, our appearance on planet earth is an accident. If it were all to happen again, we wouldn't be here. No, the heavens do not declare the glory of God, and no, God's invisible attributes are not clearly seen from God's creation. This is the upshot of theistic evolution as the design theorists construe it.
>
> William A. Dembski, "What Every Theologian should know about Creation, Evolution and Design," in *The Princeton Theological Review*, March 1996

Indeed, many evolutionists argue that Darwinian evolution leads to the conclusion that, unlike the watch in Paley's analogy, life did not have a designer.

> Paley's argument is made with passionate sincerity and is informed by the best biological scholarship of his day, but it is wrong, gloriously and utterly wrong. The analogy between ...a watch and living organism, is false. All appearances to the contrary, the only watchmaker in nature is the blind forces of physics, albeit deployed in a very special way. A true watchmaker has foresight: he designs his cogs and springs, and plans their interconnections, with a future purpose in the mind's eye. Natural selection, the blind, unconscious, automatic process which Darwin discovered, and which we now know is the explanation for the existence and apparent purposeful form of all life, has no purpose in mind. It has no mind and no mind's eye. It does not plan for the future. It has no vision, no foresight, no sight at all. If it can be said to play the role of watchmaker in nature, it is the blind watchmaker.
>
> Richard Dawkins, *The Blind Watchmaker*, p. 5

However, there is an entirely different perspective that one can adopt on this matter. Even Thomas Henry Huxley (1825-95), the principle defender of Darwinism, acknowledged that

> ...there is a wider teleology which is not touched by the doctrine of evolution... The teleological and mechanical views of nature are not, necessarily, mutually exclusive. On the contrary, the more purely a mechanist the speculator is, the more firmly does he assume a primordial molecular arrangement of which all the phenomena of the universe are the consequences and the more completely is he at the mercy of the teleologist, who can always defy him to disprove that this primitive molecular arrangement was not intended to evolve the actual phenomena of the universe... Evolution has no more to do with theism than the first book of Euclid has.
>
> *On the reception of the Origin of Species,*
> in *Life and Letters of Charles Darwin*, ref. 160, Vol. 2, p. 179

Rabbi Dessler explains how one can always trace natural processes back to a prime cause:

> Why was the world created in a way such that it appears as though it came about by way of evolution (seemingly referring to the general

development of the universe rather than specifically biological evolution—N.S.)? However, this is the way of the revelation amidst the concealment. We see a long chain of cause and effect, which is the concealment. But it is up to us to mentally climb from the last to the first until we reach the First Cause, Blessed be His Name—and this is the revelation... The path of revelation is that we should choose to see how the entire chain of causes and effects unite at their root with the First Cause, Blessed be His Name, and the deeper that the concealment is, the greater that the eventual revelation, by way of our free will, will be.

Michtav Me-Eliyahu, vol. IV, p. 113

Rabbi Aryeh Kaplan discusses aspects of chance and concludes that there is no better indication of God's existence than a seemingly mechanical universe that results in intelligent life:

How great is the concept of God when looked at in this light. He is seen not merely as the Creator of life forms, atom by atom, molecule by molecule... The chemistry of carbon, the uniquely life-sustaining properties of water, are nothing less than miraculous. God created matter so that life, culminating in man, leading to the ultimate recognition of God, would be inevitable.

Rabbi Aryeh Kaplan, *Faces and Facets*, pp. 94-96

Since, at the end of the day, there is a remarkable degree of complexity present in living creatures, then somewhere along the line we will have to invoke a designer; whether it be at the level of making the creature directly, or of making laws of nature and a world that result in the evolution of such a creature. In other words, if chance leads to remarkable order, then it obviously wasn't "chance" in the first place![1] Sir John Eccles spells out the significance of this point:

...There seems to be some purpose, some deeper meaning to it all. There must be a divine plan—the Anthropic Principle. This divine plan came through this whole immense cosmos.

---

1 One cannot argue that since there are atheists, then the world clearly doesn't point to God. There always has to be a possibility of denying God in order to preserve free will.

...The creation of planet Earth is itself a wonderful arrangement for life. The whole cosmos can be thought of as being immense in order to give time for the creation of Planet Earth and to give time for the evolution of life and eventually the creation of us in the evolutionary process. So I look upon the whole cosmic design as not being made in sheer immensity for no purpose. The sheer immensity is there in fact to get the time for the creation of Planet Earth with its immense richness of elements and then the time for it to cool down and then the time for the evolutionary process of life which took something like 3500 million years. That's the way you have to think of the time. And so this great cosmos of ours may look very extravagant in the way of material investment of mass but in order to get the long duration of the expansion you have to have this immense momentum going out in the expansion, and all this is applied to time for the solar system to exist and for earth to exist and the planets too and the earth to go right through evolution and finally create us. So that is the Anthropic Principle as I see it.

...The whole thing was wonderfully organized and planned to give the immensity, to give the size, to give the opportunity, for the Darwinist evolutionary processes that gave rise to us. So that's the Anthropic Principle. The whole process gave rise to the existence of mankind.

John Eccles, "A Divine Design: Some Questions on Origins,"
in *Cosmos Bios Theos*, pp. 161-162

Eccles is saying that the entire vastness of the universe was used by God in order to form man through an evolutionary process. At the end of the process, one can look back and see the necessity of it all. This is related to the concept in classical Jewish thought of *sof maaseh bemachshavah techilah*, the end of deed is first in thought, which explains that the final result sheds light on the entire process. In this case, it clarifies that when a seemingly meaningless process results in a highly meaningful conclusion, one looks back and sees that the apparent meaninglessness was a mere disguise for the goal, which was actually envisaged at the start of the entire process.

In summary: the secular Darwinist believes that he can explain the complexity of life in terms of the natural laws of chance mutation, and therefore feels that life came into being without a Creator. The religious

Darwinist, on the other hand, believes that if natural laws can produce something as astonishingly complex as life, then those natural laws must have been designed; the whole system was engineered to ultimately produce the results that we see today.

Chapter Twenty-Two

Darwinian Evolution
And God's Attributes

Expectations of a Creator

Part of the case for Darwinian mechanisms of evolution is made on the basis of phenomena in the natural world that are understood to raise difficulties for the notion of special creation but to be accounted for by Darwinian evolution. Some of these are also taken not to just to argue against organisms having been individually designed and created from scratch, but also against any form of creation. In case there is any doubt as to whether Darwinian evolutionists are basing themselves on such arguments, let us quote them on it:

> The case for evolution then has two sides: positive evidence—that evolution has occurred; and negative evidence—that the natural world does not conform to our expectation of what an omnipotent, omniscient, truthful Creator would have created.[1]
>
> Douglas Futuyma, *Science on Trial*, p. 198

---

1 Futuyma continues that "If the creationist replies that everything in the world, no matter how arbitrary, useless, or cruel, is just what we should expect of the Creator's infinitely inscrutable wisdom, he is… tacitly admitting that creationism can predict nothing, and so cannot be science." Although we will not advance such a reply, it must be pointed out that the fact that such a reply cannot make predictions might disqualify it from being "science," but does not disqualify it from being true!

While evolutionists are correct that this evidence indicates that God did not create each species separately from scratch, it certainly does not indicate that there is no God! It may well be that the natural world does not conform to Douglas Futuyma's expectation of what an omnipotent, omniscient, truthful Creator would have created. However, let us now explore whether it conforms to a Jewish expectation of what an omnipotent, omniscient, truthful Creator would have created.

In this section, we are not discussing whether or not phenomena that Darwinian evolutionists argue to exist do in fact exist. Rather, the phenomena of the ensuing discussions are observable facts of the natural world; the question is as to how to interpret them. Some Darwinists claim that not only does their theory give a satisfactory explanation for these phenomena, but it further provides evidence against the existence of God. In giving satisfactory religious explanations for these phenomena, we are not disproving Darwinism; instead, we are showing how it does not detract from the rationality of believing in a Creator.

Imperfect Design from a Perfect Creator

A primary argument of atheistic evolutionists is that the "bad design" of various organisms is something that is both explained by Darwinian evolution and provides evidence against a Creator:

> The theory of natural selection would never have replaced the doctrine of divine creation if evident, admirable design pervaded all organisms. Charles Darwin understood this, and he focused on features that would be out of place in a world constructed by perfect wisdom... Darwin even wrote an entire book on orchids to argue that the structures evolved to ensure fertilization by insects are jerry-built of available parts used by ancestors for other purposes. Orchids are Rube Goldberg machines; a perfect engineer would certainly have come up with something better. This principle remains true today. The best illustrations of adaptation by evolution are the ones that strike our intuition as peculiar or bizarre.
>
> Stephen J. Gould, *Ever Since Darwin*, p. 91

Stephen Jay Gould has elaborated upon this argument in his work *The Panda's Thumb*. Pandas do not have an opposable thumb that is one of the five digits, as do other animals with grasping hands. Instead, they have a modification of the wrist bone, which serves to help grasp bamboo. Such a "thumb" makes sense in light of Darwinian evolution; the thumb was already pressed into use as a finger, leaving natural selection to operate with the wrist bone. But, argues Gould, this is too inefficient a limb to be the work of a wise Creator.

There are other features of organisms that not only appear poorly designed, but are even potentially detrimental. Wisdom teeth and the lower spine are examples of each. Evolutionists correctly argue that these indicate descent from earlier species; atheist evolutionists incorrectly argue that they disprove the existence of a wise Creator.

In order to understand the correct perspective on this, we must note that, to pick one example, the panda's thumb is simultaneously being offered to prove common ancestry, natural selection, and to disprove an intelligently designed world. An assumption here is that the first two are necessarily opposed to the latter, and *therefore* disprove it. But if we posit that God created the animal kingdom using a process of gradual modification from common ancestors, it would also mean that the panda, created from an animal which already had its thumb pressed into use for a particular purpose, would have its bamboo-grasping thumb made from something else. If evolution by natural selection is an excellent system for forming a diverse range of animals, then why shouldn't the Creator have used such a system?

On the contrary—Judaism states that creation unfolds from the unity of God. We can therefore plausibly contend that He would use the simplest means to obtain the complex goal of the world in which we live. It is a mark of genius to create a system that can produce a panda from a non-panda (even at the "cost" of having an inflexible thumb), rather than having to design one from scratch. Far from being a menace to religion, Darwinian evolution assists in explaining an age-old problem of why there are so many features of living things that seem poorly designed, useless, or even harmful.

> Theologians in the past struggled with the issue of dysfunction, because they thought it had to be attributed to God's design. Science, much to the relief of many theologians, provides an explanation that

304

convincingly attributes defects, deformities, and dysfunctions to natural causes.

Fransico Ayala, "Design without Designer," in Debating Design p. 70

Gould and company are correct that there are physiological features that argue against creatures being the result of a direct design by a Creator. But they are wrong in swinging this as a club against the very idea of Creator. It simply means that He used a more sophisticated method for creation – the "creative wisdom" of which Rabbi Samson Raphael Hirsch spoke.

True, this results in a natural world that possesses various "imperfections." But Judaism has never shied away from the idea of imperfections in the natural world. Classical Jewish thought maintains that the world is not supposed to be perfect in the first place:

> "And God said, Let the earth bring forth grass, herb-yielding seed, and fruit-trees"—that the taste of the tree should be as the taste of the fruit; and it did not do so, but rather "the earth brought forth... trees producing fruit."

Rashi to Genesis 1:11-12, citing Midrash Bereishis Rabbah 5:9

Maharal explains that this flaw reflects the fundamental nature of the world:

> This does not mean that the earth deliberately transgressed God's command, as it does not possess an evil inclination that it should be able to do so; but rather, because the world is of the Lower Regions... it is perpetually lacking perfection.

Gur Aryeh, Genesis 1:11

The so-called "imperfect design" of various creatures is evidence for common ancestry and natural selection. It argues against the Creator having created every creature from scratch. But it does not present evidence against the God Who, in the words of Rabbi Hirsch, "in His boundless creative wisdom and eternal omnipotence, needed to bring into existence no more than one single, amorphous nucleus, and one single law of 'adaptation and heredity' in order to bring forth, from what seemed chaos but was in fact a very definite order, the infinite variety of species we know today, each with its unique characteristics that sets it apart from all other creatures."

305

A Vicious Struggle and a Benevolent Creator

One aspect of Darwinian evolution that some religious people see as problematic is the idea of "survival of the fittest." This contradicts the idea that "the meek shall inherit the earth" (Psalms 37:11). While that verse is speaking of human destiny rather than the pattern of nature, the ideology behind it is that God is just. The idea that nature rewards viciousness would stand in contrast with the view of how God runs the world.

In response to this, it is first worth noting that it is by no means proven that nature only promotes viciousness, as Darwinian evolutionists believe. Brian Goodwin, for example, a mathematician and biologist who is leading a new school of evolutionary thought, states otherwise:

> Darwinism sees the living process in terms that emphasize competition, inheritance, selfishness, and survival as the driving force of evolution. These are certainly aspects of the remarkable drama that includes our own history as a species. But it is a very incomplete and limited story, both scientifically and metaphorically, based upon an inadequate view of organisms; and it invites us to act in a limited way as an evolved species in relation to our environment, which includes other cultures and species... but Darwinism short-changes us as regards our biological natures. We are every bit as co-operative as we are competitive; as altruistic as we are selfish; as creative and playful as we are destructive and repetitive.
>
> Brian Goodwin, *How The Leopard Changed Its Spots*, p. xiv.

Second, it is by no means clear that it is the vicious carnivores that are the most successful. If one measures success in terms of numbers, then the meek herbivores are far more successful! They vastly outnumber the predators, both in number of species and number of individuals. The meek have indeed inherited the earth.

Yet it cannot be denied that there is an enormous amount of cruelty seen in the natural world, resulting in some animals performing acts of horrific brutality to others in order to survive. This was described by Charles Darwin as producing some of his own doubts about God:

> With respect to the theological view of the question; this is always painful to me.—I am bewildered.—I had no intention of writing atheistically. But I own that I cannot see, as plainly as others do, and

as I should wish to do, evidence of design and beneficence on all sides of us. There seems to be too much misery in the world. I cannot persuade myself that a beneficent and omnipotent God would have designedly created the Ichneumonidae (a wasp with parasitic larvae) with the express intention of their feeding within the living bodies of caterpillars, or that a cat should play with mice.

Letter to Asa Gray, May 22, 1860

Darwin identified this a major element of his difficulty with religious belief, and aggressively atheistic evolutionists, such as Richard Dawkins and Douglas Futuyma, present it today as evidence against a loving Creator. The argument is powerful. All species of animal are struggling for survival, and will stop at nothing to obtain this. Gazelles constantly became swifter to deprive cheetahs of their food, whereas cheetahs continually became stronger to deprive gazelles of their lives. This vicious competition, state Darwinists, is perfectly accounted for by evolution, but is incompatible with the idea that there is a benevolent Creator who created a harmonious world:

> Does it accord with the divine sense of harmony that male elephant seals should battle so furiously for females that great numbers of them die of bloody wounds?

Douglas Futuyma, *Science on Trial*, p. 200

The phenomenon does raise a question for the religious person to deal with. For we do indeed believe that Creation is, to use the Torah's description, "very good," and yet there is undeniably an enormous amount of pain and suffering in the natural world. The evolutionists have an explanation for this, and it is one which rewards viciousness and suffering; but what explanation does Judaism offer?

One can answer this in the same way as we answered the previous objection, that this was an inherent constraint in the otherwise extraordinary creative wisdom that God used to create life. Rambam discusses the idea that there are inherent limitations to the world that God created, which result in a certain degree of physical suffering present in the world.[1] This is the approach suggested by philosopher Michael Ruse:

---

1   *Guide For The Perplexed* 3:12.

Dawkins wants to claims that the coming of Darwin made the God hypothesis impossible. After Darwin we see that the world is simply not how it would be if an all-loving, all-powerful creator had made it (the cheetah and antelope argument). Nothing like this could possibly occur, given a loving god. But this is exactly what one would expect from blind, purposeless law. However, the appeal to blind unbroken law—things not working perfectly and pain and strife being commonplace—can be turned on its head, to yield a traditional argument protecting the possibility of... God... Having once committed himself to creation by law, everything else follows as a matter of course.

Think of trying to make physical processes entirely pain-free. Start with fire. It could no longer burn or produce smoke. But if this were the case, would it still be hot? If so, then how could this be? There would have to wholesale changes at the molecular level. If fire were not hot, how would we warm ourselves and cook our food? One change by God would require a knock-on compensation, and another and another. And even then, could we get a system that worked properly?

Once we start altering things to eliminate pain and suffering, there is no end to it—except that we would have changed humans so that they are no longer truly human. And even then, who would dare say we humans would be better situated? ...All things in the world fit into an interlocking whole. We should not assume that God could have made things in another way, avoiding instances of physical evil.

Michael Ruse, Darwin and Design, p. 332

Ruse proceeds to point out that according to Darwinians such as Richard Dawkins, who claim that natural selection is the *only* natural mechanism by which to accomplish the complexity of life on this planet, there is all the more reason not to see the vicious struggle of evolution as evidence against a Creator:

In other words, if God's process of creation is through unbroken law, then he had to do it as he did—natural selection, pain and agony, imperfection, and all... Darwinism as such does not make irresistible the argument from natural evil. It may even make the solution easier to grasp.

Ibid., p. 333

Still, this is not as satisfactory an answer as one would hope for. If the constraints upon creation via natural law result in such tremendous suffering, we may wonder if it was such a good idea in the first place. We should still look for a better answer.

What does classical Jewish thought have to say about the suffering that is present in the animal kingdom? Rabbi Yehudah HaLevi, in the *Kuzari*, discusses the harshness of life in the animal kingdom in the context of describing the wonder of its design:

> See how wonderfully conceived is the nature of the creatures, how many marvelous gifts they possess which show forth the intention of an all-wise Creator, and the will of an omniscient all-powerful Being. He has endowed the small and the great with all necessary internal and external senses and limbs. He gave them organs corresponding to their instincts. He gave the rabbit and the stag the means of flight required by their timid nature; endowed the lion with ferocity and with the instruments for robbing and tearing. He who considers the formation, use, and relation of the limbs to the animal instinct, sees wisdom in them and so perfect an arrangement that no doubt or uncertainty can remain in his soul concerning the justice of the Creator.
>
> When an evil thought suggests that there is injustice in the circumstance that the rabbit falls prey to the stoat or the wolf, and the fly to the spider, reason warns him as follows: How can I charge the All-Wise with injustice when I am convinced of His justice, and that injustice is quite out of the question? If the stoat's pursuit of the rabbit and the spider of the fly were mere accidents, I should have to assert the necessity of accident. I see, however, that the wise and just Manager of the world equipped the lion with the means for hunting, with ferocity, strength, teeth and claws; that He furnished the spider with cunning and taught it to weave a net which it constructs without having learned to do so; how He equipped it with the instruments required and appointed the fly as its food, just as many fish serve other fish for food. Can I say anything but that this is the fruit of a wisdom which I am unable to grasp, and that I must submit to Him Who is called "The Rock Whose doing is perfect" (Deuteronomy 32:4)?
>
> *The Kuzari*, 3:11

Rather than give an explanation, he states that since there is an *a priori* awareness that God created the universe and is just, and that animals are clearly designed to eat one another, then predation must therefore be planned, and it must be the product of a justice that is beyond our comprehension. Like the mystery of human suffering, the suffering of the animal kingdom is one of the ultimate, unknowable mysteries of creation.

Rabbi Avraham Yeshayah Karelitz, the "Chazon Ish" (1878-1953), gives more of an explanation, although one that is nevertheless still somewhat cryptic:

> Animals are of utility to man, such as an ox for a yoke and a donkey for a burden, and they prepare food for man, milk and eggs, and from some of them we obtain wool to wear, and some of them are themselves food for people. They were created as different kinds and as many species, and the food of each is different. Some of them people do not benefit from, such as predatory animals, and snakes, and vermin, and insects; however they possess sublime necessity and benefit. Sometimes man is punished by way of them, and sometimes man learns wisdom and ethics from them. We are already used to their existence, and we feel that without them the world would be lacking, and the world is not beautiful and perfect except when there are predatory animals in it.
>
> Chazon Ish, *Emunah U'bitachon* 1:7

Rabbi Karelitz seems to be saying that the harshness of nature, demonstrated by predatory animals, is part and parcel of the overall grand tapestry of creation. "...We feel that without them the world would be lacking, and the world is not beautiful and perfect except when there are predatory animals in it"—man somehow intuitively understands that it is part of a greater good.

A contemporary scholar, Rabbi Moshe Eisemann, makes a similar point, except that he implies that the function of the natural world may be purely to demonstrate to man the concept of there being a greater good. He explains this in the context of explaining God's description to Iyov (Job) of the behemoth and the leviathan:

> The picture with which we are left of the behemoth is that of massive strength coupled with a surprisingly benign temperament. This titan is pictured as living its life with no reference to any struggle with man. It browses on the hills, tolerates wildlife in its surroundings, stretches out to sleep in the sun and seems to be in conflict with no one at all...

The image of the leviathan is quite different. With no other introduction at all, we are immediately confronted with the picture of a bucking, pitching colossus, spitting forth man's puny tackle, fiercely resisting capture, utterly contemptuous of man's need to dominate it...

Stewardship of the world, then, is a question of balances. There is room for the behemoth and for the leviathan, for nature's victims and its snarling predators.

Iyov must understand that absolute justice in a physical world can never be more than a theoretical construct. In a real world of conflicting claims and the concomitant need for balance, the longevity and tranquility of the wicked may also contribute to a greater good which is beyond the ken of man. "All that there is, God created for His greater glory—even the wicked marking time toward the day when evil will overtake them" (Proverbs 16:4).

Rabbi Moshe Eisemann, Iyov, pp. 352-353

Thus, while Darwinian evolution does give an efficient explanation for the vicious competition found in the natural world at a physical level, religious thought has never been silent on the metaphysical perspective on this.[1] The essential answer is that such things are part of the larger picture, part of the greater good, part of God's ultimate and unknowable plan:

For My thoughts are not as your thoughts, nor are your ways as My ways, says God.

Isaiah 55:8

Indeed, Darwin himself acknowledged that this may well be the answer:

On the other hand I cannot anyhow be contented to view this wonderful universe and especially the nature of man, and to conclude that everything is the result of brute force... I feel most deeply that the whole subject is too profound for the human intellect. A dog might as well speculate on the mind of Newton.

Letter to Asa Gray, May 22 1860

---

1   The concepts that we introduced earlier of this world necessarily lacking perfection—in the words of the Maharal, "...because the world is of the Lower Regions... it is perpetually lacking perfection"—may also be relevant in explaining this matter.

But even if animal suffering is indeed a mystery beyond comprehension, let us at least attempt to give a rationale for it. One point to note when we consider the suffering experienced by animals is that it is generally the savagery exhibited by other animals which is the cause of their suffering. Although Judaism states that there are noble traits to be learned from the animal kingdom, there are clearly many undesirable traits to be found also. In fact, animals are fundamentally motivated by selfish drives. Long before this was stated by evolutionists, we find similar statements in the Talmud:

> Rav Nachman bar Rav Chisda expounded: What does it mean when it writes, "And God formed (*vayyitzer*) man" with two *yodin*? The Holy One created two inclinations, one good and one evil. Rav Nachman bar Yitzchak asked: But if so, then an animal, which does not have written concerning it, "And he formed," does not have an inclination; and yet we see that it damages and bites and kicks!
>
> Talmud, *Berachos* 61a; see Maharsha ad loc.

This would appear to be referring to animals being governed by the simple and selfish instincts of hunger and so on:

> With animals, there is no difference between the purpose of one species and the purpose of another, or between the formation of a male and the formation of a female; the intent with all of them is a single purpose, and that is the perpetuation of the species.
>
> Rabbi Yosef Albo, *Sefer Ha-Ikkarim* 3:2

There are two possible benefits to see in the selfish savagery of the animal kingdom. One is that we see that selfish drives, when focused in a broader sense, bring benefits. Animals benefit from symbiotic relationships, even though each individual is working for his own benefit. A lesson can be taken here for humans. The truth is that all actions can be viewed as selfish in motivation—even an act of charity is done for the performer to feel good about himself.[1] But it is a selfish act that helps others, rather than a selfish act that helps nobody.

---

1 Cf. Rabbi Eliyahu Dessler, *Michtav Me-Eliyahu* vol. I p. 45.

A second purpose to nature's savagery is perhaps that man should realize what he has to elevate himself beyond. Man is born as a selfish animal, but he has to learn to elevate himself to act selflessly. It is a fundamental part of God's plan for man that he should possess free will, which necessarily includes the potential to sink into an animal-like existence.[1]

> Man has choice in his deeds; he can be drawn after his intellect, to be like the uppermost beings, or after his physicality, and be like the animals and beasts... And therefore, so as to spur him on, he was created on the same day as the other animals, dwelling amongst them, with their lowly spirit and mortality; that he should not think that they are innately lesser beings than him... But the difference between them is from the perspective of the intellect within him, and therefore man should strengthen himself to distance himself from their material ways, and to devote himself to his intellect, for in this way he acquires a name and a continuation for his soul; and if he does not act thus, his end will be like that of the animals and beasts, just as they all began together on a single day.
>
> Abarbanel, Commentary to Genesis, p. 66

As we shall see later, Ramban states that man was a non-human brute before he became human. Perhaps this serves to teach us that where there is progression there can also be regression, and it is possible to sink back into the state of being a brute. Perhaps God wants man to realize that if he allows his humanity to be compromised, then all the terrible evils of which the animal world is capable could be his lot too. God's plan for creation demands that there be an animal world full of savagery in order to make man realize what lies in store for him if he allows himself to slip.[2]

A Destructive Process and a Loving God

We have discussed the matter of the deaths of individual creatures, but there is a further difficulty, centering on the concept of the evolution of

---

1 As we shall see later, Ramban in his commentary to Genesis 2:7 states that Adam was a non-human brute before he became human. Perhaps this serves to teach us that where there is progression there can also be regression, and it is possible to sink back into the state of being a brute.

2 I am indebted to Rabbi Moshe Eisemann for his assistance in developing this idea.

new species and the extinction of old ones. The history of the world shows that new species have continually come into existence, which Darwinian doctrine explains to be due to "survival of the fittest." This is claimed to stand in contradiction to a benevolent God:

> Indeed, if the world's species had been created by the wise and loving deity imagined by the creationists, why should more than 99 percent of them be extinct?
>
> Douglas Futuyma, Science on Trial, p. 121

The question is that surely a wise and loving deity would not need to use such a wasteful process in order to produce the world as we have it today. Darwinian evolution, on the other hand, does purport to account for the numerous extinctions that have taken place.

Here, yet again, the principle of the response is the same as our response to the earlier objections. Since Darwinian evolution is argued to be an excellent method of producing the diversity of life via natural means, why shouldn't the Creator use such a system? When Darwin first introduced evolutionary theory, some theists welcomed it as helping the religious worldview for this very reason. Asa Gray (1810-1888), professor of natural science at Harvard, was the most notable proponent of this "Darwinian teleology":

> Darwinian teleology has the special advantage of accounting for the imperfections and failures as well as for successes. It not only accounts for them, but turns them to practical account. It explains the seeming waste as being part and parcel of a great economical process. Without the competing multitude, no struggle for life; and without this, no natural selection and survival of the fittest, no continuous adaptation to changing surroundings, no diversification and improvement, leading from lower up to higher and nobler forms. So the most puzzling things of all to the old-school teleologists are the principia of the Darwinian. In this system the forms and species, in all their variety, are not mere ends in themselves, but the whole a series of means and ends, in the contemplation of which we may obtain higher and more comprehensive, and perhaps worthier, as well as more consistent, views of design in Nature than heretofore. At least, it would appear that in Darwinian evolution we may have a theory that accords with if it does not explain the principal facts, and a teleology that is free from the

common objections… We have only to say that the Darwinian system, as we understand it, coincides well with the theistic view of Nature.

Asa Gray, *Darwiniana: Essays and Reviews Pertaining to Darwinism*,
article XIII

Again, however, we need not limit ourselves to this response. The idea of mass destruction is not something of which Judaism has been unaware. The Midrash that we cited earlier, written well before extinctions were documented, notes that God destroyed entire worlds:

> Rabbi Yehudah bar Simon said: It does not say, "Let there be evening," but "And it was evening." Hence we derive that there was a time system prior to this. Rabbi Avahu said: This teaches us that God created worlds and destroyed them, saying, "This one pleases Me; those did not please Me."
>
> *Midrash Bereishis Rabbah* 3:7

The "loving deity" clearly manifests His love in more subtle ways than by simply letting everything live forever. Some may still ask how the idea of "trial and error" fits with the concept of a God Who knows the consequences of His actions. Still, it is clear from this Midrash that such was part of the Jewish understanding of God many thousands of years before extinctions were discovered by science. If such phenomena were always our understanding of how God works, then the explanation of the physical mechanisms via evolution cannot be said to challenge religion.

Furthermore, the pattern of the replacement of old species by newer and more advanced models is actually consistent with the theistic model of the universe and stands in conflict with the steady-state model of existence that lay in the thought-patterns of atheists until this century. It is precisely with the Torah perspective that the universe is seen as ever progressing towards the ultimate perfection of the Messianic era, as we discussed earlier.

Malbim explicitly writes that the destruction of earlier creations and their replacement by more advanced successors is what the Torah describes as "good":

> Everywhere in the creation narrative, it concludes with, "And God saw that it was good." This was meant to emphasize that notwithstanding the fact that each successive stage of creation was *yesh mi-yesh*, which

means that it came about at the expense of the destruction of what had been before—in the pattern of God creating worlds and then destroying them—and all annihilation is evil from the perspective of that which is annihilated, nevertheless, since its purpose was to effect an improvement, a higher stage in Creation, it was seen by God as good.

Malbim, Commentary to Genesis 1:4

The extinctions of nature have been part and parcel of a process that has led to more advanced forms of life, ultimately culminating in mankind. While this may present problems for the conception of God held by atheists, it is seen in the Torah, according to Malbim's explanation, as something positively good.

Chapter Twenty-Three

The Ascent of Man

The Desire For Reconciliation

Some people are mystified and horrified that anyone would want to reconcile the Torah's account of man's origins with the scientific idea that man evolved from animals. The story is often cited of the nineteenth-century Rabbi Simcha Zissel Ze'ev, otherwise known as the Alter from Kelm, who stated that had Darwin seen his saintly mentor, Rabbi Yisrael Salanter, he would not have been able to propose the theory of evolution. He argued that Rabbi Salanter was such a refined human being that nobody who encountered him could have entertained the idea that he evolved from a monkey.[1]

But those who have studied biology and anthropology—the science of human origins—find compelling reason to believe this. There are several different lines of evidence for man having evolved from apes.[2] Many of these are the same as those lines of evidence that we earlier discussed regarding the common ancestry of animals. For example, there is the fossil evidence. While there have been some infamous forgeries, such as Piltdown

---

1 Rabbi Ahron Soloveitchik, *Logic of the Heart, Logic of the Mind*, p. 55.

2 Strictly speaking, the evolutionary perspective is not that man evolved from present-day apes, but rather that both man and apes evolved from a common apelike ancestor, which in turn evolved from a more primitive mammal, and so on. However, for the sake of convenience, we shall refer to the notion of man evolving from apes; there is, in any case, no qualitative difference between an ape and an ape's apelike ancestor.

man, this does not detract from the fact that there are many authentic fossils of primitive humans. These do not conclusively prove that humans evolved from apes, but when one finds that there is a succession of bipedal humanoids over the last million years, which change from a more apelike to a more humanlike physiology, this is strongly suggestive of the idea that the latter developed from the former.

A cast of the skull of Australopithecus afarensis, *a hominid that lived over three million years ago, pictured next to the skull of a modern human.*

Another line of evidence is that people have various physiological aspects that make much more sense in the light of their having evolved from apes. We have wisdom teeth that are of no help and can cause considerable problems, but would understandably exist if we evolved from apes that possessed longer jaws. The hairs on the back of our neck stand on end when we are afraid; this is of no use whatsoever, but it would make sense if we evolved from animals that erect such a mane in order to appear larger and scare away predators. Goosebumps presently have no known function, but on a cold furry animal, they fluff up its fur and trap air for insulation. Our lower backs often cause problems by the time we reach our forties, and do not seem well-engineered for long-term upright posture, but this is understandable if the spine was originally developed for the horizontal posture of an animal. For all these aspects, there is no doubt that a sufficiently creative person could contrive some sort of function, or claim that one still exists to be discovered, but it is certainly reasonable to conclude instead that man evolved from animals.

Then there are records of ancient and primitive civilizations. In France, there are cave-paintings depicting primitive hunts that have been reliably dated to thirty thousand years ago. The aboriginal settlement in Australia dates back at least forty thousand years. These and many other such pieces of evidence indicate that man evolved from a more primitive ancestry.

Thus, while there are those who would dispute, dismiss or ignore the evidence for human evolution, there are also those who find it extremely convincing and are greatly disturbed by the seeming contradiction that this raises with the Torah account. In this chapter we shall discuss resolutions for this difficulty.

Tradition and Innovation

There is no source in classical Jewish thought which states that man is part of the evolutionary tree. Yet this should not come as a surprise; after all, medieval Jewish scholars were not confronted with fossils of primitive man or any of the other reasons to posit such a relationship. However, what we can do is to explore whether there is anything innately problematic in believing that God used an animal as the raw material from which to create man; as we shall see, Ramban and others state that man was made from a two-legged being that was qualitatively no different from an animal. Furthermore, we shall find that there is considerable *conceptual* basis in classical Jewish thought for the idea of man emerging from the animal kingdom. This means that while classical authorities did not state that man evolved from animals, they did discuss concepts that fit well with this model. Rabbi Joseph B. Soloveitchik, in a recent posthumously published manuscript that bases an extensive discussion of man's nature on such a position, argues that it has a powerful basis in ancient Jewish thought:

> Our task now is to investigate the cogency of the almost dogmatic assertion that the Bible proclaimed the separateness of man from nature and his otherness. It is certain that the fathers of the Church and also the Jewish medieval scholars believed that the Bible preached this doctrine. Medieval and even modern Jewish moralists have almost canonized this viewpoint and attributed to it apodictic validity. Yet the consensus of many, however great and distinguished, does not prove the truth or falseness of a particular belief. I have always felt that due to some erroneous conception, we have actually misunderstood the Judaic anthropology and read into the Biblical text ideas which stem from an alien source. This feeling becomes more pronounced when we try to read the Bible not as an isolated literary text but as a manifestation of a grand tradition rooted in the very essence of our God-consciousness that transcends the bounds of the standardized and fixed text and fans out into every aspect of our existential experience. The sooner Biblical texts are placed in their proper setting—namely, the Oral Tradition

with its almost endless religious awareness—the clearer and more certain I am that Judaism does not accent unreservedly the theory of man's isolationism and separatism within the natural order of things.

Rabbi Joseph B. Soloveitchik, *The Emergence of Ethical Man*, p. 6

Natural vs. Supernatural Creation

There are two basic objections to the notion that man evolved from an apelike ancestor. One is based on the literal reading of the Torah, which indicates that man was created directly from the dust of the earth. A second objection is based on the conceptual issue of man being fundamentally different from animals.

We shall deal with the latter issue first. This conceptual difficulty in turn arises from both traditional Jewish ideology, which regards man as a fundamentally different being than animals, and also from Scriptural verses such as the following:

> And God said, Let us make mankind in our image, after our likeness; and let them have dominion over the fish of the sea, and over the birds of the air, and over the cattle, and over all the earth, and over every creeping thing that creeps upon the earth. So God created man in His own image, in the image of God He created him; male and female He created them.
>
> Genesis 1:26-27

Many people consider it difficult to understand how man could be created in the image of God if he is descended from an ape. The Torah depicts man as being of the noblest creation, while evolutionists present an extremely degrading view.

Now, let us first raise a simple question to those who consider the evolutionary account of man's origins to be degrading. Such people would doubtless also find it offensive to posit that man evolved from dogs. Or rats. Or frogs. Or worms. Or mushrooms. Or dirt? And yet the Torah says that man was made from dirt!

Why is it any less degrading to say that man is made from dirt? One reason is that although dirt is not more dignified than an ape, turning dirt directly into a human requires more visible work at the hand of God than turning an ape into a human. It therefore does initially seem to be removing God from the picture when speaking of man's gradual evolution from the animal kingdom.

Yet according to the Maimonidean approach that we discussed earlier, it is in no way demeaning when God uses natural processes. On the contrary; the structure and law of natural processes are considered to testify to His greatness. While some are inspired at the idea of a man-shaped piece of clay miraculously coming to life, *golem*-style, it can be argued to be part of the grandeur of God that He instead formed man through a remarkably structured process, the "creative wisdom" of which Rabbi Hirsch spoke.

The Essence of Man

There is, however, a more profound reason why people find it degrading to state that man came from apes, but not to state that he came from dirt. There is an obvious fundamental difference between man and dirt; clearly the former could not have come from the latter without significant divine intervention. This in turn means that there was a divine component to man's creation that makes him now unmistakably different from dirt. Positing that man came from apes, on the other hand, does not suggest that divine intervention was involved and that man possesses a spiritual component that apes lack.

Yet in clarifying the objection in this way, the solution becomes obvious. Human evolution can become acceptable as long as one still maintains that there was a spiritual component to his creation. In other words, as long as man contains a spiritual aspect that animals do not possess, the origin of his physical body is of no significance.

It is this soul which makes the difference between man and animals. In fact, the soul is more than just the most important component of man; it fundamentally defines him.

> Man stands in a single category with the Higher Beings, due to his being similar to them in that he possesses an intellect as they do. When you ask about this: Surely the fact of man possessing an intellect is an exceptional feature of his category, not a classifying characteristic; since he is only similar to the Higher Regions in his possessing a communicating intellect, and is different from them in possessing life

321

like the physical life of animals, which are in his category, then how can he be grouped together in the category with the Higher Regions, when his category is different from theirs? It is for this reason that I prefaced this with saying that the true definition of man is that he is a living communicating being. My intent was that the true, fundamental essence of man is in his intellectual soul. That is to say, a human being, from the aspect of his essence and source, has no relevance to the lower regions at all, but rather to the Higher Regions. His physical body is peripheral to his identity and is not the essence of it.

Malbim, Commentary to Psalms 8:6[1]

Man's fundamental identity is his spiritual nature, not his physical body. One fascinating manifestation of this idea is seen in the laws of naming people. A person's full Hebrew name is always given together with his father's name; for example, my own Hebrew name is Nosson Nota Moshe *ben* (son of) Menachem Asher. But when a person converts to Judaism and receives a Hebrew name, his biological father's name is not included. Instead, he is called "*ben* Avraham," and a woman is called "*bat* (daughter of) Sarah," since Avraham and Sarah were the ancestors of the Jewish People. Converts are considered to be more fundamentally linked to their new spiritual ancestors than to their biological parents. This is a powerful demonstration that the significance of man is in his spiritual nature, and his biological ancestry is largely irrelevant.

The critical factor in defining man is to state that he possesses a soul that came from Above. It is perfectly legitimate to believe that God created the soul and placed it in a hominid, which then became "a living soul"—a human being. From a religious point of view, it is untenable to say that man is nothing more than an intelligent ape. But the theory that man was created by developing a soul within a hominid creature which itself evolved from earlier creatures is not qualitatively different than talking about the embryo evolving from a sperm and egg. Although a sperm and

---

1   A seemingly contrasting perspective is presented by Rabbi Joseph B. Soloveitchik, in *The Emergence of Ethical Man*, p. 9: "…We come across a duel concept of man in the Bible. His element of transcendence was well-known to the Biblical Jew. Yet transcendence was always seen against the background of naturalness. The canvas was man's immanence; transcendence was just projected on it as a display of colors. It was more a modifying than a basic attribute of man."

egg are purely physical constructs, the Torah teaches us that the human soul, with its divine spark, enters the embryo. Likewise, the human soul developed in the evolving animal when it became a man.[1]

With this in mind, let us reconsider the claim of Rabbi Simcha Zissel Ze'ev that nobody who saw Rabbi Yisrael Salanter could believe that man evolved from apes. Now, Rabbi Salanter was once nothing more than a drop of sperm and an egg, which is an even lesser being than an ape. Surely, nobody who saw Rabbi Yisrael Salanter could have believed that he developed from a drop of sperm and egg without any added spiritual component. The point is that the amazingly refined nature of Rabbi Salanter demonstrated that man is so much more than just an ape or an egg. The argument is only that man must now possess something that apes lack, not that man's body could not have originated in a lower form of life.

Rabbi Joseph Hertz makes an allusion to Darwin's book on human origins, *The Descent of Man*, and beautifully expresses the idea that man's soul makes all the difference:

> …It is not so much the descent, but the *ascent* of man, which is decisive… it is not the resemblance, but the *differences* between man and ape, that are of infinite importance. It is the differences between them that constitute the humanity of man, the God-likeness of man. The qualities that distinguish the lowest man from the highest brute make the differences between them differences in kind rather than in degree; so much so that, whatever man might have inherited from his animal ancestors, his advent can truly be spoken of as a specific Divine act, whereby a new being had arisen with God-like possibilities within him, and conscious of these God-like possibilities within him.
>
> Rabbi Joseph Hertz, *The Pentateuch*, Additional Notes to Genesis p. 194

The Evolution of Man

One significant source for the concept of human evolution is to be found in Ramban's commentary to the Torah. Although he does not propose the concept of man evolving from animals, he does expound

---

1 For an extensive discussion of the differences between man and animals in the Torah worldview, see my book *Man And Beast*.

the idea that man evolved from a lower being that was not qualitatively different from animals in any way whatsoever. Thus, it is effectively the same as if man had evolved from animals.

Ramban mentions this concept in several places. At one juncture, he discusses the dispute between Plato and Aristotle concerning the nature of the human soul, and shows that both views have support in Jewish tradition. Plato's view was that the human soul is a single indivisible entity, comprised of a vegetative-like power of growth, an animalistic life-force, and a rational intellect. Aristotle, on the other hand, took the position that these three components are distinct; in other words, a human being contains the growth-nature of a plant, the animate life of an animal, with a rational intellect superimposed on top of that.[1] Ramban explains how Scripture should be understood according to this view:

> If this is so, when Scripture states, "And the Lord God formed the man," it refers to the formation of a mobile being. Man was formed in that he became an animate being; for "formation" here refers to life and sentience, via which he became a man instead of a clump of earth. And this is in the same way as it states, "And the Lord God formed all the beasts of the field from the earth… and He brought them to man." And after He formed him with sentience, He blew into his nostrils the "soul of life" from the mouth of the High One, to add this soul on to the aforementioned formation.
>
> Ramban, Commentary to Genesis 2:7

Thus, there were two stages in the creation of man. In the first, man was formed to be an animal like any other. In the second stage, he was given a human soul that set him apart from animals. Ramban elsewhere explains that the raw material used for the formation of both animals and the physical aspect of man was the same, and only man's divine soul was made from something altogether different:

> The earth shall bring forth [man's] body from the elements, as it did for the animals and beasts… and He, blessed be He, would supply the spirit from the mouth of the High One, as it is written, "and He blew into his nostrils the soul of life."
>
> Ramban, Commentary to Genesis 1:26

---

1 Aristotle, *On The Soul* II:2.

Ramban also addresses a Midrash that expounds upon the Torah's account of the creation of animal life. Astonishingly, the Midrash states that this act of creation also includes the creation of man:

> "Let the earth bring forth a spirit of life, each according to its kind" (Genesis 1:24)—Rabbi Elazar said: "A spirit of life" refers to the spirit of the first man.
>
> *Midrash Bereishis Rabbah 7 (cf. Midrash Tanchuma, Tazria 1)*

Ramban explains that this "soul" refers to the animal aspect of man:

> ...Rabbi Elazar could not be saying that "Let the earth bring forth" refers at all to the [uniquely human] soul of the first man, but rather to that which I mentioned; to say that the creation of man's *spirit*, which is the life-force in the blood, was made from the earth in the same utterance as the beasts and animals. For all the animate life-forces were made together, and after that He created bodies for them; first He made the bodies for the animals and beasts, and then the body of man, and placed this life-force in it. And afterwards, He blew the higher soul into him, for it is because of this separate soul within him that a distinct [creative] utterance was attributed to God, Who gave it to him.
>
> Ramban, Commentary to Genesis 1:26

The Midrash even states that before man received his uniquely spiritual element, he was physically similar to an animal:

> "And man became as a living soul" (alternatively, "a beast with a soul")—Rabbi Yehudah said: This teaches that He made him a tail, like a beast, and then returned to take it away from him, for his honor.
>
> *Midrash Bereishis Rabbah 14:10*

Thus, the physical aspect of man—his body, and his being alive—is not qualitatively different in any way from that of animals, and was part of the same creation. It is only man's uniquely spiritual component that sets him apart from animals.

Ramban's explanation is also found in the commentary of Rabbi Ovadiah Seforno:

> "And He blew into his nostrils the breath of life" (Genesis 2:7)—A living soul, ready to accept the image of God... nevertheless, "and man

was as a living being"—he was still only a living creature, unable to speak, until he was created in [God's] image and likeness.

Commentary to Genesis 2:7

Ramban and Seforno were unaware of modern paleontological evidence and biological theory, and thus did not address the idea of man's body originating from animals. Yet their understanding of philosophy and Scripture led them to explain that man was first created in a form not qualitatively different from that of an animal, and only later did man receive "the image of God"—his intellectual capacity and immortal soul. From the explanations of Ramban and Seforno, it becomes clear that there can be no fundamental theological objection to man's physical body evolving from animals. As Rabbi Gedalyah Nadel notes:

> Regarding Seforno's basic point, that the creation of man in the image of God was the conclusion of a lengthy process, which began in a non-rational being under the category of animals, that processed to develop until it acquired human intellect, and also the physiological appearance of man with which we are familiar—it is reasonable that this is a correct description. The evidence of Darwin and of paleontologists, regarding the existence of earlier stages, appears convincing…

> As long as there is recognition of the Divine will that functions in nature via spiritual forces (*mal'achim*), there is no need whatsoever to negate the description of events that scientific investigation presents today. There are discoveries of skeletons of bipeds with a small skull, whose brain could not have been like the brain of the human being that we know. The man about which it is said, "Let us make man in Our image," was the final stage of a gradual process.

Rabbi Gedalyah Nadel, BeToraso Shel Rav Gedalyah, p. 100

The Wild Side of Man

Positing that man is defined by his spiritual nature does not negate the idea that man has an important physical component too. Judaism has long been aware of man's animal side.

> The Hebrew Bible is cognizant of man as a natural being found on the same plane as the animal and the plant. Indeed, such an idea is a motivating force in Jewish ethics and metaphysics. The nihility, instability, helplessness and vulnerability of man—human life and

death—are popular themes of prophets who contrast him with the eternity, unchangeability, everlasting life and omnipotence of the Creator. All those negative traits suggest the naturalness and immanence of man rather than his spirituality and transcendence.

Rabbi Joseph B. Soloveitchik, *The Emergence of Ethical Man*, p. 7

This does not mean that man does not also possess a uniquely spiritual element; but it does mean that Judaism perceives this element as existing within a physical being that is otherwise no different from animals.

Furthermore, we find that the distinctions between people and animals are not necessarily as absolute as is commonly assumed. The Mishnah discusses a view that apes may possess certain humanlike spiritual aspects:

> *Adnei ha-sadeh* is rated as an animal. Rabbi Yosi says: It causes spiritual impurity (when dead) in a building like a human being.
>
> Mishnah, *Kilayim* 8:5

The *adnei ha-sadeh* is explained by several authorities to refer to great apes such as the orangutan and chimpanzee.[1] According to Rabbi Yosi, a dead ape possesses the same degree of spiritual impurity as a dead human being. We see from this that the special status of man is not harmed by some of his traits being possessed by animals too.

We also find that many classical sources discuss the idea that God used the character traits of the animal kingdom in constructing man. This is one explanation given for the phrase "Let *us* make man"—the animals provided various attributes, and God combined them with a soul to make man.[2] If the animals are even considered to provide the character traits of man, it is certainly easy to see that they might have provided the physical components.

It is interesting to note that in the account of the six days of creation, it states that man was created on the same day as animals. One would certainly expect that man, as the most important part of creation, would

---

1 See *Perush HaMishnayos* and *Tiferes Yisrael* ad loc., Malbim to Leviticus 11:27, and this author's *Mysterious Creatures* pp. 209-217.

2 Vilna Gaon, *Aderes Eliyahu*, Genesis 1:26; Malbim; Rabbi Gedalyah Schorr, *Ohr Gedalyahu, parashas Noach*.

merit his own day to be created, rather than sharing it with animals. Yet the Torah teaches us that man is instead part of the natural order:

> Man in the story of creation does not occupy a unique ontic position. He is, rather, a drop of the cosmos that fits into the schemata of naturalness and concreteness.
>
> Rabbi Joseph B. Soloveitchik, *The Emergence of Ethical Man*, p. 12

Ran[1] and Abarbanel explain this in terms of man not necessarily being any different from animals. Abarbanel cites the verse:

> ...the difference between man and beast is nothing...
>
> Ecclesiastes 3:19

...and explains it to refer to the physical aspect of man. From a purely physical perspective, man is not superior to an animal.

> Why was there no day designated uniquely for the creation of man? ...Another answer is that all those beings that had a day dedicated to their creation had this because they possess an existing quality that is actually found with them and which cannot be separated from them. But man is not so; for his perfection is not actually born with him. He has choice in his deeds; he can be drawn after his intellect, to be like the uppermost beings, or after his physicality, and be like the animals and beasts... And therefore, so as to spur him on, he was created on the same day as the other living creatures, dwelling amongst them, with their lowly spirit and mortality; that he should not think that they are innately lesser beings than him, "for as the death of one is the death of the other, and one spirit"—of [physical] life—"is to them all, for the difference between man and animal is nothing"—in matters pertaining to their physical nature—"for all is emptiness" (Ecclesiastes 3:19). But the difference between them is from the perspective of the intellect within him, and therefore man should strengthen himself to distance himself from their material ways, and to devote himself to his intellect, for in this way he acquires a name and a continuation for his soul; and if he does not act thus, his end will be like that of the animals and beasts, just as they all began together on a single day.
>
> Abarbanel, Commentary to Genesis, p. 66

---

1 *Derashos HaRan* 1.

If man does not fulfill his spiritual potential, he remains nothing more than an animal. But if he puts the soul that was created within him to good use, then he becomes a human being.

Ramban sees fit to justify why indeed man was created with a different utterance from that used to create animals:

> "And God said, Let us make man"—A separate utterance was devoted to the making of man because of his exalted status; his nature is not like the nature of the beasts and animals that God created with the preceding utterance.
>
> Ramban, Commentary to Genesis 1:26

Man is different from animals in possessing a higher type of soul, which is why there was a separate utterance for his creation; but he is similar to animals in possessing a body with an animate spirit, which is why man and animals were created on the same day. Rabbi Yosef Gaon Mechasya, in discussing this idea, brings Scriptural support for this:[1]

> …Man is born as a wild animal…
>
> Job 11:12

A baby leads a solely physical, selfish existence—"for the inclination of the heart of man is evil from his youth" (Genesis 8:21)—only later does he acquire the capacity for intellectual and spiritual growth. When man is young, he is no different from a wild animal; he must spiritually evolve beyond that. The same idea can be applied to mankind. The real significance of man's nature does not lie in his physical origins but in how much he has transcended them.

The Opposition to Evolutionists

We can well understand the vehement opposition to human evolution by some elements in the religious community. The secular evolutionist sees man as nothing more than his physical component, and claims that there is no fundamental difference between ape and man. The prominent spokesman for evolution, Stephen Jay Gould, is unequivocal about this:

---

1 *Ginzei Kedem*, vol. 3, p. 60, cited by Kasher, *Torat HaBeriah*.

> ...An evolutionist must add the defining voice of history: You are what you have been and what your closest genealogical nexus shares. Think kinship.
>
> Stephen Jay Gould, *Dinosaur in a Haystack*, p. 400

Such dismissal of the religious outlook is baseless, quite aside from being highly offensive. The spiritual nature of man is not something that can be seen under a microscope, and positing that man's physical origins are from apes does not state anything about man's fundamental identity. In light of such strident non-scientific pronouncements by prominent evolutionists, we can well understand why many people are so reluctant to accept the scientific evidence for the physical origins of man. There is an enormous amount at stake: is man just another physical creature, or does he possess a spiritual side that renders him a fundamentally different being? If the former, then there is no objective reason for him to act any different from animals; whereas the moral calling of Judaism is predicated upon the latter view.[1] When certain evolutionists insist that a physical origin from animals necessarily rules out a spiritual side of man, we can well sympathize with those who take their word for it and deny man's physical origins in order to maintain his spiritual uniqueness.

With so much at stake, we can understand why the Torah would not explicitly state that man physically evolved from animals. It was far more important for the Jewish People to be made aware of man's fundamental difference from animals than his physical relationship to them. As we discussed earlier, not every truth can be unleashed upon mankind at once, and the best development may require the temporary suppression of certain truths in order for more important ones to be adequately ingrained in the human psyche:

> The Torah certainly obscures the [meaning of] the act of creation... What is most important about the act of creation is what we learn in regard to the knowledge of God and the truly moral life. The Holy One, who precisely measures out even the revelation of the prophets, has determined that only through the images of the stories of Genesis would mankind, with great effort, be capable of drawing out all that is beneficial and exalted in the great matters inherent in the act of

---

1   See my book *Man And Beast* for further discussion of this point.

creation… The crux of the matter is that the time of the appearance and the effects of every idea and thought is predetermined. Nothing is haphazard.

Rabbi Avraham Yitzchak Kook, Igros HaRe'iyah, letter 91

Differences in Kind, Differences in Degree

Some components of man, such as his higher soul, appear to be uniquely spiritual and exclusive to man. Other components seem to be only quantitatively different from those characteristics possessed by animals, and yet are still described in Jewish tradition as being uniquely human traits. Intelligence, potential for character growth, and the power of communication, are all found to a certain extent amongst higher order animals. Some argue that these differences in degree are actually critical differences in kind.[1] However, their fine distinctions are debatable. But as we shall now explore, the qualitative difference between man and animals in these areas can exist even if these aspects exist with animals to a lesser degree.

As noted earlier, there is a concept that existence is divided into a hierarchy of four levels. The lowest level is *domem*, inanimate matter such as rocks or water. The second level is *tzome'ach*, plants that grow. The third level is *chai*, living creatures. The fourth and highest level is *medaber*, man, the communicating being. However, as we saw earlier, all these levels are not as distinct as is commonly assumed. They all possess intermediates. We are forced to acknowledge that gradual ranges do exist and are part of God's design for the world. We must now work out how it is then possible to speak of fundamental differences between man and animals.

In describing a physical continuum from animals to man, Darwin believed that he had thereby ruled out any qualitative differences between the two:

> There is no fundamental difference between man and the higher mammals in their mental faculties... The difference in mind between

---

1 Mortimer J. Adler, *The Difference of Man and the Difference it Makes,* with regard to speech on pp. 114-118; regarding tool-making and culture, on p. 121.

man and the higher animals, great as it is, certainly is one of degree and not of kind.

Charles Darwin, The Descent of Man

Darwin thereby aroused the ire of the religious establishment. But the truth is that it was his ideological conclusion, rather than his description of biological relationships, that was heretical. Unlike Darwin, we say that there is indeed a difference in kind between man and animal regarding their mental faculties (aside from the other differences), not just in degree. Perhaps it is more accurate to phrase it as follows: Judaism maintains that a difference in degree *creates* a difference in kind.

This is a widespread concept in Judaism. Torah law is often about distinguishing black and white out of a spectrum of shades of gray.

> The Rabbis established that all produce that is harvested on Sukkos has grown one third by Rosh HaShanah… Rabbi Yirmiyah said to Rabbi Zeira: Can the rabbis really distinguish between a third and that which is less than a third? He replied, Did I not tell you, do not remove yourself from the realm of *halachah*? All the prescribed amounts of the Sages work in this way; a person may fulfill immersion in forty *se'ah*, but if it is forty *se'ah* less one *kurtuv*, he cannot immerse. The volume of an egg transmits impurity of food, but the volume of an egg less a sesame seed does not transmit impurity of food. An area of three by three (hand's-breadths) conducts *tumah madras*, but an area of three by three less a single hairsbreadth does not cause *tumah madras*.
>
> Talmud, Rosh HaShanah 13a

The fourteenth century scholar Rabbi Yom Tov Ibn Asevilli, better known by the acronym Ritva, explains:

> …It would be impossible to give a required measure for anything, for a person would always be able to be pedantic and say with any measurement that it shouldn't affect it to add or subtract a tiny quantity, and all required measurements would thereby be rendered useless…
>
> Ritva, Commentary ad loc.

Law, by its very nature, necessitates drawing strict lines, or else it falls apart. There is a continuous spectrum between day and night, and yet we say that one is Friday, and the next is Shabbos. A healthy person is prohibited from eating on Yom Kippur; a sick person is *obligated* to eat on

332

Yom Kippur. And yet there is no single objective point at which a person changes from healthy to sick. Instead, there is a continuous spectrum of physical health to sickness. Yet at one point, we draw the line, and say that a person on one side of the line is prohibited from eating, and a person on the other side of the line is obligated to eat.

There may indeed be a continuous spectrum of communication ability or intelligence from turtles through apes to man. Yet the Torah has drawn the line between them. The former are animals and the latter is man.

Adam from the Earth

The literal contradiction between the Torah's description of man's origins and the evolutionary theory that he descended from an apelike ancestor is clear:

> And the Lord God formed man of the dust of the ground, and breathed into his nostrils the breath of life; and man became a living soul.

> Genesis 2:7

The Torah, at a simple literal level, states that man was created from the dust of the ground, not from an apelike creature. Yet this is far from an insurmountable difficulty. As we noted previously, contradictions with the literal reading of Genesis are not problematic. Rambam noted that many parts of the Creation story are metaphoric in intent; Rabbi Dessler explained that it is simply written in an easy way for man to grasp.

There are two ways of interpreting this verse. One is that the entire phrase "forming man from the dust of the earth" is an abstraction of a deeper concept about the fundamental nature of man. We could relate this to the discussion of Maharal, for example, who explains that there is a fundamental conceptual similarity between man and earth. Man is named *adam*, after the *adamah*, as with both of them there is so much more than meets the eye. The earth contains the hidden potential of all the plant life that grows from it; and man contains the hidden potential of his soul, which it is his duty to fulfill.[1] It is easy to see that the conceptual relationship of man to earth is far more important to convey than the science of the formation of his body.

---

1 Maharal, *Tiferes Yisrael* 3.

But there is also a simpler way of interpreting the verse; that the "dust of the earth" is simply an idiom for "raw material":

> The description of the formation of man from the dust is by way of allegory and parable. The Holy One did not take a spoonful of dirt and knead it with water, as children do in kindergarten. The "dust" here is raw material, from which animals were also formed.
>
> Rabbi Gedalyah Nadel, *BeToraso Shel Rav Gedalyah*, p.99

Either method of interpretation is possible, and according to both approaches, the literal text of the Torah presents no reason not to accept that man evolved from animals.

If we return to looking at the overall pattern of the six days of creation, an interesting idea about man emerges:

One: Light	Four: Luminaries
Two: Sea and Sky	Five: Fish and Birds
Three: Land and vegetation	Six: Animals and man

As we noted earlier, there are parallels between the first set of three days and the second set of three days. One such parallel is that on both the third and the sixth days, there were two distinct acts of creation rather than one. On the third day, the land was separated away from the waters, and plants grew from it. On the sixth day, God created animals and also man.

But perhaps the parallel runs even deeper. The relationship between the land and plants is similar to the relationship between animals and man. Plants are what emerges from the land when it is implanted with a higher element—with the spark of life. Man is what emerges from the animal kingdom when it is implanted with a higher element—with the divine soul.[1]

---

1   Cf. Norbert Samuelson, *Judaism and the Doctrine of Creation*, p. 163: "....it might also be the case that as the vegetation crowns the work of the first unit and points to the work of the second unit, so the human crowns the work of the second unit and points to the work of the third unit. In other words, by observing the Sabbath, man transcends the creation of this world."

There may even be an intriguing allusion to this idea in the text. The simple explanation as to why man is called Adam would appear to be that it is because he was made from the *adamah*, the earth. Elsewhere, the Torah likens man to a tree in several instances—"for man is the tree of the field" (Deuteronomy 20:19),[1] "and he shall be like a tree planted by streams of water, that brings forth its fruit in its season" (Psalms 1:3). Putting these ideas together tells us that *adamah* is the raw material to which a soul is added to make man, and the final product is compared to a tree. Thus, the following pattern emerges:

Day Three: *Adamah* plus life-force => plants

Day Six: Animals plus soul => *Adam*

The animals are the raw physical material, the *adamah*. The plants and man are the raw material with a spiritual addition. The above pattern can therefore also be expressed as follows:

Day Three: *Adamah* => plants (=*Adam*)

Day Six: Animals (=*adamah*) => *Adam*

Thus, the text itself hints at the idea that man's physical component was made from animals, just as the physical component of plants comes from the earth.

The natural world is divided into four levels: mineral (*domem*), vegetable (*tzome'ach*), animal (*chai*) and man (*medaber*). These four categories contain a parallelism. The difference between vegetable and mineral is the same as the difference between man and animals. Just as vegetable emerges from mineral with an added ingredient, so too does man emerge from animal with an added ingredient.

When Was Man Created?

Having established the legitimacy of reconciling man's physical evolutionary origins with the Torah, the next question to be addressed is when this took place. According to the Jewish calendar, man was created

---

1   See *The Emergence of Ethical Man* p. 24.

5,766 years preceding the year of this book's publication, 2006. But *Homo sapiens* has been here for over 100,000 years.

One approach would be that just under six thousand years ago, God implanted a soul into one of these hominids.[1] The hominids that existed before then were human in the biological sense of the term, but not according to the Jewish definition. Adam, the first man with a soul, lived less than six thousand years ago, when civilization took off.[2]

In connection to this, it should be noted that there are many classical Jewish sources indicating that Adam was not the first human being. According to these schools of thought, there were numerous earlier acts of creation, and the one described in the Torah is merely the most recent. This is based upon the statement in the Talmud that there were 974 generations before the appearance of man described by Genesis:[3]

> Rabbi Yehoshua ben Levi said: When Moshe ascended upon high, the ministering angels said before the Holy One: Master of the universe! What is this descendant of woman doing amongst us? He said to them, He has come to receive the Torah. They replied to Him, This hidden treasure that You concealed for 974 generations before the world was created, You seek to give to flesh and blood?
>
> Talmud, *Shabbos* 88b

Rabbi Yisrael Lipschitz, author of *Tiferes Yisrael*, writes that this accounts for the fossils of prehistoric man:

> Notice that large letter *beis* that begins the Torah, and observe its four *taggin* (accent marks). It has been transmitted to us by the Kabbalists that the four *taggin* allude to our world being here for the fourth time,

---

1 This approach is taken by Schroeder, *Genesis and the Big Bang*, p. 150. A similar view is presented by Rabbi Aryeh Kaplan, in *Immortality, Resurrection, and the Age of the Universe*, p. 21.

2 Rabbi Shimon Schwab suggests that there were soul-less men living at the same time as Adam. See *Me'ein Beis HaSho'evah*, Genesis 2:26.

3 Many are of the view that this statement of the Talmud refers to generations that God thought of creating but did not actually create; cf. Talmud, *Chagigah* 13b-14a; *Midrash Koheles Rabbah* 4:3; *Midrash Tanchuma, Lech Lecha* 11, *Yisro* 9; *Midrash Tehillim* 105:3; but there is a manuscript of *Midrash Tehillim* which explains it as referring to generations that were actually created. See *Torah Sheleimah, Bereishis* vol. I section 422, for extensive discussion of this topic.

with all its hosts; and the fact that it is a *beis* (of numerical value 2), written large, indicates that the pinnacle of creation, the intelligent soul of man, now inhabits the world for the second time. For, in my humble opinion, the people who lived in the prehistoric world… that is to say, the people who were in the world before the creation of the Adam HaRishon of the present world, are identical with the 974 pre-Adamite generations referred to in the Talmud tractates of *Shabbos* and *Chagigah*, who were created in the world preceding our own.

Derush Ohr HaChaim

Rabbi Aryeh Kaplan explains further:

Adam was merely the first human being created in the latest cycle. According to these opinions, it would seem that man already had the physical and mental capacities that we possess as early as 974 generations before Adam, or some twenty-five thousand years ago.

Immortality, Resurrection, and the Age of the Universe, p. 21

Yet this explanation involves a serious difficulty. Not all the people in the world today are descended from a single ancestor who lived less than six thousand years ago. We have found evidence that there were people all over the world at that time. If only one person was implanted with a soul, which was then passed on to his descendants, this would mean that many people in the world are not human according to the Torah definition. Obviously, this is a very disturbing proposition.

A variation on this approach would be to suggest that God planted souls into everyone in the world at that time. But there is no hint of any such notion in the Torah. On the contrary; Judaism has always strongly advanced the concept that all mankind came from a common origin:

For this reason was man created alone: to teach you… whoever preserves a single soul of Israel, Scripture ascribes merit to him as though he had preserved a complete world.

Talmud, *Sanhedrin* 37a

While it may be possible to accommodate such solutions, there is an intriguing alternate possibility. The conventional understanding of the account of man in the Creation episode is that a single man was created, who subsequently sinned, was driven from Eden, and fathered Cain and Abel. Yet this is not the only interpretation given. Rabbi Gedalyah Nadel states that the references to Adam in Genesis do not always refer to the same person. Sometimes, the name Adam does not refer to a single person at all but rather to mankind in its entirety:

> When the Torah says "And God created the man" it does not refer to one person whose personal name was "Adam." "The Man," with the definitive "the," is the name of the species, as in the previous verse, "Let us make man in our image, as our form, and he shall reign over the fish of the sea etc."—"Adam" is not a personal name, but refers to the species of man. Similarly, in the continuation, "And the Lord God formed the man of dust from the earth, and He breathed the spirit of life into his nostrils, and man became as a living soul."
>
> Rabbi Gedalyah Nadel, *BeToraso Shel Rav Gedalyah*, p.99

When God says "Let us make man," it does not mean, "Let us make an individual named Man," but rather "Let us make mankind."[1] This can therefore be taken to refer to the original evolution of *Homo sapiens*, many hundreds of thousands of years ago. When *Homo sapiens* arrived on the scene, and attained the capacity for a spiritual relationship with God, man was thereby created. The Adam who gave birth to Cain and Abel was a different person.

The Man Without A Name

Rambam cryptically presents an intriguing approach to the episode of Adam that assists immeasurably in resolving the difficulties that people face in reconciling it with modern anthropology.

> The account of the six days of creation contains, in reference to the creation of man, the statement: "Male and female created he them" (1:27), and concludes with the words: "Thus the heavens and the earth were finished, and all the host of them" (2:1), and yet the portion which follows describes the creation of Eve from Adam, the tree of life, and the tree of knowledge, the history of the serpent and the events connected therewith, and all this as having taken place after Adam had been placed in the Garden of Eden. All our Sages agree that this took place on the sixth day, and that nothing new was created after the close of the six days. None of the things mentioned above is therefore

---

1 See Seforno, Commentary to Genesis 1:26.

impossible, because the laws of Nature were then not yet permanently fixed. There are, however, some utterances of our Sages on this subject [which apparently imply a different view]. I will gather them from their different sources and place them before you, and I will refer also to certain things by mere hints, just as has been done by the Sages. You must know that their words, which I am about to quote, are most perfect, most accurate, and clear to those for whom they were said. I will therefore not add long explanations, lest I make their statements plain, and I might thus become "a revealer of secrets," but I will give them in a certain order, accompanied with a few remarks, which will suffice for readers like you.

Guide for the Perplexed 2:30

As we noted earlier, numerous commentators pointed out that Rambam understood the six days of creation to be describing a conceptual hierarchy of the world rather than being a historical account of creation. In the same way, those who deciphered Rambam's cryptic clues in *The Guide For The Perplexed* note that he believed that most of the account of Adam in Genesis is not a historical account of an individual but instead a portrayal of the role of man in this world.[1]

This may seem shocking. But at the conclusion of the events involving creation and the Garden of Eden, we find the following verses:

This is the book of the generations of *adam*, on the day that God created *adam*, He made him in the image of God. He created them male and female, and He blessed them, and He called their name *adam* on the day that He created them.

Genesis 5:1-2

Here, the Torah tells us that both man and woman were called *adam*.[2] Thus, the name *adam*, at least in this context, was given to mankind,

---

1 At this point, it would be a good idea for the reader to refer back to chapter seven, and reread the material on allegory—both the dangers involved in using it, and the firm backing that it has in the works of several Rishonim. Rambam's approach will strike many readers as disturbing, because it is so different from what they have previously been taught. But although this approach has its own dangers, it is the most effective in terms of resolving the conflicts with anthropology.

2 The Midrash (*Bereishis Rabbah* 8:1) states that it refers to the first person who was created as an androgynous being. However, this is not the plain meaning of the verses;

and is not the personal name of an individual. The above verses should therefore be translated as follows:

> This is the book of the generations of mankind, on the day that God created man, He made him in the image of God. He created them male and female, and He blessed them, and He called their name "man" on the day that He created them.
>
> Genesis 5:1-2

What about the earlier accounts involving Adam? A careful study of the Hebrew text of Genesis reveals that it does not actually speak of "Adam." Instead, it usually writes *ha-adam*, "*the* man," and professional English Bibles generally translate it as such.[1]

It is extraordinary that the Torah would not tell us the name of the first man. Why would it depersonalize him? The implication is in accordance with Rambam's view that the Torah is concerned with teaching us about the nature of man as an archetype rather than telling us about the exploits of a particular person. Thus, the early references to "Adam" are speaking about the fundamental nature of man in general, rather than referring to the particular person who fathered Cain and Abel.[2]

In this vein, both Rambam and Ralbag explained the events of the Garden of Eden entirely allegorically.[3] Rambam understood that the six days of creation represent a conceptual portrayal of the world rather than a

---

and even this Midrash appears to be interpreted allegorically by Rambam (*Guide For The Perplexed* II:30).

1 In some places, it states that God spoke "*le-adam*," which some English translations render as "to Adam." But in light of the numerous previous instances, it would appear most preferable to translate it here too as "to the man" rather than it being a personal name, just as with the numerous instances elsewhere in Scripture where the word in this form clearly means "to mankind" and not "to Adam." Although Adam is apparently taken as being the personal name of the first man in Chronicles 1:1, this may be simply a convenient label in light of there not being another personal name. The same would apply to references to Adam in post-Biblical literature.

2 Rabbi Nadel even says that there was no individual woman named Eve either. Rather, "*Chavah*" means "life-giver," and refers to the essential nature of Woman.

3 Ibn Ezra, in the alternate version of his commentary printed in the back of the Mossad HaRav Kook edition of *Mikraos Gedolos*, cites Solomon ibn Gabirol as giving an allegorical interpretation of the Garden of Eden.

historical account of creation, and since the episode of man in the Garden of Eden took place during the six days (according to the Talmud), it is likewise part of the conceptual description of the world rather than a historical account. According to Rambam, the sin of eating from the Tree of Knowledge and subsequent punishment is an allegory for the perpetual struggle within man between his sensation, his moral faculty, and his intellect.[1] Ralbag gives a similar explanation:

> The "Garden" alludes to the material intellect... The allusion of this is that just as gardens contain plants for which it will give life (i.e. in potential), so too the material intellect gives life to ideas... And the matter of "planting the garden" means that tools were prepared for [man] to grasp matters... The tree that was "pleasing to the appearance and good to eat" alludes to attaining certain concepts...
>
> And it is fitting to know that Eden is a place in the inhabited [world], and to the east of it is found a garden which contains all fruits of delight... And this is part of the wisdom of this allegory, that its simple meaning is also something that is found... And the division of rivers from the garden alludes to that which the material intellect leads to other powers of the soul... And the snake alludes to the power of the imagination...
>
> "And God called to the man"—is by way of allegory, in the manner of "And God said to the Satan" (Job 1:7), "And God said to the fish" (Jonah 2:11); and so too is that matter with God's statement to the woman and with God's statement to the snake. And behold, the Torah has benefited us with a great benefit in social conduct by telling us this matter in this manner. Namely, that it is not appropriate for a judge to judge a person, if he does not verify the matter with him face-to-face.
>
> You should know regarding the serpent that we must admit it is allegorical.... However, regarding Eve, there is no compelling cause that she must be interpreted allegorically... And considering that she

---

1   See the commentaries of Crescas and *Ephodi* (Rav Yitzchak ben Moshe HaLevi) (Ibn Tibbon edition, II:30, pp. 51-52). This, too, is the explanation of Rambam given by Ralbag, the commentary Abarbanel, and Rabbi Yosef Kappach, one of the greatest authorities on Rambam in modern times, in his commentary to *Mishneh Torah, Hilchos Shabbos* 5:3. For an extensive discussion, see Sara Klein-Braslavy, *Maimonides' Interpretation of the Adam Stories in Genesis - A Study in Maimonides' Anthropology*.

gave birth to Cain, Abel and Seth. However, it appears the Rambam understood even Eve [in this context] allegorically, referring her to one of the human faculties...

Ralbag, Commentary to Genesis 2:9-3:24

Ralbag does comment on the allegory having aspects of manifestation in the physical world. However, it is clear that he does not hold that there was any physical Tree of Knowledge or snake. Likewise, he believes that none of the conversations of the Garden of Eden actually took place, except in a very abstract spiritual sense; certainly not in real time, and not between two earthly beings.

Putting all this together with Rambam's and Ralbag's explanation of the six days, it would seem that, according to this approach, the first three chapters of Genesis are, for the most part, speaking about the archetypical nature of man and his life in this world, rather than a historical account of a particular person's life. While this view is far from mainstream in Orthodox Judaism today (at least as far as people are willing to openly discuss their views), it receives interesting discussion by Rabbi Avraham Yitzchak Kook in a letter to someone who was bothered by conflicts raised by science:

> I necessarily find myself obligated to awaken your pure spirit in regard to the theories that have emerged from new research, which for the most part contradicts the literal meaning of the Torah. My opinion on this is, that anyone with common sense should know that although there is no necessary truth in all these new theories, at any rate, we are not in the least bit obligated to decisively refute and oppose them, because the Torah's primary objective is not to tell us simple facts and events of the past. What is most important is the [Torah's] interior— the inner meaning of the subjects, and this [message] will become greater still in places where there is a counterforce, which motivates us to become strengthened by it. The gist of this was already been recorded in the words of our Rishonim, headed by *The Guide For The Perplexed*,[1] and today we are ready to expand more on these matters. It makes no difference for us if in truth there was in the world an actual Garden of Eden, during which man delighted in an abundance

---

1 Part I chapter 71, part II chapters 15, 16, and 25, and part III chapter 3.

of physical and spiritual good, or if actual existence began from the bottom upwards, from the lowest level of being towards its highest, an upward movement. We only have to know that there is a real possibility, that even if a man has risen to a high level, and has been deserving of all honors and pleasures, if he corrupts his ways, he can lose all that he has, and bring harm to himself and to his descendants for many generations, and that this is the lesson we learn from the story of Adam's existence in the Garden of Eden, his sin and expulsion.

…[If we accept] the idea of evolution without any support from the past, [we] will always be under the threat that the process will stop in the middle of its path, or that the world will regress, since we have no secure source to say that happiness is the permanent nature of man [even of essential man—the spirit], let alone, for physical man as he is, body and soul together. Thus it is only man's experience in the Garden of Eden that attests for us a bright world and consequently it is fitting for it to be realistically and historically true, even though it is not essential to our belief.

And in general, this is an important rule in the struggle of ideas: we should not immediately refute any idea which comes to contradict anything in the Torah, but rather we should build the palace of Torah above it; in so doing we are exalted by the Torah, and through this exaltation the ideas are revealed, and thereafter, when are not pressured by anything, we can confidently also struggle against it.

Rabbi Avraham Yitzchak Kook, *Igros Ha-Re'iyah* 134, pp. 163-164

According to Rabbi Kook, while it is fitting for the account of Adam in the Garden of Eden to be historically true, it is not essential to religious belief. The important part of it is the lessons that the Torah teaches us. The purpose of Genesis is to teach us about the metaphysical and spiritual nature of the world, not its physical history.

Chapter Twenty-Four

In Conclusion

In the first part of this book, we learned how Judaism prepared the foundations for science, and how science in turn contributes to the goals of Judaism. It enhances our appreciation of God's handiwork, and teaches us important lessons about the lawfulness of existence. By the same token, it is a more noble way for God to create and run His world than via supernatural miracles.

In the second part, we explored what science teaches us about the development of the universe. We saw that Genesis is best understood not as a scientific account but rather as a theological cosmology. As such, it presents a powerful worldview that has accomplished amazing objectives with mankind.

In the third part, we explored the potential conflicts between different elements of evolutionary theory and religion, and saw that none of them prove to actually be points of conflict. Although in some cases, the religious view would have a profoundly different angle from the secular view, the actual scientific explanation proves never to be incompatible with religion, not even Darwinist theory. While certain inferences that some people draw from the theory do stand in conflict with religion, the actual theory itself does not.

Each generation attains new insights into both Torah and the natural world. The revelations of science, which have challenged scientists to account for the extraordinary lawfulness of the universe, have enhanced our appreciation of the wonders of God's creation. They have enhanced our grasp of the unity of existence. And they have also enhanced our understanding of the "creative wisdom" of God, as Rabbi Hirsch phrased it. There is grandeur in this view of Creation.

Bibliography

Abarbanel, Rabbi Don Isaac. Commentary to the Torah (Jerusalem: Beni Arbel 1964).

Aderes, Rabbi Shlomo (Solomon) ben. See Rashba.

Adler, Mortimer J. *The Difference of Man and the Difference it Makes* (New York: Fordham University Press 1993).

Alley, Richard B. and Bender, Michael L. "Greenland Ice Cores: Frozen in Time," *Scientific American* 278 (2) pp. 80-85.

Arama, Rabbi Yitzchak. *Akeidas Yitzchak* (Jerusalem 1953).

Ashkenazi, Rabbi Tzvi. *Shailos U'Teshuvos Chacham Tzvi* (Amsterdam 1712).

Aviezer, Nathan. *In The Beginning—Biblical Creation and Science* (Hoboken, NJ: Ktav Publishing House, 1990).

———. *Fossils and Faith* (Hoboken, NJ: Ktav 2001).

Avraham ben HaRambam, Rabbi. Commentary to Genesis (London 1958).

Ayala, Fransico. "Design without Designer," in *Debating Design* (Dembski, William, and Ruse, Michael, eds.) (Cambridge University Press 2004).

Bachya ben Asher, Rabbi. Commentary to the Torah (Jerusalem: Mossad HaRav Kook).

Bachya ibn Pakuda, Rabbi. *Chovos HaLevavos* (Jerusalem 1968).

Barber, Elizabeth W. and Barber, Paul T. *When They Severed Earth From Sky: How the Human Mind Shapes Myth* (New Jersey: Princeton University Press 2004).

Barrow, John D. and Tippler, Frank J. *The Anthropic Cosmological Principle* (Oxford University Press 1986).

Barrow, John D. *Theories of Everything* (New York: Oxford University Press 1991).

Becker, Bernd. "A 11,000-year German Oak and Pine dendrochronology for radiocarbon calibration," *Radiocarbon* 35 (1993) pp. 201-213.

Becker, Bernd and Kromer, Bernd. "German Oak and Pine 14C calibration, 7200 BC - 9400 BC," *Radiocarbon* 35 (1993) pp. 125-135.

Benamozegh, Rabbi Eliyahu. *Em LeMikra* (Leghorn 1863).

Berger, Rabbi David. "Miracles and the Natural Order in Nahmanides," in *Rabbi Moses Nahmanides: Explorations in His Religious and Literary Virtuosity*, R. Isadore Twersky ed.

Berger, Michael. *Rabbinic Authority* (New York: Oxford University Press 1998).

Berlin, Rabbi Naftali Tzvi Yehudah. *Haamek Davar* (Jerusalem: Yeshivas Volozhin 1999).

Brooks, Michael. "The Mysteries of Life," *New Scientist* 183:2463, 4 September 2004.

Brumfiel, Geoff. "Outrageous Fortune," *Nature* vol. 539, 5th January 2006.

Buchman, Asher Bentzion. "*U-Madua Lo Yeresem*," in *Hakirah: The Flatbush Journal of Jewish Law and Thought* (Fall 2005) vol. II.

Campbell, Ian. *Energy and the Atmosphere* (London: Wiley 1986).

Cantor, Geoffrey. *Quakers, Jews and Science* (New York: Oxford University Press 2005).

Carmell, Rabbi Aryeh and Domb, Cyril (eds.). *Challenge: Torah Views on Science and its Problems* (Jerusalem: Association of Orthodox Jewish Scientists/ Feldheim Publishers 1976).

Carmy, Rabbi Shalom. "The Nature of Inquiry: A Common Sense Perspective," *The Torah U-Madda Journal*, vol. III (1991-1992), pp. 37–51.

Cassuto, Umberto. *From Adam to Noah* (Jerusalem: Magnes Press 1961).

Chaim of Volozhin, Rabbi. *Nefesh HaChaim* (Bnei Brak 1989).

Cherry, Michael Shai. *Creation, Evolution And Jewish Thought* (Brandeis University, PhD dissertation 2001).

——. "Three Twentieth-Century Jewish Responses to Evolutionary Theory," *Aleph: Historical Studies in Science and Judaism* 3 (2003) pp. 247-290.

Cohen, Rabbi Dovid. "*Torat HaHitpachtut beChochmat haKodesh*," *Sinai*, Nissan 5706, vol. 19, pp. 34-40.

Cohen, Naomi. "The challenges of Darwinism and biblical criticism to American Judaism," *Modern Judaism* 4:2 (1984): 121-57.

Colp Jr., Ralph and Kohn, David. "A Real Curiosity: Charles Darwin Reflects on a Communication from Rabbi Naphtali Levy," *The European Legacy*, Vol. 1, No. 5 (August1996) pp. 1716-1727.

Darwin, Charles. *On The Origin Of Species* (London 1859).

——. *The Descent of Man* (London 1871).

——. *More Letters of Charles Darwin* vol. I (Ed. Francis Darwin) (London 1903).

Davies, Paul. *The Accidental Universe* (Cambridge: Cambridge University Press 1982).

——. *The Mind of God* (New York: Touchstone 1992).

——. *The Fifth Miracle* (New York: Touchstone 1999).

Dawkins, Richard. *The Blind Watchmaker* (W. W. Norton 1986).

De Duve, Christian. *Vital Dust: Life as a Cosmic Imperative* (New York: Basic Books 1995).

Dembski, William A. "The Intelligent Design Movement," *Cosmic Pursuit* (Spring 1998).

——. "What Every Theologian should know about Creation, Evolution and Design," *The Princeton Theological Review* (March 1996).

Denton, Michael. *Nature's Destiny* (New York: Free Press 1998).

Dessler, Rabbi Eliyahu E. *Collected Essays and Notes* (dupl.) (London 1959).

——. *Michtav Me-Eliyahu* (Jerusalem: Sifriyati 2000).

Dieudonné, J. "Modern axiomatic methods and the foundations of mathematics," in *Great Currents of Mathematical Thought*, Vol. II (New York: Dover 1971), pp. 251-266.

Dirac, Paul. "The Evolution of the Physicist's Picture of Nature," *Scientific American* (May 1963).

Dodson, Edward O. "Toldot Adam: A Little-Known Chapter in the History of Darwinism," *Perspectives on Science and Christian Faith* 52 (March 2000) pp.47-54.

Domb, Cyril. *B'Or HaTorah* 4 (Summer 1984), pp. 66-67.

Dubin, Lois. "Pe'er Ha-adam of Vittorio Hayim Castiglioni: an Italian chapter in the history of the Jewish response to Darwin." Jewish Studies 14 (1995): 87-101. Yakov Rabkin and Ira Robinson, editors.

Eccles, John. "A Divine Design: Some Questions on Origins," in *Cosmos Bios Theos* (La Salle, IL: Open Court Publishing Company 1992)

Einstein, Albert. *Lettres a Maurice Solovine* (Paris: Gauthier Villars 1956).

Eisemann, Rabbi Moshe. *Iyov* (New York: Artscroll/ Mesorah Publications 1994).

Eisley, Loren. *Darwin's Century: Evolution And The Men Who Discovered It* (New York: Anchor 1961).

Emden, Rabbi Yaakov. *Mitpachas Sefarim* (Lemberg 1870).

Eybeschitz, Rabbi Yonasan. *Ya'aros Devash* (Jerusalem: Or HaSefer 1983).

Faier, Zvi. Malbim: *Beginning and Upheaval* (Jerusalem: Hillel Press 1978).

Faur, Jose. "The Hebrew Species Concept and the Origin of Evolution: R. Benamozegh's Response to Darwin," *La Ressegna Mensile di Israel* 63: 3 (1997) pp.42-66.

Feit, Carl. "Darwin and Drash: The Interplay of Torah and Biology," *The Torah U-Madda Journal* (1990) vol. II.

Ferguson, Charles W. "Dendrochronology of bristlecone pine, Pinus aristata: Establishment of a 7484-year chronology in the White Mountains of eastern-central California, U.S.A." *Radiocarbon Variations and Absolute Chronology* (ed. I.U. Olsson) (New York: John Wiley & Sons 1970) pp. 237-259.

——. "Dendrochronology of bristlecone pine: a progress report," *Radiocarbon* 25:2 (1983) pp. 287-288.

Ferguson, Kitty. *The Fire in the Equations* (Eerdmans 1995).

Frankfort, Henri. *Before Philosophy* (Pelican Books 1949).

Friedlander, Rabbi Chaim. *Sifsei Chaim, Pirkei Emunah VeHashgachah* vol. I (Bnei Brak: Friedlander 1999).

——. *Pirkei Emunah u-Bechirah* (Bnei Brak: Friedlander 2000).

Futuyma, Douglas J. *Science on Trial: The Case for Evolution* (New York: Pantheon Books 1982).

Gershom, Rabbi Levi ben. See Ralbag.

Goldfinger, Andrew. *Thinking About Creation* (New Jersey: Jason Aronson 1999).

Golding, Joshua L. "On the Limits of Non-Literal Interpretation of Scripture from an Orthodox Perspective," *The Torah u-Madda Journal* (2001) 10 pp. 37-59.

Goodwin, Brian. *How The Leopard Changed Its Spots* (Princeton University Press 2001).

Gosse, Phillip Henry. *Omphalos* (Original publication, London: John Van Voorst 1857. Reprint, Woodbridge, CT: Ox Bow Press 1998)

Gottlieb, Rabbi Dovid. "The Age of the Universe," at http://www.dovidgottlieb.com.

Gould, Stephen Jay. *Bully for Brontosaurus* (New York: W.W. Norton, 1992).

——. *Dinosaur in a Haystack* (New York: Harmony Books 1995).

——. *Ever Since Darwin* (New York: W.W. Norton, 1977).

——. "Impeaching a Self-Appointed Judge," *Scientific American*, July 1992, 267(1) pp. 118-121.

——. *Rocks of Ages* (Random House 2001).

Gray, Asa. *Darwiniana: Essays and Reviews Pertaining to Darwinism* (New York: Appleton 1876).

Halberstam, Rabbi Chaim. *Divrei Chaim al HaTorah* (Solivia 1913).

Halbertal, Moshe. *Bein Torah le-Chochmah: Rabbi Menachem ha-Meiri u-Vaalei ha-Halachah ha-Maimonim be-Provence* (*Between Torah and Wisdom: Rabbi Menachem ha-Meiri and the Maimonidean Halachists in Provence*) (Jerusalem: Magnes Press 2000).

HaLevi, Rabbi Yehudah. *Kuzari* (Warsaw 1880).

Hamming, R. W. "The Unreasonable Effectiveness of Mathematics," *American Mathematics Monthly* 87:2 (February 1980).

Hawking, Stephen. *A Brief History of Time.* (London: Bantam Press 1988).

Hersh, Reuben. "Some Proposals for Reviving the Philosophy of Mathematics," *Advances in Mathematics*, 31 (1979).

Hertz, Rabbi J. H. *The Pentateuch and Haftorahs* (1936; reprint, Soncino Press 1960).

Herzog, Rabbi Isaac, "The Talmud as a Source for the History of Ancient Science," in *Judaism: Law, and Ethics* (London: Soncino Press 1974).

Hirsch, Rabbi Samson Raphael. *Collected Writings* (Jerusalem: Feldheim Publishers 1984).

——. *The Nineteen Letters* (ed. Rabbi Joseph Elias) (Jerusalem: Feldheim Publishers 1995).

——. *The Pentateuch* (Gateshead: Judaica Press 1989).

Hoffman, Rabbi Dovid Tzvi. *Commentary to Genesis* (Bnei Brak: Nezach 1969).

Honigwachs, Rabbi Yehoshua. *The Unity of Torah* (New York: Feldheim Publishers 1991).

Hooykaas, R. *Religion and the Rise of Modern Science* (Edinburgh: Scottish Academic Press 1972).

Hoyle, Fred. *Nicolaus Copernicus* (London: Heinemann Educational Books 1973).

Horowitz, Rabbi David. "Rashba's Attitude Towards Science and Its Limits," in *The Torah U-Madda Journal*, Vol. III, pp. 52-81.

Huxley, Thomas Henry. "The Interpreters of Genesis and the Interpreters of Nature," *The Nineteenth Century* (December 1885).

——. "On the reception of the Origin of Species," in *Life and Letters of Charles Darwin* (New York: D. Appleton & Co. 1905).

Jacobsen, Thorkild. "Mesopotamia." In Frankfort, Henri. *Before Philsophy* (UK: Pelican Books 1949).

Jaki, Stanley L. *The Road of Science and the Ways to God* (Chicago: The University of Chicago Press 1978).

Jastrow, Robert. *God and the Astronomers* (New York: W.W. Norton 1978).

Johnson, Phillip. *Darwin on Trial*, 2nd edition (Illinois: InterVarsity Press 1993).

Jones, A.T. *The Two Republics* (1891).

Kahn, Rabbi Ari D., *Explorations* (Jerusalem: Targum Press 2001).

Kanievsky, Rabbi Yaakov Yisrael. *Kraina De-Igresa* (Bnei Brak 1986).

Kaplan, Rabbi Aryeh. *Faces and Facets* (New York: Moznaim Publishing Corporation 1993).

——. *Immortality, Resurrection, and the Age of the Universe* (New Jersey: Ktav Publishing House 1993).

——. *The Handbook of Jewish Thought* vol. II (New York: Moznaim Publishing Corporation 1992).

Kaplan, Lawrence and Berger, David, "On Freedom of Inquiry in the Rambam—and Today," *The Torah U-Madda Journal*, vol. II (1990) pp. 37-50.

Karelitz, Rabbi Avraham Yeshayah. *Emunah U'bitachon* (Bnei Brak).

Kasher, Rabbi Menachem Mendel. "*Shabbos Bereishis VeShabbos Sinai*," *Talpiot* 1:2 (1944) pp. 351-422.

——. *Torah Sheleimah* (Jerusalem: Beis Torah Sheleimah 1992).

——. *Toras HaBriah uMishnas HaHitpachtut beMidrashei Chazal, Talpiot* 6:1 (1953) pp. 205-225.

Kass, Leon. *The Beginning of Wisdom: Reading Genesis* (New York: Free Press 2003).

Katz, Rabbi Tuviah. *Maaseh Tuviah* (Krakow 1908).

Kitagawa, H. and van der Plicht, J. "Atmospheric Radiocarbon Calibration to 45,000 yr B.P.: Late Glacial Fluctuations and Cosmogenic Isotope Production," *Science* 279 (1998) pp. 1187-1190.

Klein-Braslavy, Sara, *Maimonides' Interpretation of the Story of Creation*, Jerusalem, 1978; (second edition Jerusalem, 1987) (Hebrew).

——. *Maimonides' Interpretation of the Adam Stories in Genesis - A Study in Maimonides' Anthropology*, Jerusalem, 1986 (Hebrew).

Kline, Morris, *Mathematics and the Physical World* (New York: Dover 1980).

Kohn, David. "A Real Curiosity: Charles Darwin Reflects on a Communication from Rabbi Naphtali Levy."

Kook, Rabbi Avraham Yitzchak. *Igros HaRe'iyah* (Jerusalem: Mossad HaRav Kook 1985). English translation by Tzvi Feldman, *Rav A.Y. Kook: Selected Letters* (Jerusalem: HaMakor Press 1986).

——. *Orot HaKodesh* (Jerusalem: Mossad HaRav Kook 1985).

Kramer, Rabbi Eliyahu (Vilna Gaon). *Aderes Eliyahu* (Warsaw 1887).

——. *Biurei Aggados* (Warsaw 1886).

Landmann, Günter, et al. "Dating Late Glacial abrupt climate changes in the 14,570 yr long continuous varve record of Lake Van, Turkey," *Palaeogeography, Paleoclimatology, Palaeoecology* 122 (1996) pp. 107-118.

Lau, Rabbi Yisrael Meir. *Al Tishlach Yadecha El Ha-Na'ar* (Tel Aviv: Yediyot Achronot/ Sifrei Chemed 2006).

Leibush, Rabbi Meir. See Malbim.

Lerner, Berel Dov. "Omphalos Revisited," *Jewish Bible Quarterly* XXIII:3(91) July-September 1995, pp. 162-7.

Levine, Hillel. "Paradise Not Surrendered: Jewish Reactions to Copernicus and the Growth of Modern Science," in Robert S. Cohen and Marx W. Wartofsky, eds. *Epistemology, Methodology and the Social Sciences* (Holland: D. Reidel Publishing Company 1983) pp. 203-225.

Levovitz, Rabbi Yerucham. *Da'as Chochmah u'Mussar* (Brooklyn, NY: Daas Chochmo Umussar Publications 1966).

Levy, Naftali. *Toldos Ha-Adam* (Vienna: Spitzer and Holzwarth 1874). (English translation by Ardeshir Mehta 1994.)

Lipschitz, Rabbi Yisrael. *Derush Ohr HaChaim* in *Tiferes Yisrael* (Danzig 1845).

Loew, Rabbi Yehudah. See Maharal.

Lovejoy, Arthur O. *The Great Chain Of Being* (Harvard University Press 1936)

Luzzatto, Rabbi Moshe Chaim. *Da'as Tevunos* (Jerusalem 1948).

———. *Derech Hashem* (Jerusalem: Feldheim Publishers 1997).

Maharal. *Be'er HaGolah* (Jerusalem: Machon Yerushalayim 2003).

———. *Gevuros Hashem* (Jerusalem 1971).

———. *Nesivos Olam* (Jerusalem: Machan HaMaharal 1999).

Maimon, Rabbi Moshe ben. See Rambam.

Malbim (Rabbi Meir Leibush). Commentary to the Torah (*HaTorah VeHaMitzvah*) (Bnei Brak: Mosdos Chassidei Alexander 2000)..

Margenau, Henry and Varghese, Roy Abraham, eds. *Cosmos Bios Theos* (Illinois: Open Court 1992)

Margolese, Faranak. *Off The Derech: Why Observant Jews Leave Judaism* (Jerusalem: Devora Publishing 2005).

Meese, D. J. and Gow, A.J. et al. "The Greenland Ice Sheet Project 2 Depth-Age Scale: Methods and Results," *Journal of Geophysical Research*, 102(C12):26, pp. 411-26, 423.

Meiri, Rabbi Menachem ben Shlomo. *Beis HaBechirah*: Commentary to *Avos* (Jerusalem 1994).

Miller, Kenneth R. *Finding Darwin's God* (New York: HarperCollins 1999).

———. "The Flagellum Unspun," in *Debating Design* (Dembski, William, and Ruse, Michael, eds.) (Cambridge University Press 2004).

Monod, Jacques. *Chance and Necessity* (London: Collins 1972).

Munk, Rabbi Eli. *The Seven Days of the Beginning* (Jerusalem: Feldheim Publishers 1974).

Munk, Rabbi Michael L. *The Wisdom in the Hebrew Alphabet* (New York: Artscroll/ Mesorah Publications 1983).

Nachman, Rabbi Moshe ben. See Ramban.

Nadel, Rabbi Gedalyah. *BeToraso Shel Rav Gedalyah* (Maale Adumim: Shilat 2004).

Needham, Joseph. *The Grand Titration: Science and Society in East and West* (London: Allen & Unwin, 1969).

Neher, Andre. *Jewish Thought and Scientific Revolution of the Sixteenth Century: David Gans (1541-1613) and His Times* (New York: Oxford University Press 1986).

Nieto, Chacham David. *Matteh Dan* (London 1714).

Parnes, Rabbi Yehudah. "Torah U-Madda and Freedom of Inquiry," *The Torah U-Madda Journal*, vol. I (1989) pp. 68-71.

Penrose, Roger. *The Emperor's New Mind* (Oxford University Press 1989).

Petuchowski, Jakob J. *The Theology of Haham David Nieto* (New York 1954; reprint, Ktav 1970).

Planck, Max. "Wissenschaftliche Selbstbiographie," *Physikalische Abhandlungen* 3 (1948). Cited in Abraham M. Hasofer, "Jewish Mysticism and Nature," in *Fusion* (Feldheim/ B'Or HaTorah 1990).

Plaut, Rabbi Mordecai. *At the Center of the Universe: Essays on Western Intellectual Space* (Plaut 1983; accessible online at http://www.geocities.com/mplaut2/).

Rakovsky, Rabbi Azriel. *Shelemah Mishnaso* (Warsaw 1895).

Ralbag, Commentary to the Torah (Jerusalem: Mossad HaRav Kook 1992).

Rambam, Commentary to the Mishnah (Jerusalem: Mossad HaRav Kook 1989).

——. *Yad HaChazakah* (Jerusalem: Shabsi Frankel 2001).

——. "Treatise Concerning the Resurrection of the Dead," in *Iggeres HaRambam* (Jerusalem: Shilat 1995).

——. The Guide For The Perplexed/ *Moreh HaNevuchim* (Jerusalem: Mossad HaRav Kook 1977). English translation by M. Friedlander (New York: Dover Publications 1956).

Ramban, Commentary to the Torah (Jerusalem: Mossad HaRav Kook 1996).

Rashba, *Shailos U'Teshuvos HaRashba* (Jerusalem: Machon Yersuahalayim 1997).

Rashbam, Commentary to the Torah (Breslav 1882).

Rashi, Commentary to the Torah, in *Toras Chaim* (Jerusalem: Mossad HaRav Kook 1986).

Raymo, Chet. *Skeptics and True Believers: The Exhilarating Connection between Science and Religion* (Walker 1998).

Rischer, Rabbi Yaakov ben Yosef. *Shailos U'Teshuvos Shevus Yaakov* (Lvov 1897).

Ritva. Commentary to the Talmud (Jerusalem: Mossad HaRav Kook 1988).

Roizen, Ron. "The rejection of Omphalos: a note on shifts in the intellectual hierarchy of mid-nineteenth century Britain," *Journal for the Scientific Study of Religion* 21 (1982) pp. 365-369.

Rosenberg, Rabbi Yehudah Yudel. *Pri Yehudah* (Belgoria 1935); available online at http://www.rabbiyehudahyudelrosenberg.com.

Ruderman, David. *Jewish Thought and Scientific Discovery in Early Modern Europe* (Detroit: Wayne State University Press 1995).

Ruse, Michael. *Darwin and Design* (Cambridge, MA: Harvard University Press 2003).

——. The Evolution-Creation Struggle (Cambridge, MA: Harvard University Press 2005).

Russell, Robert John, (Ed.), *Chaos and Complexity: Scientific Perspectives on Divine Action* (University of Notre Dame Press 2002).

——. *Quantum Mechanics: Scientific Perspectives on Divine Action* (University of Notre Dame Press 2002).

Saadiah Gaon, *Emunos ve-Deyos* (*Sefer ha-Nivchar be-Emunos u-veDeyos*), Arabic text with Hebrew translation by Rabbi Yosef Kappach (Jerusalem: Sura 1960). In English, *Book of Beliefs and Opinions*, trans. S. Rosenblatt (New Haven: Yale University Press 1951).

Samuelson, Norbert M. *Judaism and the Doctrine of Creation* (Cambridge University Press 1994).

Sarna, Nahum. *Understanding Genesis* (New York: Schocken Books 1966).

Schneerson, Rabbi Menachem Mendel. *Mind Over Matter* (Jerusalem: Shamir 2003).

Schroeder, Gerald. *Genesis and the Big Bang: The Discovery of Harmony Between Modern Science and the Bible* (New York: Bantam 1992).

——. *The Science of God* (New York: Simon and Schuster 1997)

Schwab, Rabbi Simon (Shimon). "How Old Is The Universe?" in *Challenge: Torah Views on Science and its Problems* (Jerusalem: AOJS/ Feldheim Publishers 1976)

——. *Me'ein Beis HaSho'evah* (New York: Mesorah Publications 1994).

——. *Selected Speeches* (New York: CIS Publishers 1991).

Schwadron, Rabbi Shlomo Mordechai. *Techeles Mordechai* vol. I (Jerusalem: Machon Daas Torah 1986).

Schwartz, Dov, "The Debate over the Maimonidean Theory of Providence in Thirteenth-Century Jewish Philosophy," *Jewish Studies Quarterly* vol. 2 (1995) pp. 185-196.

Seely, Paul H. "The First Four Days of Genesis in Concordist Theory and in Biblical Context," *PSCF* 49 (June 1997) pp. 85-95.

Seforno, Rabbi Ovadiah. Commentary to the Torah, in *Toras Chaim* (Jerusalem: Mossad HaRav Kook 1986).

Shapira, Rabbi Chaim Eliezer. *Shailos U'Teshuvos Minchas Elazar* (Munkatch 1902).

Shapiro, Marc B. *The Limits of Orthodox Theology* (Oxford: The Littman Library of Jewish Civilization 2004).

Shem Tov Falaquera ben Joseph. *Moreh HaMoreh* (Jerusalem 2001).

Slifkin, Rabbi Natan. *The Camel, The Hare And The Hyrax* (Jerusalem: Targum Press/ Feldheim Publishers 2004).

——. *Man and Beast* (Jerusalem: Zoo Torah/ Yashar Books 2006).

——. *Mysterious Creatures* (Jerusalem: Targum Press/ Feldheim Publishers 2003).

Soloveitchik, Rabbi Ahron. *Logic of the Heart, Logic of the Mind* (Jerusalem: Genesis Jerusalem Press 1991).

Soloveitchik, Rabbi Joseph B. *The Emergence of Ethical Man* (New York: Toras HaRav/ Ktav 2005).

——. *The Lonely Man of Faith* (New York Jason Aronson 1997).

Sossnitz, Yosef Yehudah Leib. *Achen Yesh Hashem* (Vilna 1875).

Spetner, Lee. "Evolution, Randomness and Hashkafa," *BDD* vol. 4 (Winter 1997) pp. 25-53.

——. *Not By Chance! The Fall Of Neo-Darwinian Theory* (Jerusalem: Kest-Lebovits 2006).

Spurk, Marco and Friedrich, Michael, et al. "Revisions and extension of the Hohenheim oak and pine chronologies: New evidence about the timing of the Younger Dryas/ Preboreal transition," *Radiocarbon* 40 (1998) pp. 1107-1116.

Strauss, Leo. *Jewish Philosophy and the Crisis of Modernity* (New York: State University of New York Press 1997).

Swetlitz, Marc. "American Jewish responses to Darwin and evolutionary theory, 1860-1890," in Ronald L. Numbers (ed.) *Disseminating Darwinism: The Role of Place, Race, Religion, and Gender* (Cambridge University Press 1999) pp. 209-245.

Teitelbaum, Rabbi Yoel. *Divrei Yoel* (Jerusalem Hebrew Books)

Tzaddok HaKohen, Rabbi. *Tzidkas HaTzaddik* (Jerusalem: Har Beracha)

Van Till, Howard J. *Portraits of Creation Biblical and Scientific Perspectives on the World's Formation* (Michigan: William B. Eerdmans Publishing Company 1990).

Veneziano, Gabriele. "The Myth of the Beginning of Time," *Scientific American* vol. 16 no.1 (2006) pp. 72-81.

Vilna Gaon, see Kramer, Rabbi Eliyahu.

Wade, Nicholas. "Genetic Analysis Yields Intimations of a Primordial Commune," *The New York Times*, June 13th, 2000.

Wald, George. "Life and Light," in *Scientific American* 201(4) pp.92-108.

Weinberg, Steven. *Dreams of a Final Theory* (New York, 1993).

Weinstock, Israel. *Be-ma'aglei Ha-nigleh Ve-ha-nistar* ("Studies in Jewish Philosophy and Mysticism") (Jerusalem: Mossad HaRav Kook 1969).

Wheeler, J. A. *A Question of Physics: Conversations in Physics and Biology* (ed. P. Buckley and F. D. Peat; Routledge and Kegan Paul 1979).

Whitehead, Alfred N. 1967. *Science and the Modern World* (New York: The Free Press).

Wigner, Eugene. "The Unreasonable Effectiveness of Mathematics in the Natural Sciences," in *Communications in Pure and Applied Mathematics*, vol. 13, No. I (February 1960). (New York: John Wiley & Sons, Inc.). Also printed in *Symmetries and Reflections: Scientific Essays* (Cambridge and London: The MIT Press, 1970).

Young, Davis A. "The Discovery of Terrestrial History," in *Portraits of Creation Biblical and Scientific Perspectives on the World's Formation* (Michigan: William B. Eerdmans Publishing Company 1990).

——. "Scripture in the Hands of Geologists," *Westminster Theological Journal* (1987) 49 pp. 1-34.

About the Author

Originally from Manchester, England, Rabbi Natan Slifkin studied for many years at yeshivah in Israel and began his teaching career at Ohr Somayach Institutions in Jerusalem. He currently teaches a course in Biblical and Talmudic Zoology at Yeshivat Lev HaTorah, Midreshet Moriah Seminary and the Tiferet Center, and is a much sought-after lecturer worldwide. Rabbi Slifkin has written on the topic of Torah and the natural sciences for *HaModia*, *Yated Ne'eman*, *The Jewish Observer*, and *Jewish Action*. His pioneering work has been featured in dozens of newspapers and magazines including *The New York Times*, *The Scientist*, *The Jerusalem Post*, *The Jewish Observer* and *Mishpachah* magazine, and is described on his award-winning website, www.zootorah.com. Rabbi Slifkin's numerous other books include *Seasons of Life*, *Mysterious Creatures, Man and Beast*, and an English elucidation of the ancient Midrash *Perek Shirah* entitled *Nature's Song*. He is currently preparing a comprehensive encyclopedia of the animal kingdom in Jewish thought. Rabbi Slifkin lives with his family in Ramat Bet Shemesh, Israel.